Praise for *A Creative Approach to the Common Core Standards: The Da Vinci Curriculum*

"In this book, Harry Chaucer has done for teaching what his Da Vinci Curriculum does for learning. He has found ways to engage students in discovering meaning while they also meet common standards and create personal understanding of their role in a democracy. He invites teachers to do the same, designing learning based on big questions that cross the boundaries of the disciplines in search of defensible answers. Under this principle, teaching and learning follow the pattern of inquiry rather than compliance with prescription." —John H. Clarke, author of *Patterns of Thinking* and *Personalizing the High School Experience*

"We've always had standards in education and new standards alone won't transform our system. At best, they will make a better twentieth-century system. Chaucer is talking about a needed transformation of the system where learners confidently use what they know against what they do not know, and 'question storming' guides the way ahead. This work will bring excitement back to the learner." —Raymond J. McNulty, president, International Center for Leadership in Education

"A visionary educator and innovator, Harry Chaucer has chosen exactly the right moment in American time to offer this important, potentially revolutionary call to arms in our at-risk educational system." —Ron Powers, Pulitzer prize–winning author of *Mark Twain: A Life*; coauthor of *Flags of Our Fathers*; and collaborator on the late Edward M. Kennedy's *True Compass: A Memoir*

D1227537

A Creative Approach to the Common Core Standards

The Da Vinci Curriculum

Harry Chaucer

ROWMAN & LITTLEFIELD EDUCATION

A division of
ROWMAN & LITTLEFIELD PUBLISHERS, INC.
Lanham • New York • Toronto • Plymouth, UK

Published by Rowman & Littlefield Education
A division of Rowman & Littlefield Publishers, Inc.
A wholly owned subsidary of The Rowman & Littlefield Publishing Group, Inc.
4501 Forbes Boulevard, Suite 200, Lanham, Maryland 20706
www.rowman.com

10 Thornbury Road, Plymouth PL6 7PP, United Kingdom

British Library Cataloguing in Publication Information Available

Library of Congress Cataloging-in-Publication Data

Chaucer, Harry.
  A creative approach to common core standards : the Da Vinci curriculum / Harry Chaucer.
    p. cm.
  Includes bibliographical references.
  ISBN 978-1-61048-672-9 (cloth : alk. paper)—ISBN 978-1-61048-673-6 (pbk. : alk. paper)—ISBN 978-1-61048-674-3 (electronic)
  1. Education, Secondary—Curricula—United States. 2. Education, Secondary—Standards—United States. 3. Curriculum change—United States. 4. School improvement programs—United States. 5. Leonardo, da Vinci, 1452-1519. I. Title.
  LB1628.5.C43 2012
  373.190973—dc23
                                                                        2012000353

♾️™ The paper used in this publication meets the minimum requirements of American National Standard for Information Sciences—Permanence of Paper for Printed Library Materials, ANSI/NISO Z39.48-1992.

Printed in the United States of America

Contents

~

Figures and Tables

A Creative Approach to the Common Core Standards—The Da Vinci Curriculum

~

Preface

How to Read This Book

This book is about the new Common Core State Standards and an intellectually vibrant seventh–twelfth grade core curriculum called the "Da Vinci Curriculum." The Da Vinci Curriculum embraces the challenging new standards. The Da Vinci Curriculum (and its related instructional and assessment practices) is an example of biographical curricula—curricula stimulated from the life and work of admired historical figures and grounded in history.

I have written this book for educators looking for engaging secondary school models that embrace the new Common Core State Standards. Readers may be teachers (public, charter, or independent), change agents and school leaders, or education students at the undergraduate or graduate level—anyone interested in schools that are full of passionate inquiry.

This book calls for fundamental change in the secondary school curriculum. The author views the new standards as an opportunity to reexamine and radically—fundamentally—change the curriculum. The Common Core calls for bold change, for standards that are "robust and relevant to the real world."

This book presents an alternative in detail and builds a case for other schools to adapt similar practices, to create their own biographical curricula, or to create other bold alternatives to the twentieth-century high school curriculum. This books calls for nothing less than a renaissance in secondary education.

At the heart of this book are two simple premises: we human beings are wired for learning, and every single part of the universe is inherently fascinating. We are good at learning, and learning is intrinsically satisfying for us. Learning is our central purpose, and we are skillful learners. Millions of years of evolution and thousands of years of culture have tuned our brains to acquire knowledge, to create questions, and to imagine ideas. Most importantly, learning is deeply rewarding to us.

The Common Core is nothing more than sensible standards that guide us on our journey as teachers and as learners. This text is about the marriage of these standards with engaging curriculum that stimulates deep intellectual work, the kind of work that humans are uniquely good at when the lifeblood of learning is allowed to flow.

In the coming years, educators will have a choice. We may choose view the Common Core State Standards as something imposed by bureaucrats so that we can half-heartedly integrate the Common Core into our existing practices. If we do so, we will have missed an opportunity to fundamentally rethink the central intellectual purpose of learning. We will have released high school 1.1, a slight modification of high school 1.0, and an utter mismatch with student 2.0, the connected and concerned student of today.

In contrast, this text recommends that we embrace the Common Core and use it to create a renaissance in our thinking about school, learning, students, and the central purpose of adolescence. This is high school 2.0, a deep rethinking of what is meaningful intellectual work in the middle and high school years.

This is a book that arose from practice. The text has a strong theoretical base, but the practices described here have been tested over many years with real students, faculty, classrooms, books, and parents. This book comes from the classroom rather than the ivory tower.

The text advocates for curriculum that is rooted in the history of ideas and that has at its core a central organizing purpose. Leonardo da Vinci, a symbol of the Italian High Renaissance, embodies the central purpose in the core curriculum named the "Da Vinci Curriculum."

After presenting the Common Core, chapters 2 through 9 present aspects of the Da Vinci Curriculum that reflect the wide-ranging inquiry of a person like Leonardo. Some chapters stress curriculum and its relationship to the Common Core (chapters 2, 3, and 5–7), and others emphasize instructional practices (chapters 4, 8, and 9 especially). Chapter 10 presents a summary of Leonardo's life and suggests other men and women from whom biographical curriculum might be designed.

Chapter 11 examines other programs needed to address the learning needs of today's students and chapter 12 discusses briefly aspects of the change process in secondary schools.

Whether you are a public or private school educator, a college or graduate student, a school leader or a charter school advocate, this text will help you integrate "robust and relevant" new standards so that your students can pursue lives of passionate inquiry.

~

Acknowledgments

To the following great teachers:

- Mr. Mihm, my high school physics teacher—simply an inspiration;
- Mr. "G," who created advanced biology courses for students who needed them;
- The social studies department staff at Glastonbury High School—they were decades ahead of their time;
- Bob Jervis, a college professor with whom I did field work that covered half of the country;
- David Rice, a great educator;
- Dave Wolk, a college president with a big heart;
- Ted Sizer, a world-class educator who is irreplaceable;
- Esther Gailer—simply the reason why I am a teacher;
- Every student, teacher, and staff member who devoted themselves to creating Da Vinci Moments at Gailer;
- My critical readers: Dr. Judy Miller, Mr. Bill Petrics, Dr. Jim Schuman, and Dr. Bob Stanton. There is no way to thank you all enough. Of course, I take full responsibility for the final text;
- All the folks at Rowman and Littlefield—I am indebted;
- And, to my very best teachers: my lovely wife, Kathleen, and our kids.

~

Introduction

I have been impressed with the urgency of doing. Knowing is not enough; we must apply. Being willing is not enough; we must do.

—Leonardo da Vinci

I wanted a school that would be a tailwind for my education—not a headwind.

—Student

Real education should consist of drawing the goodness and the best out of our own students. What better books can there be than the book of humanity?

—Cesar Chavez

"Disscepolo della sperientia" or "Disciple of Experience"

—Title of Leonardo da Vinci's last self-portrait

Leonardo da Vinci was a genius. Not the run-of-the-mill type who showed us all up in high school, or even the once-in-a-lifetime type who makes the cover of *Time* magazine. He was a once-in-a-thousand-years genius who could *see* each tiny detail of the world precisely as it was and knew light like a blind person knows sound. His eyes could stop the wings of birds in mid-flight or the rearing of horses. He could see the similarity between the curl in a woman's hair and the turbulence of streams. He could see with such utter clarity what *was*, and was therefore able to visualize in his mind's eye *what*

1

could be. He could create the unforeseen because he had the patience to truly see what was before him.

He was so disciplined that he would copy from his mind's eye to chalk until he could recite his visual image perfectly. He was curious not in the way that you and I are about some things—he was curious about everything that he encountered. Yet he could direct his curiosity and creativity as needed.

He was a free man who could not be contained by tyrants, heads of state, patrons, men of position, or women of means. His personal renaissance did not so much recall the great men of Greek and Roman life as it did the gods on Mount Olympus. He was more Thor and Apollo, even Athena or Aphrodite, than he was Sophocles or Aristotle.

Leonardo is worthy of a curriculum that strives to understand and emulate his best qualities. A school could spend a century trying to understand this one life, drinking deeply from the waters of this spring. The lessons are endless like the Arno River of his youth that is recharged by spring runoff.

In this text, I ask you, the reader, to create a curriculum that is so compelling that you yourself cannot resist your own call to renaissance. The Common Core gives you the legitimacy that you need to break from the routine and strike off on your own. Leonardo, or some other extraordinary life around which you chose to design your curriculum, will lead the way. This is the time for action. Spread out your paints and a large canvas in your bottega (an early Renaissance workshop) and begin. Let your beginning and the beginnings of others spawn a renaissance in American education.

Premise

This book is built on the premise that *every single corner* of the universe is inherently fascinating and that *all* students have the capability to learn about, appreciate, find meaning, and contribute to that universe. Meaning is key to education and to a life well lived.

To find meaning in their world, students must be taught well within the context of a meaningful curriculum guided by challenging standards. This book is about using the Common Core State Standards to drive deep-rooted secondary school change that is meaningful to all students.

This book is also written on the premise that democracy demands a citizenry educated in the liberal arts. "Liberal arts" in this context implies that citizens have a broad background in the arts and sciences from which to think critically and fair-mindedly about issues. It means that citizens have the intellectual capacity to reason ethically beyond their narrow self-interests and ideologies (Paul and Elder 2009).

It is also written on the premise that if America is to continue to play a central moral and economic leadership role in the next quarter of a century, our schools must paradoxically become both highly *personalized* in order to engage students and must bring students together in a *common* study of our species and human culture—study guided by common standards. Each student needs to know who *he or she* is, and must understand who *we* are. The need is urgent because our problems are urgent. The need is urgent because, with a 30 percent national dropout rate, we are losing an increasing percentage of our students who view their studies as irrelevant. Far too many suffer from malaise and are disengaged from the hard, but rewarding, work of understanding their world.

Culture

Human life differs from the lives of non-human species in that our lives are not contained within our life span. We build upon others' lives. As Leonardo said, we are "disciples of experience," but not just our own experience—we are disciples of the human experience. Each of us has to learn a language, but we do not have to invent one.

Although most animal behavior is innate, some is learned, but nothing like the richness of the human experience—no libraries or museums fed by creative urges that, in our times, exponentially increase our cultural and intellectual treasures. Schools are faced with the awesome responsibility of being agents of humanity's collective cultural wealth. This book presents one successful model for comprehensive change. It is by no means the only model.

My Laboratory

Having taught the sciences for thirteen years, in 1989 I started my own school—as Leonardo suggested, "to apply and do." I named my school the "Gailer School" after my great aunt who founded her own school early in the last century in New Haven, Connecticut. I wanted a laboratory in which I could freely experiment with whole school change.

I wanted to create a school that would take seriously the awesome responsibility of being a cultural agent—a school centered on the "book of humanity." I wanted a place in which my colleagues, my students, and I could discover our voices. I wanted my school to be a "tailwind" for my students. Leonardo da Vinci, who called himself a "disciple of experience," moved me as an experiential educator.

I started a school because education was moving so painfully slowly. I felt that I was watching Darwin's finches evolve in real time—there was progress, but I didn't have millennia to wait until something measurable occurred. I had the impatience of youth. Today, I am driven by the impatience of maturity—I want to see the talk turn to action—real change in the lives of children in schools.

I want to see the heart and soul of schools change, not just their structures. I have seen enough of blue-ribbon committees telling educators what and how to teach. Too frequently those committees fail to include even token educators.

Make no mistake, there has been progress. We have standards in most states and the Common Core State Standards will soon unify those standards. We have a robust special education system that is skilled at identifying and addressing students' needs. Thanks to the work of the DuFours, and many others, we have excellent guidance regarding school leadership. Howard Gardner has helped us achieve an understanding of the multi-faceted nature of human intelligence. With the development of sophisticated scanning devices, we are beginning to achieve an understanding of how the human brain learns (Bransford and Jernstedt). Thanks to Daniel Pink (2009) and his intellectual predecessors, we have an understanding of human motivation.

Today, each state has a system for assessing student learning. The NECAP (New England Common Assessment Program), for example, is good at assessing aspects of thinking and collaboration as well as calculation and literacy skills. Educators have tools for differentiating instruction (Tomlinson 1999; Tomlinson and McTighe 2006), documenting curriculum (Jacobs 2004, 2009), and formatively assessing instruction (Stiggins 2005; Popham 2008). The table is set, but the main course is missing. The "main course" is a meaningful curriculum upon which students can direct their intellectual enzymes.

The Problem

Most schools have brilliant teachers and programs, but they are scattered like watermelon seeds throughout a melon. In too many classrooms, too few students are engaged in their education. We have not replaced meaningful farm work of the nineteeth century with meaningful schoolwork of the twenty-first (Powers, personal communication 2003). Grant Wiggins (2011) says that until teachers treat students with greater intellectual respect, nothing will change, and that until school ceases to be as needlessly boring as it is, standards can *never* be raised.

Too many students do not see their education as important to them or to the future of their community. They are passive recipients of knowledge rather than active inquirers striving for insight. Their role in school is analogous to an old transistor radio that receives occasional moments of coherent transmission through the static of their lives. Many students say that their real lives begin at 3:00 p.m. when they get home on their electronic devices and connect with their online friends. Here they feel powerful and engaged. Here they feel intellectually alive. We must bring this life-affirming power of engagement to our schools.

Biographical Curriculum

I wanted something solid at the core of my school—something more akin to the pit of an avocado than those scattered watermelon seeds. I wanted something that my educational community could hold in common, something that we could say we stood for. As I searched, I decided to build my school around a historical figure's life and works.

I chose Leonardo da Vinci due to my regard for his wide-ranging intelligence that so effortlessly crossed the divide between the arts and the sciences. I wanted my students to do the same—to think, behave, question, and create that way. I wanted my students and faculty to strive for insight—something well beyond information retrieval. I wanted my school to be experiential and, like Leonardo, I wanted my students to be disciples of experience. I wanted my school community to strive for world citizenship and to be rooted in history. I saw the Renaissance as a metaphor for the period of change that a person undergoes during adolescence.

Who Was Leonardo, and What Was the Renaissance?

These are the two overriding questions that drove my quest while on sabbatical in the summer and fall of 2010. I wanted to understand his wide-ranging intelligence and his humanity. I wanted to understand this man as you might hope to understand a friend. I felt closest to him in France in the manor home in which he died and in Windsor Castle studying his drawings with a magnifying glass.

I also wanted to better understand Medieval Europe and its transition to the Renaissance. I wanted to understand the Scientific Revolution and the Enlightenment that gave birth to our American Democracy. I was particularly interested in identifying the factors that caused the ice of the medieval world to break up and relent to the waters below.

Did the Renaissance slowly rot and transform like a snowman melts or did it "go out" one night as ice does on familiar Lake Champlain—one day it's there and the next day it's gone? Was the transition like slowly turning up a dimmer switch or like suddenly flicking on the lights in a dark room?

Of course, in Europe, when you scratch the surface and discover Roman ruins, you only have to dig deeper to find relics of Etruscan, Greek, Egyptian, Assyrian, Minoan, Phoenician, and scores of others. It is hard for us in America to understand the depth and layers of civilization in much of the rest of the world. In short, as an educator, I wanted to educate myself.

What part did Leonardo play in this transition? As the man so often called the "Renaissance Man," was he an instigator, a participant, or an emblem of the rebirth of the Western world? What role does his signature Vitruvian Man drawing serve? Why has this drawing been so closely associated with both Leonardo and with the Renaissance? What would all this mean to my historically based curriculum? Could learning about a period of profound change like the Renaissance help me to better understand our era of unprecedented change? Could the Renaissance serve as a model for radical change that so many aspire to in American education yet so few achieve? Chapter 10 presents the lessons of Leonardo's life in depth.

I hope that you, as an educator, actively pursue your *Odyssey*, wherever that might take you. As educators we must first and foremost be insatiable learners. We must learn to see the world through our own eyes. We must cultivate our curiosity. We must build our own worldview and ask questions that drive our continued inquiry. To do otherwise is to abandon our intellects to the textbook publishers, consultants, and trade journals.

Other Biographical Curricula

Could a teacher build a school around another historical figure? Yes. Susan B. Anthony, Thomas Jefferson, Margaret Mead, Nelson Mandela, Rachel Carlson, Albert Einstein, Emily Dickenson, Mohandas Gandhi, and Sojourner Truth come to mind. A school's culture and curriculum can be designed around any of these formidable people and fully address the Common Core and other standards.

A school based around any of these men or women—and a hundred others from all of the world's nations—could meet academic standards like the Common Core, address what is unique in the life and work of any one individual's biography, and focus the school's attention on the five "minds for the future"—the disciplined, synthesizing, creating, respectful, and ethical minds—that Howard Gardner identified in 2006. The point is that there would be *something* at the core of the enterprise—some intellectual driver at the wheel. Imagine a school with Susan B. Anthony's dedication to equality:

Men their rights and nothing more; women their rights and nothing less. (www. greatwomen.org/women-of-the-hall/search-the-hall/details/2-13-Anthony)

Or Margaret Mead's commitment to the scientific study of cultures and to human empowerment:

Never doubt that a small group of thoughtful committed citizens can change the world. Indeed, it is the only thing that ever has. (www.quotationspage .com/quotes/Margaret_Mead/)

Or Thomas Jefferson's belief in liberty:

I have sworn on the altar of God eternal hostility against every form of tyranny over the mind of man. (http://jpetrie.myweb.uga.edu/TJ.html)

Or Rachel Carson's early insights into environmental issues:

We stand now where two roads diverge. But unlike the roads in Robert Frost's familiar poem, they are not equally fair. The road we have long been traveling is deceptively easy; a smooth superhighway on which we progress with great speed, but at its end lays disaster. The other fork of the road—the one less traveled by—offers our last, our only chance to reach a destination that assures the preservation of the earth. (http://womenshistory.about.com/od/quotes/a/ rachel_carson.htm)

At the heart of my argument is the assumption that although *all* schools have to meet the standards for *all* students, there are an infinite number of ways of doing so. We need a diversity of programs and schools to match the diversity of interests and personalities of our students. Although all students must meet the standards, and all students must cultivate the five minds that Howard Gardner refers to, there are many ways to imaginatively do so.

Humanity faces unprecedented problems and issues today. Therefore we need to cultivate a diversity of talents to address those problems. Einstein said, "We can't solve problems by using the same kind of thinking we used when we created them." We need to create new thinkers. We need students to think differently from each other—not the same. We need a rich intellectual gene pool to draw from in our rapidly changing political, social, and physical environment. Adaptation requires diversity.

Biographical schools, based on the unique values and character of different human beings, are a way of creating a society of people who think *divergently*. The urgency and complexity of our problems calls for intrinsically motivated students who approach problems with a wide range of views.

As Daniel Pink makes clear (2011), choice is fundamental to motivation. Choice also fosters diversity.

Travel Vignettes

My goal on a recent sabbatical was to get closer to the man around whom my school was designed. I wanted to understand him, see as many of his works as possible, and understand the times in which he lived. My travels began in Windsor, England, the repository for the Windsor Codex, where I was able to closely examine approximately 150 of Leonardo's drawings. In the museums of Europe, I was able to see twenty-one of his twenty-six paintings and frescos (both figures are approximate, depending upon whom particular works are attributed). I was able to visit most of the places important to his life: Vinci, where he was born; Florence; Milan; Venice; Rome; and Amboise, France, where he died.

To better understand the context of his life, I wanted to see as much of Medieval and Renaissance Europe as possible—places like Sienna, Rome, Pompeii, Herculaneum, Athens, Heraklion (Greece), Rhodes (Greece), and the ancient city of Ephesus (Turkey). Stories and reflections are sprinkled throughout this narrative. The reader may indulge in those writings or simple skip over them to focus on the curricular issues. The reader may choose to develop a Da Vinci–like school within a school or to create a different biographical curriculum. Either way, I hope that you will find yourself collecting your own stories.

Gailer Stories

Similarly, I have included a few stories from my years at the Gailer School. I include them to give the reader a flavor for the venture—the taste and color of the school. As with the travel vignettes, these stories may be read or passed over. Following this introduction, the book is written in the third person with the exception of some of the vignettes.

The Gailer School

After founding the Gailer School in 1989, I was head of the school for twelve years. I grew the school to eighty-eight students, the design being for about ninety-six. It was a place where you could smell the sweat of athletics, hear arguments in seminar, and see tears and laughter at candid evaluations.

The school had a diverse population of students and cost about the same as our local high school. I kept these constraints because I wanted to see if I could provide a richer experience to an average group of high school students without spending more.

After leaving Gailer, I moved on to a professorship at a small state college in Vermont. Gailer moved to a smaller community, and downsized as the economy declined. I have drawn ideas, especially curriculum, from the many gifted teachers and students with whom I had the pleasure to work over the years.

For its twenty-three years, Gailer remained Gailer. You would have seen an ongoing commitment to the original mission, "Insightful World Citizenship," and to the core idea of interdisciplinary "Da Vinci" Curriculum.

Gailer will close in the spring that this book is published, both events not far from Leonardo's birthday. Gailer succumbed to the recession and demographics. My Great Aunt Esther's school closed when she passed away. To every season . . .

I have the great pleasure of hearing what former students are doing, meeting their children and spouses, and hearing their recollections of their days at Gailer. An even greater pleasure comes from watching our own children become parents as they begin to teach their kids to be insightful world citizens.

Gailer Story #1

The Writer Within

Eban believed that he could not write. He was sure of this. It had been confirmed in school many times. I recall four times that his faculty proved him wrong.

While claiming incompetence, Eban wrote three creative pieces that I will always remember. In one, he and his brother lay beneath their porch listening to his parents' "adult talk" while rocking on the porch swing. He would see glimpses of them through the floor planking as the swing moved. The image of a pair of brothers listening in to the world of adults was a powerful one.

In another story, he talked about haying a field. Beginning at the outside, the tractor slowly cut the grasses, leaving a progressively smaller unmowed rectangle. At some critical point, wildlife ran, flew, and slithered from the tall grass at the center away from the dangerous mowed field and tractor. When the protection of the ever-shrinking field failed to provide them with shelter, the concentration of life exploded into the surrounding newly mown grasses. He told this story as a rural boy who had experienced this moment many times.

In another story, Eban described his father and himself working their way ever deeper into a handcrafted Italian race car that they were working on. After hours of work, they discovered the punch mark of the builder. He felt like he had deciphered an ancient text or peered for the first time into an ancient funeral crypt.

In another assignment, the teacher asked Eban's class to choose an ancient city and write about life there. She wanted them to invest themselves in another time, place, and culture. She wanted them to imagine what it might have been like to live in other times.

Eban chose Çatalhöyük, one of the oldest (7500 BC to 5700 BC) Neolithic settlements in the world. Çatalhöyük is in what is now the nation of Turkey. She wanted him to wrap his thoughts around this ancient place. She wanted him to think about the people, their lives, their distance, and their closeness to our own lives.

Eban drew a blank. "I can't do this. I don't like history. I can't write."

However, Eban was a budding artist—he is a respected practicing artist today. Knowing this, the teacher found an artist's conception of a scene from Çatalhöyük. She asked, "What is this boy doing? Is that his father? Who is this man? Is that person dead? Why would a dead body be buried beneath a hearth in a home? Tell us a story based on this picture." Eban wrote. And more importantly, he proved himself wrong. He was a writer.

CHAPTER ONE

~

The Common Core as Unprecedented Opportunity— Renaissance or Reform?

Contemplation is vital, thinking is vital: he who thinks little, errs much.

—Leonardo da Vinci (Les Pensees, p. 28)

He is a poor disciple who does not excel his master.

—Leonardo da Vinci

Chapter 1 examines the Common Core State Standards as a unique opportunity for deep-rooted change—nothing less than a renaissance—in American secondary schools. The chapter examines the importance of historically based and biographical curricula in a democratic society and the relationship between curriculum, the Common Core State Standards, and ethics.

American education is at a crucial juncture. Educators have been pummeled by calls for reform since 1984 when the *Nation at Risk* claimed that the American education system was so inadequate that the nation might as well have unilaterally disarmed (then ironically, the report prescribed more of the same). Many say that it was no more than a political exercise. Going back a quarter of a century earlier to the *Sputnik* era, reforming education has repeatedly been identified as a solution to America's threats. To a new teacher, education can seem like a gauntlet of qualifying tests and regulations—the usual response to calls for reform.

Education is also faced with extraordinary budget pressures, yet hidden within these forces is an unprecedented opportunity. That opportunity lay

11

hidden in the curriculum reform that will inevitably parallel the implementation of the Common Core State Standards, America's first nationally agreed-upon curriculum standards. The National Governors Association Center for Best Practices (NGA Center) and the Council of Chief State School Officers (CCSSO) has sounded the alarm—existing state standards are inconsistent and fail to prepare students for college or the contemporary workplace. At this writing, thirty states have agreed to one of two common assessments and forty-five to the Common Core itself.

Educators have a choice: faced with our first national standards and assessments, we can choose to make minor curriculum changes in each state and local curriculum to align what is taught with the new standards, or we can fundamentally reshape the curriculum in order to make it coherent, meaningful, engaging, and relevant to today's students. We can respond to the alarm, or we can hit the snooze button. This choice is unique and unlikely to present itself again within the next twenty years.

In *Catching Up or Leading the Way* (2009), Yong Zhao, critical of America's rush to imitate the traditional rigidity of Asian schools, puts it this way:

> We thus face a choice of what we want: a diversity of talents, of individuals who are passionate, curious, self-confident, and risk takers; or a nation of excellent test takers, outstanding performers on math and reading tests. (p. 59)

Introduction to the Common Core State Standards

Standards-Based Reform

Before the 1980s, students in U.S. schools tended to be compared to their peers. This could be seen in some teachers' "curved" grading practices (with student outcomes fitted to a predetermined statistical curve), in the norm-referenced SAT exam, or in the emphasis on class rank. How well the student did depended upon the cohort with which he or she studied. The student's cohort was the norm against which his or her progress was judged.

Since the 1980s, school, state, and national curriculum groups setting standards for all students have characterized education reform in the United States. These standards are criterion referenced. Rather than being compared to each other, students are compared to an objective standard—a criterion. With criterion-referenced assessment, all students can succeed if taught well. A familiar example of criterion-referenced tests is the driver's education test. It does not matter how others performed. In both the written and driving aspect of the driver's test, each student is compared to an objective standard.

The Common Core State Standards are an effort to create new criterion-referenced standards.

The Common Core State Standards (CCSS)

The Council of Chief State School Officers and the National Governors Association for Best Practices convened a working group in July of 2009 to create a draft of Math and English Language Arts (ELA) standards. By March of 2010, the group released the first public draft of the standards. Along the way, the group solicited and incorporated feedback from a broad range of stakeholders. The CCSS work group claims to have based its work on national and international education best practices and research. The CCSS has scores of partners, including most major educational groups. In short, the Common Core State Standards focus on fewer concepts while stressing deeper learning and understanding. The CCSS is designed to prepare students for both higher education and the workplace. The word "state" is used in the CCSS title to emphasize that the initiative arose from the governors and chief state school officers, not the federal government.

The Common Core mission is to

> provide a consistent, clear understanding of what students are expected to learn, so teachers and parents know what they need to do to help them. The standards are designed to be robust and relevant to the real world, reflecting the knowledge and skills that our young people need for success in college and careers. With American students fully prepared for the future, our communities will be best positioned to compete successfully in the global economy. (National Governors Association 2010).

Emphasis on Complex Text

Through its research, ACT (the college entrance exam center) determined that "performance on complex texts is the clearest differentiator in reading between students who are likely to be ready for college and those who are not. And this is true for both genders, all racial/ethnic groups, and all annual family income levels" (ACT 2006). According to the ACT, "Relationships, Richness, Structure, Style, Vocabulary, Purpose—none of these 'RSVP' aspects is described in detail anywhere in any state's prior reading standards."

Similarly, the Common Core website states the following:

> Evidence shows that the complexity of texts students are reading today does not match what is demanded in college and the workplace creating a gap between what high school students can do and what they need to be able to do. The Common Core State Standards create a staircase of increasing text

complexity, so that students are expected to both develop their skills and apply them to more and more complex texts. David Coleman, architect and author of the standards states that "the entire ELA (English Language Arts) structure has been radically mis-focused. That is, we have not concentrated on what matters in terms of kids' literacy growth. Eighth grade NAEP results are flat—a wall. We should shift to a 50/50 fiction/informational text mix from 80% fiction in elementary schools. (National Governors Association 2010)

The Common Core has been adopted by forty-five states as of this writing. Two states have not joined the initiative (Texas and Alaska), and three states have joined, but not yet adopted the standards (Minnesota, Montana, and Nebraska). The CCSS have been embraced rapidly, in part, because President Obama's *Race to the Top* legislation required adoption of the CCSS in order for states to apply for significant competitive federal support. The CCSS are scheduled for implementation by 2014. It remains to be seen whether enthusiasm will hold once federal incentives decrease.

Nutritional and Flavorful Curriculum

Why not simply update and align current curricula to the Common Core? To answer this, it is worth exploring an analogy between eating nutritional foods and learning from an engaging curriculum. In both cases, we have standards to guide us.

With nutrition, we know how many calories we need to energize our body and mind; how much protein, fat, and carbohydrates we require; and what vitamins and minerals we need. We understand the risk of eating too much fat, sugar, or salt. We can get the nutrients we need efficiently by consuming one of the better energy bars or protein drinks. Sometimes that is the best way to proceed—a quick bite before a sports event, in the car between meetings, or getting into a campground late at night. Energy bars meet many of the nutritional standards.

However, we know that sound nutrition provides more than a certain number of grams of protein or milligrams of sodium. We know that there are less tangible areas of nutrition, such as fiber, texture, color, odors, and flavor. We know that how foods are presented and combined makes a difference in how they are enjoyed. We know that eating is a profoundly satisfying social process—a central event in the life of families, in marriages and friendships, and in the development of children. Eating with others is an important part of a fulfilling human life.

Imagine the absurdity of a couple going out for a romantic candle-lit evening and sitting down to a couple of *Cliff Bars* and a bottle of *Ensure*. Yet, ironically, the *Cliff Bars* and *Ensure* meet most of the nutritional standards.

Our American curriculum is analogous to the energy bar. It meets the standards, but often does so in an unimaginative and unengaging fashion. Except for those students with strong intrinsic motivation, many curricula fail to engage and satisfy today's students. Whether in a job setting or in higher education, as Leonardo said, "Thinking is vital—he who thinks little, errs much." Thinking is so often compromised in the interest of content acquisition.

The Conventional American Curriculum (CAC), as documented in textbooks and high school curriculum documents, leaves it to the imagination of the individual teacher to figure out how to make a socially, emotionally, and intellectually satisfying meal out of a protein bar.

Our new Common Core State Standards provide us with an opportunity to reexamine our curriculum—the intellectual food that we create to provide our students with a nutritious intellectual diet. We have an opportunity to make our classrooms into rich, satisfying across-the-dinner-table conversations—the kind of conversations that are the basis for family-like relationships—the kind of conversations that are the essence of powerful learning and lives well lived.

The analogy can be taken further. Imagine sitting down to a simple hors d'oeuvre—a wedge of sharp cheddar and some crackers. The cheese contains protein that our digestive systems break down into its amino acids. We then reassemble those amino acids into the proteins that we need to build and run our bodies. We assemble the amino acids that we got from cheese, and ultimately from cows, into our own proteins—we make them ours.

The standards are analogous to amino acids—not very useful in their own right. Yet as our bodies have biochemical machinery, our minds can be taught to have intellectual machinery to disassemble and recombine core knowledge and skills to make them ours. We do this via meaningful instructional practices, engaging curriculum, and authentic assessment.

Unfortunately, given the pressure of standards and testing, many classrooms never get to the point of recombining learning outcomes into personally meaningful understanding. Too often, the bits and pieces of learning—the standards—are never recombined into ideas, skills, dispositions, and knowledge that we can personally use. Much learning falls shy of insight. Many of our students graduate with an intellectual protein deficiency. Learning may fail to be "robust and relevant to the real world." Despite the heroic efforts of well-prepared teachers, too much of our secondary school learning is unsatisfying and ineffective.

This book is about creating meaningful curriculum that engages both teacher and student. It is about curriculum that has a meaningful structure. It is about curriculum that allows all students to exceed rigorous standards. It is about curriculum that engages all students in intellectually rich activities whether they are bound for college, technical training, or the workplace. It is about curriculum that addresses how students learn as well as what they learn.

The word "intellectual" is important. As teachers, although we are comfortable with Howard Gardner's use of the term "multiple intelligences," we shy away from "intellect" or "intellectual" as if those words connoted activities that are exclusive—beyond the realm of the ordinary classroom or ordinary students.

As educators we should embrace our intellectual capacities and the capacities of every single student we encounter, regardless of their status, ability, or aspirations. As educators, we are literally micro-neurosurgeons creating physical links between the neurons in our students' brains. This is photographically documented in other mammals and is certain to be the case with humans as well. The connections we make in our thinking result in dendrites connecting in our brains (Jernstedt 2008).

Democracy and Citizenship

The *Oxford English Dictionary* defines "intellect" as "that faculty . . . of the mind or soul by which one knows and reasons (. . . distinguished from *feeling* and *will*); power of thought." *Every* student who enters our classroom must exit with the ability to know and reason on the job, in their continuing education, and as citizens.

Think of one of your least capable students. His or her vote in our republic is absolutely equivalent to your most prepared student—and to your own! If our democracy is to flourish, *all of our citizens* must be able to distinguish between their feelings and their reasoning. They must all be adept at acquiring knowledge and using their knowledge to reason. It is the "power of thought" that fuels the democratic process. Our citizens must be *insightful* citizens. As educators, the human intellect is our province and we should embrace it without apology.

In 1748, the French philosopher and political thinker Montesquieu said, "The tyranny of a prince is not so dangerous to the public welfare as the apathy of a citizen in a democracy."

Public education and democracy were inextricably linked in the eyes of the American founders, particularly for Thomas Jefferson, who in 1816 famously wrote, "If a nation expects to be ignorant and free, in a state of civilization, it expects what never was and never will be." His plan for education asserted four principles:

1. Democracy cannot long exist without enlightenment.
2. It cannot function without wise and honest officials.
3. Talent and virtue, needed in a free society, should be educated regardless of wealth, birth, or other accidental condition.
4. The children of the poor must be thus educated at common expense. (as cited in Padover 1952, p. 43)

In 1788, founder and president James Madison stated that "knowledge will forever govern ignorance, and a people who mean to be their own Governors must arm themselves with the power knowledge gives" (www.constitution.org/jm/jm_quotes.htm). In our times, Norman Cousins said, "In a democracy, the individual enjoys not only the ultimate power but carries the ultimate responsibility" (www.brainyquote.org). Freedom and responsibility are inextricably linked in our American democratic vision. Public education is our defense against the tyranny of apathy. Enlightenment is a necessary condition for a free and democratic people. People are the "depository of the ultimate powers of the society," and if they fail to act with discretion, they need only to be better informed.

Rarely do students practice democratic principles in schools today. Educational reform should increase students' experience with democracy. Educational renaissance and robust standards will create schools with governance structures that will invite—even require—democratic participation, schools in which students are encouraged to speak and write with informed conviction. Practicing democratic principles is part of a wholesome and nutritional educational diet. As G. K. Chesterton said, "Democracy is like blowing your nose. You may not do it well, but it's something you ought to do yourself."

In this view of education, the Common Core provides the building blocks. Yet curriculum should engage students beyond these building blocks. Memorable study is both personal and universal. Our students are crying out for this. It has been over a quarter of a century since *A Nation at Risk*. It's time we delivered the goods. It is time to stop reforming and to begin a renaissance!

How Is the Conventional Curriculum
Misaligned with the Common Core?

A student entering seventh grade in the year 2012 will graduate from high school in the year 2018—*if* he or she graduates at all. One student drops out of an American school every twelve seconds (Big Picture Learning 2011). There are several reasons why the conventional curriculum is inadequate for contemporary students, whether they are preparing themselves for the workplace, a technical job, or for college and graduate programs. Regardless of the role of formal education in their lives, all of our students, from the most adept to the most challenged, will become citizens of our democracy and will be asked to perform increasingly complex tasks in the workplace.

The conventional curriculum was designed for the industrialized twentieth century. There used to be a division between brains and brawn. For example, the 1950s telephone repairman needed to have the ability to climb a telephone pole and the docility to do what the diagnosticians in the home office asked. Today's repairperson *is* the diagnostician who must know how to use sophisticated computerized diagnostic tools. Except for out lowest-level service jobs, our workforce must be far better educated than ever before. A passive curriculum does not prepare our students for this reality. What else is ineffective in the secondary curriculum?

1. Narrow Focus on the Academic Disciplines

The Conventional American Curriculum (CAC) is organized according to academic disciplines. "What's wrong with that?" you might ask. The problem is that the disciplines are an academic convention—an artificial way to view the world. Limited disciplinary thinking will not reach the common core mission of being "robust and relevant to the real world." Real world problems are interdisciplinary. A fraction of the students in biology classrooms became biologists; veterinarians; or doctors, nurses, or other medical practitioners. For the large majority, the biology that they learn improves and enriches their lives.

Over their adult lives, high school graduates will be faced with thousands of actual problems that do not present themselves within neat disciplinary boundaries. In their own lives, they have had to make decisions that involved medical ethics, human sexuality, and disease. They have read about bio-medical advances and, if their teachers have done their jobs well, have the background to understand what they have read. The real world is unpredictable and chaotic—it does not obey the rules, as we might like. We need to prepare them for the world in all of its chaotic glory. For a powerful critique on the structure of American schooling, see Sir Kenneth Robinson's YouTube video titled "Changing Educational Paradigms."

2. Little Horizontal Organization

When we teach disciplinarily, there is some vertical organization in the curriculum (through the disciplinary sequence of courses that students take within disciplines), but no order horizontally (within each year of a student's program). Perhaps this is an artifact of our allegiance to academic departments. Since there is no order horizontally, there can be no coordination or discussion across disciplines. The student's annual experience is fragmented and lacking in context. Each student is on his or her own schedule marching toward graduation (or, for about 30 percent, marching toward dropping out).

The math teacher is discouraged, curricularly, from talking with the literature teacher about the different languages—two different forms of literacy—that they teach. They share students only by coincidence, not by design. Numerical and English literacy are taught as distinct and unrelated subjects. We fail to understand the human development of literacy as, perhaps, a unique phenomenon of our species.

Some authors attribute the following quote to Leonardo:

Principles for the development of a Complete Mind: Study the science of art. Study the art of science. Develop your senses—especially learn how to see. Recognize that everything connects to everything else. (Attributed to Leonardo by Atalay and Wamsley 2008, 96. Shorter version attributed to Leonardo [Les Pensees, p. 32]. Attribution questioned by Martin Clayton, Librarian, Royal Library at Windsor Castle, personal communication, 2010).

Regardless of whether these words were written by Leonardo or not, there is something to be learned from them. Seeing was fundamental to Leonardo. Connections were also. His art and his science were indistinguishable—he illustrated his science and he approached his art experimentally (not always to his benefit—his experiments in color fixative failed with the *Last Supper*, leaving us a muted, but strikingly beautiful result).

The CAC fosters separation of art from science—in many schools the disciplines are arranged on different tracks for different students. Yet we want students with "complete minds" who can understand the "art of science" and the "science of art" to be robust in their understanding.

3. Lack of Historical Context

There is limited development of historical context in the CAC. History is an occasional sidebar in the textbooks that guide the CAC. Why is historical context important? For the simple reason that all human knowledge was created within the context of time, place, people, and culture.

For example, as a society, most people today value science. We do so because of our intellectual heritage. Twenty-six hundred years ago, in Greece, a man named Thales said, "One does not have to attribute natural phenomena to the whims and vagaries of the Gods, but rather to look for causes through natural law" (Atalay and Wamsley 2008, 160). Some say that Thales was the first scientist, and that the quote above is the first record of a person beginning the long tradition of explaining phenomena with natural causes rather than godly intervention. Can this historical understanding help ward off superstition today? How can our understanding of science be complete without understanding its intellectual tradition?

For example, it is fine to know that the earth revolves around the sun and that the planet Jupiter has sixty-three moons, but why was Galileo Galilee put under house arrest for the last decade of his life for identifying the first four moons of Jupiter and the moon's mountains? Why was this knowledge such a threat to the Church?

Historical context makes it clear. Galileo, in turning his telescope skyward and reporting on what he saw, threatened Church authority. In claiming that Jupiter has moons, he was also saying that the heavens, previously the exclusive domain of the Church, were now accessible to unordained people using simple lenses. Heaven—or, at least, the heavens—were no longer the sacred and exclusive domain of specially trained clergy. And the heavens were imperfect—the moon was pocked with craters—not the perfect Godly sphere that the Church had said it was.

The story reveals the importance of Galileo's work—its controversial and forward-looking nature. It has been said that we get our word "revolution," meaning to make a dramatic change, from the revolutionary Copernican concept of the earth *revolving* around the sun.

In contrast to the Renaissance, which connotes rebirth, the *Oxford English Dictionary* tells us that the Protestant Reformation implied that religion would be "restore(d) or change(d) back . . . to an original form or state, or to a previous condition." Our choice in education is simple: rebirth or restoration—renaissance or reform?

The story—the narrative—is what is memorable. As teachers, we are in the business of making learning memorable. Stories—rich, interesting, historical narratives—help us teach effectively. And it is important that we know our story—as a species living on a planet with cousin species. It is who we are. We have the great privilege as a species to be able to inquire and comprehend our journey.

In *The Call of Stories* (1989), Robert Coles, a doctor, recalls having been lectured by a senior physician: "The people who come to us bring us their stories. They hope they tell them well enough so that we understand the truth of their lives. They hope we know how to interpret their stories correctly. We have to remember that what we hear is their story" (p. 7).

Cole's physician mentor is talking about patients, but the same is true of our students. Good teachers, like good doctors, listen for their students'

Gailer Story #2

The Airship

When I began planning my school, the Gailer School, I found myself thinking back to my Great Aunt Esther Gailer. "What would Esther do?" became a frequent question. She (a math and writing teacher for the older students) and her sisters, my Aunt Bessie (an early childhood educator) and my Grandmother Mae (a history and literature teacher), were all educated in normal schools. They were Russian immigrants whose father was a tailor for Czar Nicholas II, the last Emperor of Russia.

As I designed my school I was taken with the idea of contacting some of Miss Gailer's school students. My father recalled a few names. With those as a starting point, I started writing letters. I wanted to understand the school that, you might say, gave birth to my school; so I asked them for stories—any recollections that these older men and women might have had about their schools days. One stood out.

He recalled May 5, 1937. This student, probably six or seven years old or so at the time, recalled "Miss Bessie" taking them on a field trip from the school on Bishop Street in New Haven, Connecticut, to cross Whitney Avenue. They often went there to play in the open field. Today, there is now a Yale University parking lot with a linear accelerator underneath.

The kids sat with their lunches and impatiently waited for an airship to pass overhead. The dirigible never showed up, and the disappointed children eventually walked back to school. That airship had been facing headwinds as it crossed the Atlantic. The dirigible, the *Hindenburg*, exploded as it attempted to land a day late in Lakehurst, New Jersey. The children heard the famous Herbert Morrison broadcast the following day. The disappointingly empty sky was this student's memory of that tragic event.

stories. Good teachers find ways to ask, "What is important in your life?" and build from there. Great teachers do more. Their teaching enriches their students' stories. Great teachers help their students learn that their personal stories are part of a much larger human drama that crosses cultures, time, and continents. These students know that they are not alone despite the particulars of their personal narrative.

Ironically, to teach exclusively within disciplines makes the discipline itself harder to understand as a human enterprise. It is a forest-and-tree phenomena. When so enmeshed in the discipline of science, for example, it is too easy to lose perspective on science as a human activity that developed over time. Paradoxically, the structure of the disciplines (Posner 2004) becomes more apparent in interdisciplinary learning in which disciplines illuminate concepts as if each discipline shined a unique wavelength of light on the concept being examined.

When learning physics as a body of conclusions rather than a process of human understanding we fail to see how hard-won our current worldview is. For example, physics teaches us that force equals mass times acceleration ($f = ma$), but what did other people in other times think about the concept of force? We fail to understand when and where science developed. While dutifully applying the laws of physics, we may fail to ask if science has progressed toward an ever-greater understanding, or if it has moved in fits and starts, or even moved "backward" at times, having lost knowledge as civilizations have foundered. To be well educated is to understand how human knowledge has developed in the world's cultures over time. Without this historical perspective, we are simply passive vehicles for our own cultural transmission.

4. Difficulty of Learning Decontextualized Content

Learning simple ideas (facts and skills) out of context is more difficult than learning complex ideas within a meaningful context. Our minds are built to create meaning, not to memorize out-of-context information that we might someday use in a meaningful way.

The Common Core writers ask us to "include rigorous content and application of knowledge through high-order skills." The facts—core knowledge—are a means to a much larger end. See below for more on the Common Core's assumptions; the International Center for Leadership in Education (ICLE; Bill Daggett and Ray McNulty); and the Rigor—Relevance Framework (Daggett 2011). The Common Core Assessments will be fully implemented by 2014–2015.

5. Convergent Nature of the CAC

The CAC does not inherently support heterogeneity. It promotes sameness. Standards are often interpreted to mean standardization. To accommodate students' diverse needs, the disciplinary approach to curriculum fosters tracking and leveling of students. A real world investigation is so multifaceted that it encourages each student to find a niche while learning to expand his or her horizons. Real world studies are inherently divergent, calling on many different skills and talents.

Renaissance

After so many years of calls for change and (some would say) so little actual change, could public secondary schools embrace a renaissance in the next decade? Several factors argue that schools can, must, and will embrace a deep-rooted renaissance.

New teachers have more content and pedagogical training in their initial licensure programs than their predecessors. They have had to pass GPA requirements and content assessments, such as Praxis, and to fulfill rigorous general and major requirements. In many teacher education programs, rigorous liberal arts classes—the same classes taken by mathematicians, historians, scientists, and writers—have replaced "soft" education courses. The new generation is also well prepared in special education, brain-based learning, and formative assessment. As occurred in medicine over the last 150 years, education is becoming research based.

There is widespread dissatisfaction both within the teaching ranks and in the general public. It is widely believed that we can do far more than we are with students at the secondary level. Students recognize this and are ready for change.

The Common Core nationalizes the Standards Movement. The times are ripe for change. In two to four years, there will be substantial curricular shifts due to the implementation of the Common Core. Federal money and federal sanctions will leverage change.

People need models to make sweeping change. Florentine architect Brunelleschi imitated Rome's Pantheon, one of the most beautiful buildings in the world, to envision the Duomo in Florence. Similarly, models of secondary school change exist today and can be emulated. This text focuses on one such model. In the last twenty years, the middle school movement converted thousands of junior high schools into effective middle schools. High schools are next in line.

Travel Vignette 1

Thoughts En Route from Rhodes, Greece, to Heraklion, Crete

I wonder if the Roman Catholic Church survived the Renaissance because it was able to adjust and accept stylistic change as long as fundamental doctrine went unchallenged. This is in contrast to Galileo, whom the church did not accept. The church viewed the Galileo telescope as a challenge to the church's exclusive heavenly domain.

There are parallels to the challenges that the Roman Catholic Church faced in the fifteenth century and the challenges that the church faces today. Will the church be able to preserve itself as an institution, given its drop in membership and clergy and the worldwide abuse scandal?

The Roman Catholic Church has had an admirable ability to stay on message and adjust to local conditions and changing times. I had always known that the Roman Catholic ritual was rich, but I had no sense of the depth of the history, ritual, and symbolism of Christianity. Following Saint Paul from Damascus to Rhodes, seeing the cave in which Saint John wrote revelations, visiting Greek Orthodox churches, seeing the place where the Virgin Mary is thought to have lived the last part of her life, and hearing from many guides for whom the stories of Christianity are important impresses upon me the rich, consistent, and flexible narrative of Christianity and the resilience of the church as an institution.

Witnessing the resilience of this institution, I find myself asking what is fundamental and nonnegotiable in public education? What are our core values, our stories worth preserving? Who are our Galileos and how should we respond to them?

The Critical Importance of Ethics in Secondary Education

Wall Street firms did not need to be bailed out because the leaders did not understand mathematics. The American real estate market did not collapse because banks and realtors did not understand contracts and agreements. General Motors did not need to be saved because its engineers did not understand engineering. Our environment is not threatened due to our lack of scientific understanding. In each case, factors such as lack of will, excessive greed, poor judgment, unchecked self-interest, and a variety of rationalizations led to short-term personal gain at the cost of long-term societal good. These are ethical issues, not issues of skills and traditional content. At the core of unethical action is egocentric (selfish) thinking (Paul and Elder 2009).

The secondary school curriculum *must* engage students in important ethical issues. Ethics is not a murky and personal exercise. Ethics is a form of reasoning that can be taught and applied (Paul and Elder 2009). Teachers must learn ethical reasoning and must have a curriculum that fosters ethical thinking.

The Da Vinci Curriculum, by engaging students in historical and contemporary issues, invites ethical reasoning. Similarly, students must be *practiced* in ethical decision making. We do not expect students to become effective automobile drivers without driving, and we do not expect them to become chemists without working in a lab. We should not expect students to become citizens who can make decisions well without practicing making decisions of importance. This should take place within the curriculum (in a structured and limited way) and in decision making in the school. There is no reason why students cannot be fully involved in policy matters of direct importance to their school lives, such as the evaluation and selection of their faculty (See chapter 7, satellite programs).

Chapter 1 Summary

The Common Core as Unprecedented Opportunity—Renaissance or Reform?

- The Common Core State Standards present an opportunity for deep-rooted change in American public schools.
- In a democratic society that depends upon an educated citizenry, curriculum matters. It must be full-bodied, intellectually rich, and satisfying as well as meet the new Common Core Standards.
- The conventional secondary school curriculum is limited because of its disciplinary focus and its lack of horizontal organization (across courses within a student's year). It is limited because it lacks historical context and meaningful overarching concepts. It does not inherently support heterogeneity since the work of students is convergent, asking much of the same from all students.
- To be effective citizens, secondary students must be practiced in systematically confronting ethical issues.

~

CHAPTER TWO

The Da Vinci Core Curriculum in Light of Contemporary Educational Theory

History is a vast early warning system.

—Norman Cousins

Be not false about the past.

—Leonardo da Vinci (Les Pensees, p. 29)

Those who fall in love with practice without science are like pilots who board a ship without rudder or compass.

—Leonardo da Vinci (Atalay and Wamsley, 2008, p. 192)

It was the artist who taught the scientist "how to observe."

—Atalay and Wamsley describing Leonardo (2008, p. 241)

There is nothing quite as practical as good theory.

—Kurt Lewin

There is nothing quite as theoretical as good practice.

—John Dewey

Chapter 2 examines the historically grounded Da Vinci Curriculum in light of John Dewey's belief that students should participate in the preservation and enhancement of human culture. The chapter also presents four other educational theorists in the context of the Da Vinci Curriculum.

What alternatives to the Conventional Secondary School Curriculum unite theory and practice, teach students to observe closely, and are true to the past? There are many alternate curricula. For example, the MET School in Providence, Rhode Island (Big Picture Learning 2011), helps students find the intersection between their interests and the standards that society dictates. Many Coalition of Essential Schools programs (www.essentialschools .org/) around the country provide thoughtful alternatives to conventional schools while adhering to ten broad principles such as "learning to use one's mind well" (as contrasted with mindlessly covering content).

Many "alternative schools" and technical centers are rich sources of excellent secondary school practice. The same is true of independent and charter schools. The National Association of Independent Schools promotes four freedoms for independent schools, including "The Freedom to teach the truth, as each school sees it" (NAIS Trustee Handbook 2003, p. x). Imagine how different public schools would be if they embraced such a freedom? Public comprehensive high schools have much to learn from independent and charter schools and vice versa.

The focus here is on the "Da Vinci Curriculum,"* or DVC. The idea is simple: organize the secondary school curriculum horizontally *and* vertically. The vertical organization (through the student's years of study) is the flow of geological, biological, and human history. Historical time is the driver in this curriculum. History allows students to engage with the development of ideas over time and to develop the historical "early warning system" that Cousins referred to. The horizontal organizers are the disciplines that illuminate each era of history. Simple. Each student is on a path of understanding that begins at the beginning, the creation of the universe, and ends with predictions about the fate of our universe, planet, species, and culture. See Table 2.1.

Each of the disciplines shines its own wavelength of light on each yearlong study. History, archeology, science, mathematics, writing, literature, geography, politics, economics, religion, ethics, and art all illuminate the histori-

---

*Leonardo's name, "Leonardo da Vinci," means Leonardo from Vinci. The "da" is not capitalized in this context, but, as a formal name of a curriculum, I have capitalized it. Hence, the "Da Vinci Curriculum" or "DVC." Leonardo's name is variously spelled "Lionardo" (according to his grandfather's birth record) or "Lyonardo" (used more by his French patrons). His full name, in English, is "Leonardo di Ser Piero da Vinci," reflecting his father, Ser Piero. "Ser" is roughly equivalent to our "Sir."

Table 2.1. Da Vinci Curriculum Overview

Grade Level	DV Curriculum and Historical Dates
Grade 7	Creation (Origin of Universe–10,000 BCE)
Grade 8	Into Civilization (10,000 BCE–200 CE)
Grade 9	The Age of Faith (200 CE–1400 CE)
Grade 10	Encounter and Change (1400–1700)
Grade 11	Rise of Liberalism, Industrialism, and Globalism (1700–1900)
Grade 12	Twentieth and Twenty-First Century— The American Century, The Ascent of Asia and Revolt in the Middle East, Imagining the Future

cal study. There are other historically organized curricula. For example, the Saint John's College curriculum is historically oriented around classic texts.

The DVC is the core curriculum. Students have other needs (for example, to create service learning projects). See chapter 11 for brief descriptions of Da Vinci satellite programs.

The Common Core contains the standards that undergird the curriculum. History is the organizer that gives purpose to those standards. One might visualize the historical study of several cultures as a strip of Velcro that the students sew into their neurons over the six-year study. That Velcro will serve as an intellectual infrastructure upon which all future learning will stick. And stickiness is what teachers are after—educators want learning to be memorable. Learning that is meaningful is memorable. And ultimately, teachers want students' knowledge to add meaning, efficacy, capacity, and richness to their lives.

Many, perhaps a majority, of secondary students do not know why they are studying what they are studying, why it is relevant to their lives, or why it has a larger importance than their own lives. It is no surprise that states have to coerce students to learn. Too many students are passive and resistant because they do not believe that their schoolwork is important. Many do not see their intellectual work as being part of the larger human story. They do not see their understanding of the world as having arisen over time, passed on and enriched with each mind, each culture, and each historical period that has shaped human understanding.

They do not view themselves as active carriers of humanities' intellectual heritage. They do not see themselves as striving for insight or truth. They do not see themselves as preparing for citizenship. They do not feel that their work is relevant beyond the narrow purpose of preparing them for admission to college or the work force, and being able to support them in a satisfying lifestyle. They do not see their work as being part of a larger meaning-conferring context. Yet meaning cannot be imposed by coercion (Pink 2009). It is intrinsically intrinsic.

John Dewey: Our Responsibility as Educators

In contrast, in *A Common Faith* (1934), John Dewey wrote of the larger role that we each play in the human drama:

> The things in civilization we most prize are not of ourselves. They exist by the grace of the doings and sufferings of the continuous human community in which we are a link. Ours is the responsibility of conserving, transmitting, rectifying and expanding the heritage of values we have received that those who come after us may receive it more solid and secure, more widely accessible and more generously shared than when we received it.

Many students do not see themselves as being part of a larger human community, a grander cultural heritage. For many, school is not inherently satisfying. But it should be. It can be. If our democracy, our economic system, and the ecosystems upon which we depend are to flourish, *schools must be*.

Nel Noddings (2008) said it this way:

> The point is to appreciate the topics that matter in real life and encourage thinking in each area. This is not accomplished by first teaching everyone algebra—thus developing mental muscle—and *then* applying that muscle to everyday matters. (emphasis in original)

Yet the conventional secondary school curriculum operates in precisely this manner. Global marketing executive Elisa Moses (quoted by Intrator in Seymour 2004) is even more dire: "Do not bore this generation or it will abandon you." Daniel Pink (2009) and Alfie Kohn (1993) write about the importance of intrinsic motivation and the pitfalls of incentives. Grant Wiggins says that schools are "needlessly boring" and that we do not treat our student with "intellectual respect."

Conversation across the Disciplines

In the conventional curriculum, the Spanish teacher cannot ask students to compare the language that they are learning in algebra with the language they are learning in Spanish. Algebra is reduced to a series of sequential skills, devoid of the historical context—the heritage—in which human beings developed mathematical skills and thinking. At best, the history is reduced to textbook sidebars that mention things like the development of algebra in Babylon and the Arab world. Human issues like history and diversity are given only lip service rather than central emphasis.

Application has become more common in math texts and in math classrooms, but applications still sit as islands of meaning surrounded by a sea of decontextualized, disarticulated content. The disciplines appear to the student as isolated patches of tundra left behind on high mountain peaks after the last glaciation. The curriculum discourages them from seeing the connecting terrain.

Veronica Boix Mansilla and Howard Gardner (2008) recognized this when they explained, "Subject-matter learning may temporarily increase students' information base, but it leaves them unprepared to shed light on issues that are even slightly novel. A different kind of instruction is in order, one that seeks to discipline the mind." Mansilla and Gardner distinguish between the *conclusions* of each discipline ("subject matter") from disciplinary *thinking*.

Contemporary problems—the Middle East conflict, global warming and solar dimming, conflict over oil and water, global economic trouble, for example—are vexing, inherently interdisciplinary, life-and-death issues. Technology, culture, religion, politics, history, human greed, and hubris are inseparable. We would be foolish to overlook the past in helping us understand the present and create our future. We limit our understanding if we confine our inquiry to narrow disciplinary boundaries. Conventional secondary curriculum leaves this to chance. Mansilla and Gardner (2008) note that "cross-disciplinary transfer proves elusive."

The Da Vinci Curriculum (DVC) organizes the curriculum differently and makes different assumptions about the purpose of human learning and the centrality of meaning to human learning. This curriculum asks all students to achieve a broadly defined cultural literacy and expects nothing less of students than that they engage deeply in inquiry driven by essential questions. The DVC asks students to actively apply the wisdom of humanities' past to the urgent environmental, international, and social problems of the present and foreseeable future. The DVC fosters broad abilities such as Gardner's "disciplined," "synthesizing," "creating," and "respectful" and "ethical" minds. Notice that in describing the "five minds" that we will need to be successful as a species, Howard Gardner does not mention "content packed mind."

The Da Vinci Curriculum asks students to recognize that "the things in civilization we most prize are not of ourselves." The DVC is designed to reflect the "continuous human community in which we are a link." Through its related instructional process, the DVC asks students to "conserve, transmit, rectify and expand the heritage of values" that they have inherited so that those who come after them "may receive it more solid and secure, more widely accessible and more generously shared" than when they received it.

The DVC ensures that a wide range of students will achieve the Common Core. It is a memorable curriculum that fosters a hunger to learn. A curriculum that builds upon our greatest resource—intrinsic motivation—to create the kind of minds that Howard Gardner predicts we will need to flourish as a nation and as a species.

Our Heritage

Dewey refers to the "heritage of values" that we have received. These values include freedom, liberty, democracy, the right to elect representatives, the right to pursue happiness, and free speech. Our forefathers secured many of our fundamental rights in the first ten amendments to the Constitution. These amendments form the "Bill of Rights." The Bill of Rights is part of our heritage. Today, thousands of people in the Arab world are fighting for these basic human freedoms. Dewey asked us to do four things with our precious heritage.

As part of a continuous human community, he asks us to *conserve* our values. To do so, we, as educators, must review and understand our intellectual heritage. Regardless of our licensure specialty, as part of the human community, as citizens, and as teachers, we are obliged to educate ourselves broadly (i.e., liberally).

Second, he asks us to *transmit* these values to our students. Dewey would, I am certain, want us to do so in an engaging fashion, "constructivisticly." Third, he asks us to *rectify* our heritage. The founding fathers wrote our founding documents over two hundred years ago when the former British Colonies had a largely rural population of 2.5 million people concentrated on the East Coast. Today our population is over 300 million and considerably more diverse, complex, and technically equipped. Our founders could not imagine the Internet, interstate highways, air travel, space exploration, or global threats to the economy and environment. Our heritage of values may need to be rectified given this and all of the other changes that have occurred in our country and the world.

Similarly, Dewey tasked us with *expanding* our heritage of values. Students might do so by arguing Supreme Court cases, debating election issues, adding pages to Wikipedia, or creating artistic representations that capture our heritage in their mind's eye. They might consider, for example, a core freedom such as the protection against unreasonable search and seizure in our electronic world today. These four activities invite our students to be an active part of the human community rather than passive recipients of culture—to create as well as absorb culture.

Curriculum Decisions in Secondary Schools

Mankind is by no means agreed about the things to be taught, whether we look to virtue or the best life. Neither is it clear whether education is more concerned with intellectual or with moral virtue. The existing practice is perplexing; no one knows on what principle we should proceed—should the useful in life, or should virtue, or should the highest knowledge be the aim of our training; all three opinions have been entertained. (Aristotle, *Politics*, Greece, Fourth Century, BC)

Great thinkers since the time of Aristotle have been perplexed by curriculum. Should we teach virtue and good living, intellectual stimulus and highest knowledge (what today we call a "liberal education"), or practicality? The disagreement continues, yet in the last decade, the weight given to international math comparisons; national and state standards; and reading, writing, math (and, recently, science) skill and knowledge testing indicate that the "useful in life" has predominated American thinking. But consider Ralph.

Ralph was a corner office, Madison Avenue advertising executive—he was a "Mad Man." Late in his career, he lost his enthusiasm for advertising. His art background came to the fore and he found himself influenced by Joseph Campbell and Robert Coles's call for stories. Stories. Narratives. What could be more central to the human experience? Ralph became a storyteller. Over time, he developed personas—Gowen the Green Night, a Norse Warrior, an Egyptian funerary priest.

Ralph opened a study of ancient Greece with the *Odyssey*. It was late fall in the school's first year. Ralph stood at a podium relating the story of Homer's wily Odysseus. He spoke for ten days, several hours each day. Each night, students read from Homer what they had heard that day. At the end of the two weeks, every student spontaneously stood and applauded the storyteller who bowed graciously, shock of gray hair falling over his face. What curricular questions does Ralph's *Odyssey* reading bring to mind?

Why might a teacher choose to have her students read Homer's *Odyssey*? Is it part of the "heritage of values" that Dewey wrote about? Does it meet the

Common Core's criteria of being a "work of exceptional craft and thought" offering "profound insights into the human condition" and able to "serve as a model for students' thinking and writing"? What educational purpose (in Aristotle's view: moral lessons, practicality, or intellectual stimulation?) will students accomplish by reading this text? Should the Greek *Odyssey* be balanced with other cultures' epic tales such as the Indian Mahabharata or the ancient Sumerian tale of Gilgamesh? How broad is the "heritage of values" that Dewey refers to—American? Western? Human? The *Odyssey* also brings instructional questions to mind.

Should *all* students read the Odyssey? If read by all, how will the epic be made accessible to a wide range of students? If read in a literature class, how much historical context should the teacher provide? Should the epic be read in its entirety? Is it enough to get the gist of the story through an anthologized excerpt? How does the teacher choose which translation to read—a poetic form or prose? Should the story initially be presented as a written work, given that it was originally a story heard from oral storytellers? Can an ancient tale from another land be made relevant to contemporary American students? And most importantly, how can the teacher build a meaningful intellectual context within which students will engage their minds in reading the *Odyssey*?

The Common Core offers more guidance on the range, content, and purpose of student readings:

> Along with high-quality contemporary works, these texts should be chosen from among seminal U.S. documents, the classics of American literature, and the timeless dramas of Shakespeare. Through wide and deep reading of literature and literary nonfiction of steadily increasing sophistication, students gain a reservoir of literary and cultural knowledge, references, and images; the ability to evaluate intricate arguments; and the capacity to surmount the challenges posed by complex texts.

Teachers make difficult curricular decisions dozens of times each week. These decisions are at the heart of the teaching profession. How would a "Da Vinci teacher" approach these questions? What ideas guide the Da Vinci teacher's decisions?

Cultural Literacy

There are several contemporary ideas that guide us with these choices—with our own odyssey as educators. E. D. Hirsch's 1987 call for "cultural literacy" (*Cultural Literacy: What Every American Needs to Know*) helps us separate the wheat from the curricular chaff. Homer, Hirsch might say, is nutritious wheat because his writing has endured for many centuries, explores universal themes, and is fundamental to Western thought. In Hirsch's thinking, a person cannot claim to be educated in Western literature if he misses a reference to Helen, whose beauty was such that it could "launch a thousand ships."

Hirsch argues that such missed references are impediments to reading. He argues that rich intellectual content—texts like the *Odyssey*—are essential to learning; and that broad skills like critical thinking need something substantive—like good literature—to think about.

Critics call for a broader definition of cultural literacy, one more inclusive of women and minorities—Eastern, African, and Meso-American thought, for example—an argument for the Mahabharata or Gilgamesh. The Common Core includes such a list of "texts illustrating the complexity, quality, and range of student reading 6–12." The *Odyssey* is given as an exemplar of a ninth to tenth grade complex literary text. The list is intended as text exemplars. It is too early to tell if it will become the new school canon.

Differentiated Instruction

Few would argue today that a text like the *Odyssey* should not be made available to all students. *How* is another question. Tomlinson's (1999) concept of Differentiated Instruction provides us with strategies that help us make Odysseus's travels accessible to all students.

In order to reach *all* students in the Da Vinci classroom, a Da Vinci teacher chose to bring in Ralph, who, by retelling the *Odyssey,* provided *all students* with an entrée into the challenging poetic reading. Her reasoning was that humans have heard stories around campfires for millennia, yet reading is a relatively newly acquired skill. (The first mass-produced book was printed in Europe in 1454.) Why not give less-skilled students unabridged CDs of the *Odyssey* and require them to follow the text while listening?

The Common Core makes it clear: reading complex text is important for all students and all disciplines must support the process whereby students are progressively asked to read more complex material. Every student should read this text and be able to participate in a seminar about the *Odyssey* and other seminar works. All students should hold their heads up high while being stretched intellectually. Like all good teachers, Da Vinci teachers are shameless when it comes to engaging all students in rewarding intellectual content, building meaningful context, and developing intellectual skills.

Multiple Intelligences

Howard Gardner's work on multiple intelligences in *Frames of Mind: the Theory of Multiple Intelligences* (1983) provides educators with a theory of intelligence that guides them as they differentiate instruction. Gardner views intelligence as being complex and multifaceted. The teacher may have to differentiate instruction to reach a less capable reader, but that student may excel at graphic imagery, music, or interpersonal communication. Each person has something to offer. Special educators are expert at differentiating curriculum and appreciating each student's gifts. The diverse, unpredictable, and unforeseeable problems facing humanity argue for fostering diverse intelligence.

Understanding by Design (UbD)

Wiggins and McTighe (2005) highlight the ideas of "Understanding by Design," backward design, and essential questions. The point, they might say, is not to "cover" Homer but to uncover his wisdom. There is some reason why Homer captures the Western mind—some reason why it is a part of our "heritage of values." There is something enduring about two countries warring for years over something relatively trivial, like Paris's love for Helen.

There is something universal about traveling in the unknown for years only to find one's self returning home. This has meaning today for adolescents who might be called to fight in a foreign war. Wiggins and McTighe would have us identify these essential questions, then plan our lesson accordingly. In their world, "What are we doing in class today?" is the result of a teacher's thoughtful curriculum process.

The Missing Element

Even when driven by essential questions, drawn from a demonstrably important canon and differentiated to reach every student, the conventional secondary school curriculum lacks coherence, context, and interdisciplinary linkages. The intellectual heritage is fragmented, the values unclear, and the job of the student passive and uncertain.

How does one engage in "conserving, transmitting, rectifying and expanding the heritage of values we have received that those who come after us may receive it more solid and secure" when we are examining only disarticulated parts of the whole? Our students have the right to study an integrated rather than a disintegrated curriculum—to understand the inseparability of human knowledge. This text documents one coherent and integrated curriculum. There are other ways to create curriculum that integrate knowledge in a meaningful way.

UbD, DI ("Differentiated Instruction") and Meaningful Curriculum are parts of a coherent whole. Tomlinson and McTighe demonstrate the relationship between UbD and DI (2006). Without a curriculum such as the

Da Vinci Curriculum, the questions—regardless of how essential they might seem to be for individual teachers—lack the authority of the flow of history; of a larger and more enduring meaning—of Dewey's "heritage of values." The DVC provides a natural organization to the curriculum, a ready springboard for understanding and differentiation. In the DVC, as in UbD and DI, coverage is trumped by understanding. Interdisciplinary connections are valued as are connections to the present day.

Academic Disciplines in the DVC

The work of a science teacher is not just to teach the specifics of science, but it is to teach about the scientific enterprise and how scientific ideas have developed over time in different cultural-historical settings. To be well-educated science students, students must understand how science developed and how it works. They have to understand science's fundamental assumptions and become deeply familiar with scientists who shaped scientific thinking into what it is today. They have to learn how science differs from nonscience. To understand the scientific enterprise, they have to learn "disciplinary thinking" (Mansilla and Gardner 2008).

For example, in *Interdisciplinary Curriculum: Challenges to Implementation* (Wineburg and Grossman 2000), Kathleen Roth describes an exercise in which fifth grade students are told that scientists develop explanations whereas historians develop interpretations. Directing students to primary sources, the Da Vinci teacher might ask if this is true and might also ask what the difference is between an explanation and an interpretation.

Do scientists ever interpret and do historians ever explain? How is it that the *Oxford English Dictionary* uses the word "explain" so often in its definitions of the word "interpret"? Interpretation seems to imply making or bringing out meaning—it implies an intellectual addition to the original idea. However, the word "explain" comes from the concept of flattening, smoothing out (like a wood plane)—it implies "to make plain or intelligible; to clear of obscurity." To interpret seems to add meaning, whereas to explain seems to remove that which clouds understanding.

Is the work of a historian to add interpretations and the work of scientists to reduce to simplest meanings? The Da Vinci class might then look for these generalizations in a variety of scientific claims and historical interpretations. In doing so, the students are thinking about history and science as human endeavors. They are creating meta-understanding. In pursuing these larger insights, content is acquired.

The Importance of Stories in the DVC

The sciences developed over time, influenced by people from different cultures in different places. Time, place, culture, natural events, and people are naturally held together by narrative—that is, stories. Stories have been the glue that has made learning memorable and meaningful throughout thousands of years of human prehistory. Stories do more than reveal the *result* of an inquiry such as evolutionary theory in biology or the equation that relates force, mass, and acceleration in physics.

Stories tell us about human ambition, imagination, competition, uncertainty, failure, resiliency, and pride. Stories illustrate how human thinking about science has changed over time and how science itself has changed. In historical stories, there are causal links, evolutionary developments, progress, and regression. The narrative makes science accessible to *every* student because every student can identify with the human attributes that underlie the stories that make up the scientific enterprise.

In the Da Vinci Curriculum, the stories that make up different cultures' worldviews became the Velcro upon which knowledge and skills naturally adhere for the student's life. Historical time became the natural binder for the curriculum. This natural historical organization makes learning memorable. The curriculum is preparatory in that it prepares a scaffold for the student's future learning.

Thinking in the DVC

Natural context does not provide us with all that we need. History can provide the backbone, but each rib remained disconnected from the next. The disciplines have ways of thinking in common. To a greater or lesser degree, all disciplines analyze large concepts into components, synthesize generalizations from data, and create new ways of viewing the world. Analysis, synthesis, and creative thinking are found in all fields although some stress one way of thinking more than the others (see criticalthinking.org).

Science is more inductive, creating hypotheses from data, whereas mathematics is more deductive, deriving conclusions from assumptions. Art is more creative, yet art historians analyze art as well. If history is the backbone, then thinking—analysis and synthesis—is the common sinew that connects the ribs. Thinking and other skills like communication and ethics transcend the disciplines. Some of these universal skills (especially the interpretation of complex text) are emphasized in the Common Core.

The Da Vinci teacher views the world as inherently interdisciplinary. The academic disciplines are human constructs—attempts to simplify and understand the world—traditions that had developed over time.

The synthesizing mind (as described by Howard Garner) demands mental dexterity as well as sheer analytical power. As we ascend the exponential growth curve for our species, problems are likely to become more complex and global, interactions more frequent, the need for communication across cultures more necessary. The global war on terror and global warming have borne this out. The struggle for food, fuel, and water will only become more challenging. This calls for new curriculum.

A meaningful and coherent curriculum is necessary if Hirsch's cultural literacy, Tomlinson's differentiated instruction, and Wiggins and McTighe's understanding by design are going to be as powerful as they could be. Dewey's identification of a "heritage of values" demands that the story of the universe and humankind be told in a coherent way. Without rich, curricular context, these educational ideas remain adrift in a sea of random curriculum.

The Table 2.2 shows an overview of one macro (multi-disciplinary) unit of the Da Vinci Curriculum. The curriculum engages students over six

Table 2.2. A Single Macro Unit of the Eleventh Grade Da Vinci Curriculum. Unit 1—North America: From Colonies to Nation (1700–1850)

Discipline	Content
Historical Texts	Early colonial documents, treaties with Native Americans, documents from French-Indian war, Declaration of Independence (concentration on U.S. history)
Science (with DV Science Teacher)	Russian Scientist Mendeleev's work on periodicity of elements initiates a course in chemistry, also gunpowder's impact on the frontier, photography
Math History	Amerindians and number (chapter 2 of McLeish), quipu and calendar. From Galileo, Brahe, Kepler, Napier, Descartes, and Newton/Leibniz to mathematics as abstraction—Gauss, non-Euclidean geometry, and the development of mathematical societies.
Writing	Expository and creative essays on Huck Finn, the American Revolution
Literature	The *Adventures of Huckleberry Finn*, Paul Revere's ride, excerpts from pioneer women.
Geography	Geopolitical divisions of Colonial N. America, examination of the balance of power between France, England, and Spain in North America
Religion and Ethics	Protestantism, Anglicanism, and the diverse spirituality of Native American nations; Manifest Destiny and colonialism
Art	Art of the new world, functional art of the new world, paintings by John Copley

years from prehistorical through historical time. A "Da Vinci Humanities Teacher" and a "Da Vinci Science Teacher" work hand-in-hand to create curriculum, deliver instruction, and assess student understanding.

A Sample Multidisciplinary DVC Unit

Eight disciplines conspire to create a window into each period, culture, and place. The underlying belief is that any one point of view would be inadequate to reach a full and satisfying understanding. Thinking differs in each discipline. "Cross-disciplinary transfer proves elusive" (Mansilla and Gardner 2008), therefore students need to be taught to think disciplinarily in several disciplines and consciously (metacognitively) apply different ways of thinking to common issues. In Mansilla and Gardner's words, teachers need to "invite their students to think about important problems in multiple ways—a mental agility that characterizes the disciplined mind."

Events, or their artifacts, are used as entrées into new ways of thinking. For example, in the Da Vinci Curriculum, Mendeleev's creation of the periodic table—his perceiving the very existence of periodicity in the known elements—spawns a study of chemistry.

Eleventh grade Da Vinci Chemistry has a greater than usual emphasis on gunpowder (a crucial technology in the clash between native people and European-derived people at the frontier) and photography (that allowed the Civil War to be documented in a way that wars had not been previously) as well as the usual cover-to-cover high school chemistry lessons. Da Vinci Science Teachers stress Mendeleev's insight into the elements through his vision of periodicity. Periodicity is the foundation for our contemporary understanding of electronegativity, electron configurations, and properties of the elements. Mendeleev's view of the elements can be related back to simpler views of the elements in Aristotle's time.

This raises questions about the humans striving to comprehend what is elemental. This search leads us to charmed quarks, anti-matter, and other strange modern concepts. It leads us to ask about the quest for one unified force or Theory of Everything. In the world of Da Vinci, the study of chemistry comes from a natural and informative historical context and leads us to new thinking.

This style of thinking about history provides Da Vinci students with intellectual tools conventional students achieve by chance, if at all. In all probability, the neural architecture is different for someone who is practiced in triangulating in on a subject from many disciplines compared to someone who is not. It stands to reason that neural pathways are more complex and that memory is accessible through a stronger web in someone whose brain is used to thinking interdisciplinarily.

Historical context provides students with constant ways to elaborate their learning. Similarly, cross-cultural thinking builds empathy and understanding; crucial attributes in our increasingly diverse, densely populated, and globally communicative world. A "flat" world (flattened by technology) needs different skills from a round one (Friedman 2007). Building context is a form of elaboration, and elaboration makes learning memorable.

Mansilla and Gardner (2008) state that "quality pre-collegiate education should ensure that students become deeply acquainted with a discipline's fundamental perspectives on the world by developing four key capacities." They describe these capacities as

- understanding the purpose of disciplinary expertise (how the disciplines impact on today's life),
- an essential knowledge base (a conceptual toolkit that can be used in novel situations),
- inquiry methods (methods used to vet claims made within a discipline), and
- discipline-specific forms of communication.

The Da Vinci Curriculum is a powerful tool for creating these disciplinary capacities.

In the Da Vinci Curriculum, curriculum is inseparable from instructional practices and assessment. Students learn by creating knowledge. They are taught to make inferences inductively, from the bottom up (Clarke 1990). They identify rich information sources, such as tables, graphs, poems, paintings, novels, recordings, primary source historical records and experiments, and use "inductive towers" (Clarke 1990). Then they mine the data source, transform the data (by grouping, noting irregularities, and comparing data), and draw generalizations. See chapter 3.

They become powerful learners by becoming adept at asking what is important to know and what information sources are likely to be intellectually rich. *They* create the essential questions that drive their study. The quality of their questions—their insights—is a key focus of assessment. Some students make inferences conservatively linking their conclusions tightly to their database. Others will make bold assertions that are less closely linked to the data. The teacher's assessment task is to reflect upon the student's

Differentiated Instruction

Assumes that all students will reach
the same enduring understandings
while providing different
instructional experiences for different
students depending upon needs.

The Da Vinci Curriculum

Provides context, and coherence;
identifies times, places and cultures
that stimulate enduring understanding
by encouraging students to create
questions that explicitly connect
lessons learned from history to
present-day issues.

**The
Common
Core**

Insures that all students meet key
standards regardless of the state,
district, school, or teacher

Understanding by Design

Focuses the student on essential
questions, deep understanding,
transfer of knowledge into authentic
situations, and authentic assessment
of understanding

Figure 2.1. Visualizing UbD, DI, DVC, and the CCSS

thinking—to help students understand how their minds works. This is detailed in chapters 3, 7, and 8.

How do Understanding by Design, Differentiated Instruction, and a powerful curriculum such as the Da Vinci Curriculum interrelate and support the Common Core State Standards? Figure 2.1 shows the relationship between UbD, DI, the DVC, and the Common Core.

At the core is the Common Core. Yes, standards, properly differentiated to facilitate understanding by design, are adrift without a meaningful curriculum like the DVC. When all is said and done, history endures.

Chapter 2 Summary

The Da Vinci Core Curriculum in Light of Contemporary Educational Theory

- The Da Vinci Curriculum is historically oriented and based on the multi-disciplinary thinking of Leonardo da Vinci and his passion for observation.
- As Dewey urges us to do, the Da Vinci Curriculum conserves, transmits, rectifies, and expands our "heritage of values."
- Historical context is crucial to today's learners.
- A powerful core curriculum is what is missing when Understanding by Design (UbD) and differentiation are in place.
- Science and the humanities must be united in to one coherent core study.

~

CHAPTER THREE

The Da Vinci Core Curriculum—Student, Teacher, and the Common Core

The more intelligent the question you ask of Mother Nature, the more intelligent will be her reply.

—Sir Charles Sherrington, Nobel Prize winner who discovered the function of the neuron (1932)

This chapter demonstrates how the Da Vinci Curriculum engages students in high-order skills, communication, and artistic creation as recommended by the Common Core Standards and inspired educators.

The Student's Role in Da Vinci Instruction—Questions

In the Da Vinci Curriculum, essential questions *arise from* the curriculum rather than being viewed as *drivers* for the curriculum. These intelligent questions can then be pursued by looking more deeply into the information sources or can result in creative outcomes. Consider Figure 3.1 (modified from Clarke 1990)

Figure 3.1 represents a Tower of Inquiry or what John Clarke calls an "Inductive Tower" (Clarke 1990). "Inductive" because this exercise asks students to make inferences inductively, that is, by using facts to create generalizations. At the base of the tower (level #1) are the Common Core and other Standards. The Common Core guides teachers in the areas of English language arts (including ELA in social studies and science) and in math.

Figure 3.1. From Standards to Artistic Representation—Towers of Induction. *Note:* **Clarke represents levels 3–5 and various refinements of these levels.**

Other state and national standards capture the skills, knowledge, and dispositions in other disciplines not yet detailed in the Common Core.

Standards, on their own, do not give the teacher, team, school, or district what they need to create daily lessons and units. The standards are analogous to the skeleton—essential, but lacking flesh. Between the standards and daily practice is the curriculum. In this illustration, the Da Vinci Curriculum fleshes out the standards with cross-disciplinary units, texts and other references, and assessments. This is level #2.

Any particular lesson from the curriculum will highlight certain cultural or scientific artifacts from which Wiggins and McTighe's (1998) "essential questions" and "enduring understandings" are likely to arise. These are artifacts of Dewey's "heritage of values." At this stage, culture is conserved and transmitted. The standards identify the skills and information, whereas the teacher identifies (or helps the student identify) the questions and meaning.

In the world of the Da Vinci Curriculum, these artifacts will be primary sources, whenever possible. In the world of the Common Core, these will be increasingly complex texts with an increasing reliance on informational rather than fictional texts from seventh grade to senior year. The Da Vinci Curriculum encourages a wide range of two- and three-dimensional artifacts as well as text.

Level #3 represents facts drawn from the curriculum's primary sources. The facts may be data from an experiment, allusions or metaphors from a poem, events from an historical era, or observations from an artifact. As with professional scientists, art historians, archeologists, or others, different students will emphasize different facts—they will see different facts to be of different importance.

The next level (#4) asks students to transform or organize the facts. Can they be grouped meaningfully? Are there contrasting groups or identifiable patterns?

Level #5 invites students to consider using the facts that they have organized to create conclusions, hypotheses, value statements, questions, or generalizations. Students ask, "What do the facts tell us?"

The very top of the tower asks students to create something artistic that represents their conclusions. In doing so, they are "expanding the heritage of values" that they have inherited. They are creating something fresh from their work. This is a form of authentic assessment. Beginning with the standards, students have engaged in an inferential process that has led them to represent their newly found understanding. Yet in reality, the human mind can operate in two distinct ways.

The mind can gather facts and draw conclusions. We call this induction or inductive thinking. An example is Charles Darwin sailing for five years on the *Beagle* gathering specimens and then decades later presenting his conclusion that species evolve by means of natural selection.

In contrast, when scientists today test Darwin's theory of evolution by looking for evidence of natural selection, they are engaged in a deductive process. They are asking if other parts of the fact base support Darwin's theory.

In the Da Vinci Curriculum, the emphasis is on inferring generalizations from a base of facts, often artifacts, and primary sources that are systematically examined. Essential questions and enduring understandings result from the inductive exercise carried out by students rather than deducing answers from the teacher's essential question, as UbD encourages. The Da Vinci Curriculum provides another approach to instruction, one that is inherently differentiated since different people or groups will emphasize different aspects of the fact base, draw different conclusions, ask different questions, and create different representations of their understanding. Insight is the ultimate goal. Every learner—whether a strong or weak reader, whether gifted or challenged, regardless of intelligence profile or wealth—is capable of personally meaningful insight.

For example, in the seventh grade year, after examining the origin and evolution of life, Da Vinci students study the evolution of the human species. They begin with a series of high-quality casts of prehistoric African and European crania. Their first task is to determine what traits are worthy of observation and measurement. They often miss important traits like the angle at which the brain stem enters the skull through the foramen magnum. Experts interpret this as an indicator of upright posture. The teacher fills in the missing pieces once students have exhausted their resources.

They then systematically observe and measure the traits in their skulls. After doing so, the teacher takes out rolls of newsprint. Students must solve a two-dimensional puzzle. The teacher gives them one dimension, time. Students are told the age of each cranium. They have to propose relationships between the species based on their observations. In doing so, they are proposing generalities based on evidence. They are making inductive inferences. For details, see chapter 4.

In this seventh grade study, Louis Leakey—who asked who he was and where he came from—inspires students. Students are encouraged to ask their own essential questions and to consider Dr. Leakey's.

Aside from a shift from a fundamentally deductive process to an inductive one, the work of the student and of the teacher shifts. In a conventional model (didactic or direct instruction), it is the teacher's job to *impart* knowledge and skills ("subject matter learning"). In a UbD model, it is the teacher's job to *identify* key understandings and essential questions, to then consider evidence of mastery (assessment), and only then to create activities that will support learning. In a Da Vinci model, the faculty work together to identify intellectually rich historical moments from different cultures, subjects, and times, creating a continuous curriculum.

Teachers then create activities that will provide the student with artifacts and experiences from which he or she will induce questions, hypotheses, generalizations, and value statements. In the Da Vinci classroom, the student is routinely engaged in disciplinary *and* interdisciplinary thinking.

After arriving at a question or generalization as a community, the class then has several options. One option is to test their hypotheses, pursue the questions further, and delve more deeply into their insight. This means reentering the fact base. This may mean either revisiting the existing data or creating or locating more data. This process is essentially deductive since an idea is being tested (moving from the general to the specific). Working as scientists, students are then participating in a wheel of inference making, from inductive to deductive and back to inductive again. With the crania, for example, the class will read and compare expert opinion to their propositions. They might decide to pursue one thread such as the relationship between Neanderthals and *Homo sapiens*. They might ask how Cro-Magnon cave painters differed from contemporary humans.

Similarly, during the first Gulf War, when hearing storyteller Ralph tell of the travels of Odysseus, one student said, "General Schwarzkopf expressed the same hubris that Odysseus did when he said that God was on our side." Other students simultaneously exclaimed, "Da Vinci Moment!" They understood the value in applying what they were learning from literature and history to the present day. They understood that authentic history was contemporary, that understanding was quite different from recitation. They understood that it was their work to "rectify" and "expand the heritage of values" as well as to "conserve" and "transmit" them. They had become Da Vinci students.

Gailer Story #3

New Eyes

The following is a graduation speech given by Courtney Dozetos in June of 2007. Courtney describes her changing relationship to learning over her seven years from application to graduation. Courtney was an exchange student in Germany for one year.

Seven years ago, when my parents and I were trying to figure out what my seventh grade year would look like, I had heard from several sources that the Gailer School was a place for people who love to learn.

Not good. Very scary.

My mother was awfully excited about the place, claiming she had been wanting me to go to there since I was in Kindergarten, so we visited.

The place scared me half to death. These people liked learning. I was not like them, they were smart, confident, happy, mature, and respectful. I wasn't worthy. I loved the idea of acting and being treated with respect like an adult, and I loved everything Gailer was about; but I was not one of them. I wasn't as intelligent or as learned as these people.

But I had to make them think I was, because I had to go to Gailer. They were just having such a good time over there . . . I certainly didn't like to learn. Learning, as I understood it, was burying one's self under a heap of textbooks and memorizing their entire contents. No. I did not like learning. I did not like school. Learning was memorizing the multiplication tables and being able to do all of them in less than 30 seconds. I hated learning.

I would have to fake them out. Lead Gailer's admissions office into thinking I was like their students. Trick them into accepting me. And I totally fooled them! I got my acceptance letter a few weeks after applying. I knew how to act like one of those smarty pants Gailer geeks in my application . . . oh, yeah.

The first weeks at Gailer were like summer camp. I kept waiting for the learning to start. Then, a few days later, the whole school year had gone by, and I hadn't learned a thing. How was this place allowed to stay open when the kids weren't learning anything?

For three years I had myself absolutely convinced that I didn't belong at Gailer, that I was really just a stowaway . . . making a break for freedom on the fun ship. They hadn't kicked me out yet because my disguise was so good. I think it was in the tenth grade when I finally realized what they were all talking about when they referred to "loving to learn."

I figured out that learning was not a torture device, like I had thought. It had been concealed from me that learning was, in reality, everything I had ever loved and ever will love until the day I die. Learning was sitting at my desk for hours drawing floor plans when I was eight, and playing with the sound-editing program on my computer when I was ten. Learning was traveling to places I had never been. Learning was making movies, people watching, and singing, having conversations, taking pictures, and acting in plays.

With my newly enlightened perspective on learning, I became fearless. I became hungry for knowledge. I took my admiration and curiosity for human language as an opportunity to grow myself. Gailer, having known all along that I really was a true Gailer student, knew exactly what I was up to and encouraged me to keep it up. During my eleventh grade year I went to Germany to learn German, and I was given all the freedom and support I could have ever needed to take full advantage of my surroundings. Not only did I discover that learning is fun; I figured out that learning is vital to improving our world. . . .

My life's ambition is to never stop expanding my horizons. I do that through my love, my irretrievably boundless love of learning.

As Marcel Proust puts it: The real voyage of discovery consists not in seeking new landscapes, but in having new eyes.

Courtney captures the sentiments of many students. School is too often a fearful place and learning is thought of as torturous. Yet, as a species, we are wired to learn. Something so fundamental to our survival cannot have evolved to be unsatisfying.

An Introduction to the Da Vinci Teacher's Job

The conventional teacher has traditionally been a lecturer, a deliverer of information, and a transmitter of skills. Before movable type, this was an efficient way to transmit and preserve knowledge, much of which was contained in rare manuscripts. Many writers have questioned that method and encouraged teachers to be coaches rather than a "sage on the stage." In contrast, like Leonardo himself, the Da Vinci teacher (DVT) is a fellow learner.

The DVT *has* to be a fellow learner because there is no single "correct" interpretation of the transition from Middle Ages to Renaissance, the development of calculus, the development of our species, or the differences between Western and Eastern thought. Da Vinci students think big thoughts and ask big questions—intelligent questions that bring intelligent replies. They inquire. They use particular knowledge and skills to inform that thinking. The Common Core Standards, therefore, are a means to an end.

In fact, many of the really big questions—did the universe exist before the big bang, what is the long-term fate of the universe, where was I before birth and where will I be after death, how can matter have come alive in the first place, how did human consciousness come about, are there other sentient beings either on earth or on other planets, is there some higher force that created the universe—are probably not answerable in the sense of finding scientific agreement between people of different faiths. These questions are inherently interesting to most people. They motivate learners.

In public schools (less so in private) we duck these questions—"I am a biologist; I can't speak of life beyond the molecular, cellular, and ecological levels. I am not a philosopher or a clergyman." Perhaps we should be. Einstein said, "There are two ways to live: you can live as if nothing is a miracle; you can live as if everything is a miracle." Perhaps there are two ways to teach as well.

Teachers are called to do more than import and export knowledge. They are called to think and wonder, to be awed by the sheer majesty and awesomeness of the universe. This moves students and is the best defense against teacher burnout and student disinterest. Imagine, by contrast, teaching chapter 3 of Holt-Reinhardt *Modern Biology* for the third time that day after twenty-five years. That is chapter 3 for the seventy-fifth time. Compare that to the expectation that you are a Da Vinci teacher and you are expected to advance your investigation, your understanding of the breadth and depth of the study of life every year. And imagine if your colleagues are engaged in the same intellectual exercise. You might respond: you don't know my kids—they are not intellectuals and don't come from intellectual homes. Nonsense! If dad is a plumber, he is using his intellect every day to solve complex problems. If mom is a doctor, she is involved in complex diagnostics every day. These are intellectual exercises.

The Common Core

How does the Common Core fit into this? There are six aspects of the Common Core that inform our discussion. The Common Core

- intends to "include rigorous content and application of knowledge through high-order skills";
- focuses in the areas of mathematics, reading, writing, speaking, and listening;
- focuses on reading complex texts with increasing independence (versus with scaffolding) and proficiency in preparation for college, technical, and citizenship-related reading through question answering (as distinct from higher order interpretive skills);
- is based on the assumption that there may one day be modes and methods of information delivery that are as efficient and powerful as text, but for now there is no contest;
- contends that to grow, our students must read lots of "complex" texts—texts that offer them new language, new knowledge, and new modes of thought (Adams quoted in appendix A);
- "must be partnered with a content-rich curriculum and robust assessments" (www.corestandards.org/—see 'Download the Presentation' for a clear presentation of the Common Core).

Let's look at these five aspects of the Common Core.

1. Common Core: "Rigorous Content and Application of Knowledge through High-Order Skills"

Consider Figure 3.2, the International Center for Leadership in Education's (ICLE) Rigor/Relationship Model, modified to include artistry (modified from Daggett 2011).

The vertical access displays Bloom's Taxonomy of Knowledge (Bloom 1956) from the simplest awareness of knowledge at the bottom, to high-order skills like analysis, synthesis, and evaluation at the top. The horizontal access displays the ways in which knowledge can be applied from the simplest (in one discipline, in a contrived environment like a classroom) to the most complex (applying to real-world, unpredictable environments).

A typical driver's education classroom is an example of a contrived environment as contrasted with the on-the-road aspect of driver's education. The young driver soon discovers that the real world is messy and unpredictable. According to Daggett and NcNulty, the Holy Grail is section "D,"

Knowledge Taxonomy		Knowledge in one discipline	Apply to discipline	Apply across disciplines	Apply to real-world predictable situations	Apply to real-world unpredictable situations	Ability to imagine and create novel situations
Design and Creation							**E** Artistry
Evaluation / Synthesis / Analysis / Adaptation	**C** Assimilation			**D** Adaptation			
Comprehension (and Empathy?) / Knowledge Awareness	**A** Adaptation			**B** Application			
Application Model		Knowledge in one discipline	Apply to discipline	Apply across disciplines	Apply to real-world predictable situations	Apply to real-world unpredictable situations	Ability to imagine and create novel situations

Figure 3.2. Rigor/Relevance/Artistry Model (modified from Daggett)

which they call "Adaptation." We teach students to drive not so that they can do well on driving exams, but so that they can drive safely on real roads in unpredictable situations. So much schooling ends with quadrant "A," knowledge acquisition. And learning out-of-context knowledge is inherently difficult.

By contrast, consider the Common Core goal of "application of knowledge through high-order skills." This is section D, and this is what the Da Vinci Curriculum is all about.

An Example—Hiroshima Models

Having completed an in-depth study of President Truman's decision to drop an atomic bomb on Hiroshima, twelfth grade Da Vinci students were invited to donate their carefully constructed models of Hiroshima to the Hiroshima Memorial Museum. They were faced with the real world and unpredictable problems of securing funding for their trip, making travel arrangements, travel per se, acting as diplomats while traveling, and explaining their models. Although they began by *reading* history, they were now faced with *being* diplomats. They had moved from A to D on the ICLE model.

Their project included inviting to their classroom a witness to the events of August 6, 1945. They presented their models—one of Hiroshima before the bombing, one immediately after, and a contemporary one—to Kashua Campbell, their Japanese visitor. They explained what they had read about the physics, politics, and ethics of the atomic bomb. They then heard Kashua tell her story. Kashua wept as she pointed to her uncle's home and her school on the students' models. Considering Bloom's Taxonomy of Knowledge, these students had not only amassed knowledge and achieved comprehension across several disciplines, they had analyzed their knowledge and synthesized their knowledge into ethical and political critiques. Their week in Hiroshima was a meaningful synthesis.

Artistry

Daniel Pink (*A Whole New Mind*, 2006), Yong Zhao (*Catching Up or Leading the Way*, 2009) and Ray McNulty (personal communication, 2009) argue that there should be a higher goal, something beyond adaptation. They would argue that creativity is the Holy Grail. Building on the ICLE schematic, creativity fits into their model as shown in Figure 3.2. "Design and creation" extend the knowledge taxonomy to include creating knowledge or art. The "ability to imagine and create novel situations" extends application into the creative realm. "Artistry" is the result.

Here, as a *creative* synthesis, students are challenged to imagine and create novel situations in which they are free to design and create characters, settings, and ideas based on their intellectual synthesis. For example, students might be asked to create two opposing American presidential campaign advertisements expressing their view of the world in 1952 had Truman decided not to drop the atomic bomb on Hiroshima and Nagasaki. Students might be asked to write an accompanying paper explaining how the single decision in 1945 created the world as seen through their two presidential campaign advertisements.

Daniel Pink would argue that assignments such as this stimulate "R-directed" (right-brain-directed) thinking skills such as aesthetic, contextual, metaphoric, and synthetic functions that foster skills that cannot easily be outsourced such as design, narrative, symphony (the ability to see the big picture), empathy, play, and meaning (Pink 2006). As quoted by Yong Zhao, "Human creativity is the ultimate source of economic resource, the ability to come up with new ideas and better ways of doing things is ultimately what raises productivity and thus living standards" (economist Richard Florida 2002).

At the top of an inductive tower, Da Vinci students create artistic representations of questions, hypotheses, generalizations, or value statements. This is not an inference-making process; it is a creative process. However, this artistic representation can be used to assess the degree to which the student has effectively interacted with and understood the historical events in question. This artistic representation can be used to assess a student's understanding as well as creative expression.

As Dewey recommended, the teacher asks the student to *expand* our heritage by creating art. This design work is supported by Daniel Pink's advocacy for a more right-brained approach to learning in *A Whole New Mind* (2006) The Da Vinci teacher puts the learning as much as possible in the hands of his students. This is a fundamental shift in roles. It is a shift toward disciplinary, synthesizing, and creative thinking, three of Gardner's *Five Minds for the Future* (2006).

Elliot Eisner (www.arteducators.org/advocacy/10-lessons-the-arts-teach) lists ten lessons that the arts teach. For example, "The arts make vivid the fact that neither words in their literal form nor numbers exhaust what we can know. The limits of our language do not define the limits of our cognition." This is why Da Vinci teachers put the arts at the top of the tower; having exhausted logic and language in the lower four tiers of the tower, in the top tier symbolism and poetry take over. As Leonardo said, "Art is the queen of all sciences communicating knowledge to all generations of the world" (Atalay and Wamsley 2008, 215).

As Dewey suggested, through the Da Vinci instructional process, students are "conserving, transmitting, rectifying and expanding the heritage of values we have received." In doing so, they are involved in important work "that those who come after us may receive it more solid and secure, more widely accessible and more generously shared than when we received it." They are cultural agents rather than cultural consumers. They don't just receive (conserve and transmit) knowledge, they also "rectify" and "expand" our human heritage. They are part of something much larger. Something imbued with meaning. They are creating culture and knowledge. Their work is important. See chapter 4 for more on inductive learning. What are the other four principles of the Common Core?

2. Common Core: Focused on Mathematics, Reading, Writing, Speaking, and Listening

These skills are what we typically associate with the left hemisphere of the brain. Traditional school skills such as communication and mathematical reasoning remain fundamental to the twenty-first century (necessary, but not sufficient).

The Partnership for 21st Century Skills recognizes these core skills as does the European Union (EU) in their Parliament and Council's list of eight core "competences." Communication takes two forms in the EU core—communication in the mother tongue and communication in foreign languages. The

Common Core views content through the lens of communication. Scientist Francis Bacon said it this way: "Reading maketh a full man; conference a ready man; and writing an exact man." We want full, ready, and exact men and women. Communication is central to nurturing students to become so.

3. Common Core: Focus on Reading Complex Texts with Increasing Independence through Question Answering

This means that plot, setting, and characters in fiction, or the flow of premises and arguments in expository writing, must be understood before higher-order interpretation can proceed competently. We must know what we are talking about before we speak. The Common Core asks that readers become progressively more independent and able to read progressively more difficult material over the course of their schooling.

A teacher was frustrated when his students could not understand *Guns, Germs, and Steel* (Diamond 1997). He accused them of not studying. In fact, after many conversations with students and parents, it became clear that he was assigning material that his students simply did not have the skills to master. He took for granted his students ability to work with complex arguments presented in texts.

4. Based on the Assumption That Text Is More Efficient Than Other Modes of Delivery

Perhaps this is one of the more controversial Common Core Claims. Some will argue that digital technologies are "as efficient and powerful as text," are on the rise, and that digital technologies are crucial if educators are to speak the language of today's young people, to capture their imagination, and to motivate them to learn. Like so many either-or issues in education, the prudent answer is probably that contemporary literacy must embrace text *and* the digital world.

5. Common Core: Complex Texts That Offer New Language, Knowledge, and Modes of Thought

Again, the emphasis here is on increasingly complex texts—a "staircase" of increasing complexity. The Common Core, although recognizing other media, makes it clear that text is central.

One highly respected Business Roundtable leader said, "Do you know where I learned to be a businesswoman? In literary criticism classes—that's where I learned to think." This leader was endorsing a liberal arts education for every student, regardless of whether they are immediately headed for a career or have further schooling before doing so. She was anticipating the Common Core's call for complex text interpretation.

The Da Vinci Curriculum supports the Common Core, but it asks two additional things of its teachers. The DVC asks teachers to take all those "works of exceptional craft and thought" that extend across cultures and centuries and create a curriculum that engages students in "profound insights into the human condition" by having students encounter those works in a systematic and meaningful fashion, that is, historically.

The second aspect of the Da Vinci Curriculum that is not highlighted by the Common Core is creativity. The Common Core seeks to be focused, lean. Creativity is often seen as fat to be trimmed. Creativity is central to our lives and to our economic future. There was a wonderful cartoon years ago showing Cro-Magnon figures painting caves, dancing, and drumming. In the foreground were two Cro-Magnon administrators. One was saying to the

---

Travel Vignette 2

Aegean Blue
(On a ship crossing the Aegean Sea)

There is no blue like the Aegean. It is not the Atlantic blue of the breakers off Cape Cod's National Seashore and not the blue-green of the Pacific. It is not the tidal flush blue of Long Island Sound and not the deep gray-green of Lake Champlain. There is more purple in this blue than the blue of oceans or even the Mediterranean. The Aegean is a legendary blue, a blue of ancient tales of Greek ships and the sirens who coaxed them to their rocky shores where blue abruptly stops. It is a blue imbued with lapis from the cargo of ships lost at sea. It is the blue of raw glass globes and fine Phoenician plates. It is a blue infused with wines from a thousand amphorae that silently fell to the ocean floor having dropped from screaming ships at the violent surface. It is a blue that a thousand octopi dance through each night as they hunt for prey. It is a blue that Odysseus stared over for ten years hoping to one day see his green olive groves and family again. It is the blue of mosaics at Pompeii and Rome, Delphi and the Venetian Harbor on Crete. It is a blue brought back to decorate masks in Venice and paintings in Florence. It is a blue that was carried by traders to the souks of Damascus and Palmyra. It is Leonardo's blue, and Raphael's. It is the blue of a hundred queens' dresses and the drapery of their chambers. It is royal, elemental. It is a blue that predates the eyes of the first human to migrate from Africa. It is a blue that carries salt and plankton as it has for millennia before mankind or even squid.

other, we have a budget crunch—everything has to go except for the basics, art and music.

6. Common Core: Partner with a Content-Rich Curriculum and Robust Assessments

Creating curriculum assessments (and engaging instructional practices) is the community's, the school's, and ultimately, the teacher's job. The Common Core framers were clear: the standards are not curriculum anymore than the food pyramid—now, "MyPlate"—is the recipe for wholesome food. Both are benchmarks.

Chapter 3 Summary

The Da Vinci Core Curriculum—Student, Teacher, and the Common Core

- Intelligent questions are central to good learning.
- Inductive learning is a powerful teaching tool that fosters adaptation.
- The Da Vinci teacher is a fellow learner.
- At the core of any curriculum is the Common Core.
- The Common Core focuses on higher order skills in math and written and verbal communication.
- The Common Core calls for students to become less teacher-reliant as they interpret increasingly complex text over their school years.
- Artistic creation is the ultimate creative synthesis.

CHAPTER FOUR

~

Using the Mind Well—Inductive and Socratic Instructional Practices

Becoming Disciples of Experience

Write arguments to support claims in an analysis of substantive topics or texts, using valid reasoning and relevant and sufficient evidence.

—Common Core English Language Arts Anchor Standards

One does not have to attribute natural phenomena to the whims and vagaries of the Gods, but rather to look for causes through natural law.

—Thales of Miletus (seventh century BC)

If a man will begin with certainties, he shall end in doubts; but if he will be content to begin with doubts, he shall end in certainties.

—Francis Bacon (1561–1626)

Chapter 4 examines the Western empirical tradition resulting in the Common Core's call for reasoned arguments based on evidence and compares that tradition to earlier ways to create inferences. Following the introduction, the chapter presents two instructional techniques—inductive towers and the Socratic Seminar. Both methods are powerful strategies commonly used to realize the Common Core in the Da Vinci classroom.

In 1620, a group of English merchants called the "London Adventurers" chartered a vessel named the *Mayflower* to deliver the first Pilgrims to the new world. In that same year, English scientist Francis Bacon published a stinging indictment of Western intellectual method. His treatise was titled *Novum Organum*, or "New Method." His new method was what we now teach in seventh grade classrooms as "the scientific method." As the quotes above testify, it rekindled a tradition of learning that was based on doubt and data—on experience—rather than the "vagaries of the Gods." Words of certainty were falling out of fashion and a new world, a scientific world, was being born.

Deductive Reasoning

Bacon, a seventeenth century English gentleman, was born into a world that revered Greek intellectual traditions. Yet Bacon questioned the method by which Aristotle, and more so Aristotle's teacher, Plato, established truth. The ancient Greeks viewed truth as being built from a logical process called "syllogism." For example, consider the following argument:

1. All humans are mortal.
2. Socrates is human.
3. Conclusion: Socrates is mortal.

This is an example of a syllogism: a logical argument beginning with a general statement believed to be true that leads inevitably to a specific conclusion. This form of logic is *deductive*, meaning that specific facts (Socrates is mortal) are inferred from general premises. Logic ties the premise to the facts. The medieval world continued this intellectual tradition, even as the new guilds called "universitas" (that we know as universities) developed in cities like Paris and Bologna. Thinking deductively, Saint Anselm of Canterbury wrote, "I believe that I may know, I do not know in order to believe" (quoted in Boorstin 1998).

If his form of thinking seems rigid and unfamiliar, it is because we do not generally think in this deductive fashion. We do not think this way (or teach our students to learn this way), in part, because Francis Bacon questioned this way of thinking.

Inductive Reasoning

We think more scientifically today. In *Novum Organum*, Bacon argued that science must begin with observation from which conclusions arise from a process of *inductive* reasoning. Inductive reasoning begins with facts and through a process of inference-making establishes generalities. The scientist

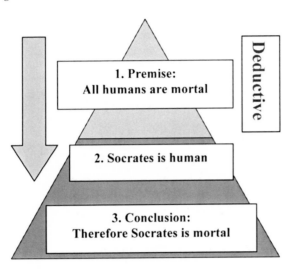

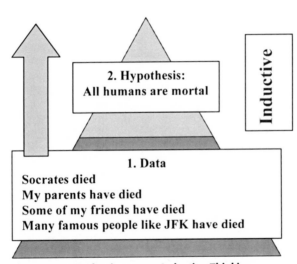

Figure 4.1. Deductive versus Inductive Thinking

"by slow and faithful toil gathers information from things and brings it into understanding" (Farrington 1964, 89).

The first pyramid shows deductive thinking. The general statement about human mortality leads one to conclude that a specific human, Socrates, is mortal. The second pyramid shows inductive thinking. Specific evidence about people the investigator has known or known about who have died leads the person to conclude that all people die. The person does not know this for sure—he has not observed all people and does not know for certain that all will die, but the evidence is strong and he accepts the statement "All humans are mortal" as a truth that he lives by.

We could test this hypothesis by asking doctors, mystics, philosophers, and healers from around the world if they know of exceptions to this hypothesis. This second part of the cycle is deductive since it begins with a generality (all humans are mortal) and suggests places in which to search for more facts (e.g., doctors, and so on). The two combine in a cycle of inference-making from inductive to deductive and back again. This is scientific thinking, a hallmark of the Western intellectual tradition. We contemporary humans are so steeped in science that it is difficult for us to imagine a world in which scientific thinking—"our" thinking—did not exist.

Bacon's "new method" turned science on its proverbial head. It was central to what historians call the "English Renaissance." Today we call this kind of thinking "empiricism." Consider this 1830 quote from the great chemist Michael Faraday: "Chemistry is necessarily an experimental science; its conclusions are drawn from data, and its principles supported by evidence derived from facts" (Jackson et al. 1996). This was the new method in action.

Yet, recall that before Aristotle, Thales said that natural phenomena were the result of natural laws and not the whim of the gods. Two thousand five hundred years later, Charles Darwin, arguably the writer of the greatest scientific synthesis of all time, tormented over the death of his eldest daughter, was torn between faith and science as he struggled to write the *Origin of Species*. Although we are scientific thinkers, the intellectual struggle that Thales considered is within each of us today. Faith and science continue to struggle for dominance in our thinking. This is what makes the study of the history of ideas profoundly relevant.

Empirical thinking—thinking from evidence—is central to our world today. We live in an empirical world in which we expect that claims to knowledge will be substantiated by evidence. For example, when we give grades to students, they expect to be able to see some correlation between tests, quizzes, and homework and the grade that they get. Teacher authority is not good enough. When we use a medication, we expect that clinical trials have been done that substantiate the pharmaceutical company's claims. When a car mechanic tells us that our car needs a new alternator, we expect that tests have been done, data analyzed, and a reasoned conclusion has been made.

The same is true when a lawyer presents a case in court—we expect that evidence will be brought forth and that logic will connect that evidence to conclusions that a jury will understand. When a doctor makes a diagnosis, we expect that he or she has examined a wealth of tests and examined data that corroborate his or her diagnosis. Sometimes we do not accept the first diagnosis and ask for a second opinion. In the same way, science must replicable to be believable.

This cycle of inductive thinking underlies our entire culture. It is the currency of schooling. Writing academic papers is central to success in high school and college. Writing term papers is no more than skillfully defending a thesis with evidence. The thesis is the top of the inductive tower and the evidence is at the bottom. Logic relates evidence to the thesis.

The Common Core supports this in several standards, such as expecting students to "write arguments to support claims in an analysis of substantive topics or texts, using valid reasoning and relevant and sufficient evidence." It is not good enough to simply state what they believe—they must use evidence and logical argument. They must do so because these analytical skills underlie our working world. The Da Vinci Curriculum operationalizes the Common Core's call for logical argument based on evidence.

We are empiricists. Yet we can be influenced by narrow self-interest rather than evidence, logic, and concern for the greater good. Richard Paul and Linda Elder of the Foundation for Critical Thinking would call these tendencies "egocentric" or "sociocentric" thinking—thinking that is limited to our own selfish interests (egocentrism) or to the narrow limits of our culture (sociocentrism). Paul and Elder argue that thinking can be taught; people can be moved from being unreflective thinkers to master thinkers (2009).

We are empiricists, yet the average student may graduate from high school never having heard the terms "inductive" and "deductive" reasoning. Many texts and teachers teach the "scientific method" as a series of steps to be memorized and obediently followed—a rote process—that one uses to write a lab report rather than as a hard-won philosophical stance that is a hallmark of Western (and, today one might argue, global) thinking. The context of the scientific method and the development of science as a way of thinking—as a human enterprise—may be lost. The Da Vinci Curriculum strives to rebuild historical context so that learning is meaningful and therefore memorable.

The average student may never realize that when her English teacher says, "Can you give me a quote from the text that substantiates your claim that Captain Ahab sought revenge from Moby Dick?" she is asking that the student engage in the same inductive process that her science teacher does in another wing of the building. Evidence. Substantiation. Inductive reasoning.

Reasoning Standards

The *National Science Education Standards* (National Research Council 1996) embraces reasoning standards:

> The new vision includes the "processes of science" and requires that students combine processes and scientific knowledge as they use scientific reasoning and critical thinking to develop their understanding of science. Engaging students in inquiry helps students develop
>
> - understanding of scientific concepts,
> - an appreciation of "how we know" what we know in science,
> - understanding of the nature of science,
> - skills necessary to become independent inquirers about the natural world, and
> - the dispositions to use the skills, abilities, and attitudes associated with science.

As introduced above, the first two Common Core English Language Arts Anchor Standards include the following:

1. Write arguments to support claims in an analysis of substantive topics or texts, using valid reasoning and relevant and sufficient evidence.
2. Write informative/explanatory texts to examine and convey complex ideas and information clearly and accurately through the effective selection, organization, and analysis of content.

In the Common Core area of Science Literacy, Integration of Ideas, we find ninth to tenth grade standards such as these:

1. Assess the extent to which the reasoning and evidence in a text support the author's claim or a recommendation for solving a scientific or technical problem.
2. Compare and contrast findings presented in a text to those from other sources (including their own experiments), noting when the findings support or contradict previous explanations or accounts.

Claims, reasoning, evidence, and analysis are central to the Common Core vision of the educated person ("college or career-ready"). Although the terms "deductive" and "inductive" are not used in the Common Core

Standards, the Common Core strongly supports the idea of using evidence (or analyzing the evidence used) to support claims. This is a strong thread in the new standards.

Bloom's Taxonomy and Webb's Depth of Knowledge Classification

However important, reasoning is only part of what our brains can do. In 1956, Benjamin Bloom developed a classification of levels of intellectual behavior in learning. This taxonomy contained three overlapping domains: the cognitive, psychomotor, and affective, which roughly translate into knowledge (cognitive), skills (psychomotor), and dispositions (affective). Within the cognitive domain, he identified six levels: knowledge, comprehension, application, analysis, synthesis, and evaluation. Others have updated Bloom to include the psychomotor and affective domains (www.humboldt.edu/celt/topics/student_learning_outcome/).

More recently, Norman Webb (2007) created a four-tiered Depth of Knowledge (DOK) taxonomy used to characterize levels of learning. The DOK has become popular in many schools. Webb's levels include I (recall), II (skills and concepts), III (strategic thinking), and IV (extended thinking).

Extended thinking (Webb) or higher order skills (Bloom) and dispositions are every bit as important in human learning as are the lower reaches of the cognitive realm, but traditionally schooling has focused on knowledge.

Attitudes and dispositions are equally important but oftentimes valued as an afterthought (like the attitude or effort grades that may be given to students but do not count in a GPA). Yet dispositions are important. It is one thing to understand cognitively the relationship between freedom and responsibility in a democracy; it is an entirely other thing to believe and practice this balance. Consider Eleanor Roosevelt's words:

> Our children should learn the general framework of their government and then they should know where they come in contact with the government, where it touches their daily lives and where their influence is exerted on the government. *It must not be a distant thing, someone else's business*, but they must see how every cog in the wheel of a democracy is important and bears its share of responsibility for the smooth running of the entire machine. (Trust for Representative Democracy 2011, emphasis in original)

Benjamin Bloom's six levels of knowledge are often considered to be sequential. Teachers may assume that an extensive period of knowledge acquisition must be obtained before comprehension can be achieved. Perhaps there is a bit of America's Puritan past embedded in this assumption—dessert is a reward for eating healthy vegetables.

Survey courses, for example, are often encyclopedic overviews of knowledge. Upper level classes are where the action is. Educationally, the problem with thinking that the "lower" order of thinking must proceed the higher is that accumulating raw knowledge without some reason to have that knowledge is not motivating for most students. Higher order thinking skills (analysis, synthesis, and evaluation) are inherently motivating because they are powerful and power—human efficacy, the ability to impact upon the world—is a fundamental human need (Glasser 1986).

Instructional Technique #1

Inductive Towers (Clarke 1990)

When using inductive towers, the student begins with knowledge—facts are the base of the tower. But before the class period has ended, the student is comparing, grouping, and ordering information (comprehensive skills), then moving on to making inferences, a higher order analytic skill; generalizing, a synthetic skill; and developing and testing new hypotheses, examples of evaluative skills. In other words, students move seamlessly throughout Bloom's levels of reasoning, developing their reasoning skills as they ask questions, interpret artifacts, and solve problems.

Whether using Bloom, Webb, or some other classification, the Da Vinci teacher views thinking as a natural process that moves throughout the taxonomy. The Da Vinci classroom explicitly teaches reasoning, both inductive and deductive, although there is a bias toward inductive reasoning because it puts students closer to the intellectual action. It requires them to engage their minds. (See the Smithsonian websites, www.smithsonianeducation.org/idealabs/ap/index.htm and www.smithsonianeducation.org/educators/lesson_plans/idealabs/artifacts_analysis.html for guidance on using artifacts in teaching.)

By contrast, traditional, contemporary schooling calls on deductive thinking to the near exclusion of inductive inference-making. For example, textbooks tend to be encyclopedias of generalizations and rarely guide students through the inductive process by which those generalities were made. Rarely do conventional classrooms trace the historical development of ideas over time in different cultures.

Deductive work in classrooms often comes down to memorizing abstractions and teaching is frequently didactic. For many students, particularly those for whom abstraction was not a part of dinner time conversation, memorizing abstractions plays to their weakest suit, yet every student—regardless of class, ethnicity, income, race, gender, or parental educational level—can observe and create inferences from observations.

Induction is inherently inclusive. Induction is inherently differentiated because different students can bring their strengths and challenges to the artifact that they observe and to the transformations and conclusions that they make. "Objects naturally invite high-level thinking and provide an authentic context in which to cultivate it," notes Shari Tishman (2008). Tishman describes the accessibility of artifacts to all students:

> Looking carefully at something and trying to discern its features is a form of cognition with an intrinsically rewarding feedback loop. The more you look, the more you see; the more you see, the more interesting the object becomes.
>
> Moreover, examining objects directly . . . is something most students can do. Regardless of background knowledge, learning style, or skill, almost all students can notice features in an object, ask questions about it, and generate ideas and connections. Students' responses may differ, but those differences contribute to the conversation rather than detract from it.

"Differentiated instruction focuses on whom we teach, where we teach, and how we teach. Its primary goal is insuring that teachers focus on processes and procedures that ensure effective learning for varied individuals" (Tomlinson and McTighe 2006). Using artifacts and systematic inductive exercises are powerful processes that make rigorous curriculum accessible to all students. They are essential tools of the differentiation trade.

Working from artifacts to create understanding begins with experience. The Da Vinci teacher uses a process that John Clarke calls "Inductive Towers" (Clarke 1990). Similarly, Leonardo da Vinci spoke of "experience and perception" leading to "knowledge and wisdom."

A Penny for Your Thoughts—An Example of an Inductive Tower

For example, in an effort to understand the nature of human civilization in an eighth grade classroom, Da Vinci students observe a penny as if it were the only known artifact from a civilization. Using inductive towers, they create generalities about the culture from which the artifact has been found (for a detailed description of this in the Da Vinci classroom, see Wiggins and McTighe 2005, 214–15). Examining a penny, students arrived at the tower shown in figure 4.2.

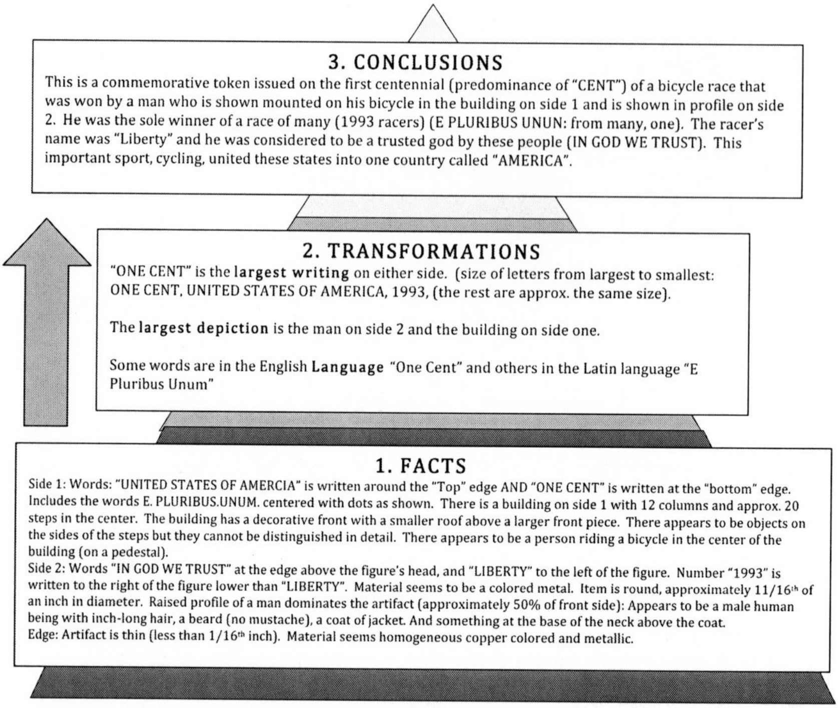

Figure 4.2.   Student-Created Inductive Tower Using a Penny as an Artifact

From their inductive tower, these students hypothesize the following:

This is a commemorative token issued on the first centennial of a bicycle race that was won by a man who is shown mounted on his bicycle in the building on side 1 and is shown in profile on side 2. He was the sole winner of a race of many (1,993 racers). The racer's name was "Liberty" and he was considered to be a trusted god by these people. This important sport, cycling, united many states into one country called "AMERICA."

Interesting. From this experience—from being archeologists—the students see that one artifact is far too few from which to draw reliable conclusions and that it is easy to be led astray or to misinterpret what is seen. They see that cultural context is very important to an archeologist. When doing this work with students, teachers see how some students or groups of students tend to stay very close to the fact base. Their conclusions are rock solid and defensible. Others take bold leaps in their generalities. They are more creative in their thinking, but less tied to the facts. Their conclusions may be more interesting but harder to defend. Students' thinking becomes visible, and therefore can be discussed. Students gain metacognitive skills—the ability to understand their thinking process.

Inductive towers are a method to teach content while teaching about thinking. They are a way to engage students in Francis Bacon's "new method." They are a method to get students closer to the action—to *be* archeologists, art historians, and scientists in the service of learning about archeology, art, history, and science. Inductive towers are a way to engage students in rich content as called for by many studies such as *Breaking Ranks* (1996), *Breaking Ranks II* (2004), and *High Schools on the Move* (2002). Inductive exercises are a way to engage students in literacy, which is at the core of the Common Core. From the Common Core website:

> Students who meet the Standards readily undertake the close, attentive reading that is at the heart of understanding and enjoying complex works of literature. They habitually perform the critical reading necessary to pick carefully through the staggering amount of information available today in print and digitally. They actively seek the wide, deep, and thoughtful engagement with high-quality literary and informational texts that builds knowledge, enlarges experience, and broadens worldviews. They reflexively demonstrate the cogent reasoning and use of evidence that is essential to both private deliberation and responsible citizenship in a democratic republic. In short, students who meet the Standards develop the skills in reading, writing, speaking, and listening that are the foundation for any creative and purposeful expression in language. (www.corestandards.org/the-standards/english-language-arts-standards)

Induction is a way for students to raise their own essential questions from which they can become backward designers in their studies (see chapter 2). Backward design, if left exclusively to teachers, remains one more teacher-directed strategy that leaves silent student interests, thoughts, and questions. In the Da Vinci classroom, students help to drive instruction. This is empowering and motivating. Students develop their voice, their thoughts, their beliefs, and their interests as they develop their knowledge and skills. Whether preparing for college or for technical training, it is important that students think about what is important for them to learn and how they will most effectively learn that which they have determined to be important.

Shifting from a deductive approach to an inductive one is also our best defense against prejudice. For example, a racist person might begin with the false and racist belief that African Americans are lazy. He might then apply that belief to a person that he meets, prejudging that new person as being lazy. This is false deductive logic based on a false and racist premise.

An open-minded person begins with the person they meet and draws conclusions from their experience with that person. Some people are lazy, and others are not. Race does not correlate with laziness. Open-minded people do not fail to distinguish between good and bad—they discriminate based on inferences made from the evidence that people present them with, not on preconceived and prejudicial beliefs. If we look at people for what they are rather than apply preconceived beliefs to those we meet, human diversity becomes a thrilling opportunity rather than a reinforcement of our prejudices.

Context

As students shift from subject matter thinking, to disciplinary thinking, to interdisciplinary thinking, the more they are driven to carefully consider the *context* in which they work. Similarly they are more likely to arrive at complex, context-dependent, shades-of-gray answers that mirror the real world than oversimplified black and white responses that fail to explain the real world in all its complexity.

Knefelkamp (personal communication, 1999; Knefelkamp 2003; Perry 1999) determined that as students progress through liberal arts programs, they tend to mature in their thinking from a simplistic model of the world as right and wrong or true and false to a contextual and complex intellectual view. Given a curriculum that nourishes and rewards such growth, this kind of intellectual transition can occur far earlier than college. Da Vinci teachers witness this transition occur as early as the seventh and eighth grade in the Da Vinci classroom.

In 1999, the National Academies (Science, Engineering, Institute of Medicine, and National Research Council) published a book titled *How People Learn*. It was the result of a two-year study designed to "better link the findings of research on the science of learning to actual practice in the classroom" (Bransford et al. 2000). In 2000, the work was expanded and updated. *How People Learn* helps us understand the fundamentals of learning and why a curriculum such as Da Vinci is powerful.

One of the key findings of *How People Learn* is that competence requires far more than factual knowledge (although accurate factual knowledge is crucial). "Understanding facts and ideas in the context of a conceptual framework" is also necessary. Oftentimes learning in schools ends with the acquisition of facts and ideas. The conceptual frameworks within which facts are developed (logically and historically) are not made explicit to the student. A student is unlikely to commit to the hours it takes to master a subject if he or she is not convinced that mastery is possible or desirable; mastery demands commitment.

Yet according to Chase and Simon (cited in Bransford 2000), world-class chess mastery requires fifty thousand to one hundred thousand hours of practice, which is the equivalent of fifty to one hundred years of schooling! Learning how to think inductively links fact acquisition to concepts that are more memorable and more inherently satisfying. Understanding is powerful. Feeling powerful feels good and builds intrinsic motivation.

A study carried out by Schwartz and others in 1999 described in *How People Learn* shows the importance of handling information *and* being presented with unifying theory. Students were broken into three groups. One group read and summarized a text on a subject then heard an organizing lecture. They performed poorly on a subsequent task that demanded understanding of the material. The second group learned best. They actively compared data to establish a base of understanding and then were given the organizing lecture. They did well—over twice as well when asked to apply what they had learned. The last group had twice as much time to work with the data but did not have an organizing lecture. They did slightly less well than the first group.

The take-home lesson is that deliberate practice ("elaboration"), coaching, *and* theoretical understanding are necessary. Inductive towers provide all three, when followed by a skillfully led seminar, insightful lecture, or some other kind of sense-making activity.

The Cycle of Induction and Deduction
Having established a conclusion from their inductive tower, students naturally ask questions about their data and their conclusions. For example, having concluded that the penny was a commemorative token celebrating a bicycle race won by a man named "Liberty," they might seek other artifacts from the culture that would either substantiate or refute their claims. In doing so, they are engaging in a deductive process, beginning with a generalization (a hypothesis) and looking for specifics to defend or refute the hypothesis.

With something to look for, imagine the richness that one other artifact provides. Imagine the liveliness of the conversation between this group and another group who concluded that the penny represents a coin made by a people who believed that "liberty" was established by brain washing many people and their diverse "states" of mind into one ("unified," "Unum") way of thinking and that this brainwashing was carried out in a columned building (the ONE CENT building) represented by a single man (the one right thinker) under the eye of a god who was trusted with this process. The two groups chose to emphasize different aspects of the fact base, transformed the data differently, and drew different conclusions. They would look for different information to substantiate their initial hypothesis. Lively discussion is inevitable.

Thinking and Words

The National Paideia Center has "come to define thinking as the ability to successfully explain and manipulate complex systems. By system, we mean a set of interrelated ideas often represented in a human artifact." Paideia director and associate directors Terry Roberts and Laura Billings (2008) describe the fundamental interdependence between thinking and literacy: "we think only through the medium of words," hence the centrality of literacy in the Common Core. They link aspects of thinking, reading, speaking, listening, collaboration, and writing to the Paideia seminar, a seminar format that closely resembles the Da Vinci seminar.

Da Vinci students are taught to write and speak with precision, to listen well, to build upon others' words, to create, and to ground one's thoughts in evidence appropriate to the discipline. Artists and others might define literacy and human thinking far more broadly than "the medium of words."

One former student who years later returned and became a Da Vinci teacher recalls:

> Students as creators is an important idea at Gailer. They should be able to create research papers, lab experiments and well-reasoned arguments, but maybe more important is the creation of poems, plays and opinions. I don't feel stress over the students who have trouble expressing themselves dramatically, but I encourage them and I allow them to give it a shot. Anyone outside of Gailer who happens upon the plays I bring home is shocked at the fact that the authors are all 8th graders. Perhaps this is because our students are gifted creators and writers, but perhaps it is also because we simply give them an opportunity not commonly given to young people, and we expect them to pick it up and try it on.

He goes on to describe the centrality of drama in the lives of adolescents and the importance of schools using this to curricular advantage:

> The dramatic work that has come directly out of classroom material is perhaps more special. What strikes me as most valuable about our use of drama is the voice that it gives to young people. Yes, I "make" my students write plays (and we spend a good bit of time with a professional playwright practicing the elements of characterization, conflict and dialogue), but when they must sit down and write a play about anything that they want, then you have an equation for revelation. More than any other creative enterprise, when we create "imaginary action," it springs directly from what is going on in our minds and our worlds. I get to see a side of students that doesn't come up even in our

progressive, student-centered classrooms. The freedom to express the entire range of human conditions and emotions in a visual, tangible way is something that many people never experience. And I love to read them and share them with the community.

According to Webb this use of drama in the classroom "extends thinking." For Bloom this is an act of synthesis. For a Da Vinci teacher, it is a way to create a "tailwind" for adolescent learning.

Gailer Story #4

Creation Myths

"We have a situation here." I'd never said anything like that before—not even sure where the words came from. As we hiked Mount Marcy in the Adirondacks—in the freezing rain—John refused to wear his hat. Now he was in the early stages of hypothermia. He had brought a down parka, useless in this kind of weather. I distributed tasks to the other adults and students, got John into dry clothes, hefted his pack onto his back and mine on my own, then we headed off. His coordination was good, he was lucid, and we were going to get his core temperature up by hiking out.

We had spent the last two days hiking in and then telling Creation stories around the campfire at Marcy Dam. I wanted them to be in the midst of Creation with the firelight flickering on the lean-to wall. I wanted them to feel these stories deeply before we launched into our study of Stephen Hawking and *Red Giants and White Dwarfs*. I wanted to reach them emotionally as well as intellectually. Ralph had prepared them. He taught them how to take in a story so that they would not have to refer to notes. He taught them where to embellish, and where to leave it sparse. Hearing the stories this way seemed right—fire on our faces and cold at our backs.

This tradition of taking the seventh grade out into the wilds for Creation myths stood the test of time. For over a decade an expert teacher took her class each year to a camp in New Hampshire. To the Creation myths, she added high ropes challenges and swimming. As Head of School, I always went on this trip—it was important for me to work mostly with the seventh grade students. I wanted them to know that they were important. By getting to know them in seventh grade, I had established the base for a six-year relationship with them. And they're fun.

By the time I got John down and to the nearest small hospital, he was flush—perhaps a little hyperthermic. I got a call in to his family and got him home late that night. We both learned a couple of lessons that were not in my plan book.

The Internet as a Museum—a Source of Inductive Content
The word "museum" originated in the seventeenth century. It comes from the Greek word *mouseion,* which meant the seat of the muses. Early museums were called "cabinets of curiosity" with cabinet indicating a room rather than a piece of furniture. This was a time when curiosities were being brought back to England and Europe. Museums, at that time privately owned, were places to display the spoils of wealth. Science did not have unifying theories such as plate tectonics, evolution, chemical bonding, or relativity. Phenomena could be observed and artifacts representing the richness of the world could be collected. Narwhal tusks were mistakenly identified as unicorn horns, but the scene was set for collections that were purposeful, such as Darwin's or Alfred Russell Wallace's collections that revealed the underlying theory of evolution.

So, where is our "cabinet of curiosities" today?

The Internet is more than a depository of data. It is an interactive museum of primary source artifacts that can be accessed in fractions of seconds. Take, for example, that anyone with a computer and Internet connection can access one of Leonardo's studies for *The Last Supper* at the Library of Windsor at www.royalcollection.org.uk.

Here we see that Leonardo has not yet broken from the tradition of placing Judas across the table from Jesus and his other apostles. Leonardo, after all, advises us, "Although nature commences with reason and ends in experience it is necessary for us to do the opposite; that is to commence with experience and from this to proceed to investigate the reason." Seeing this draft of *The Last Supper* is an experience that helps students understand Leonardo, the creative process, their drafting process, and the final painting of *The Last Supper* itself. The Internet provides them with electronic primary source experience.

Although there are millions of websites that serve an infinite number of purposes, there are four kinds of websites worthy of our examination.

1. Museums That Allow Electronic Entry
Most major museums display some part of their collection electronically today. The Louvre, the British Museum, and the National Gallery in Washington are good examples. The British Museum has nearly two million objects that can be searched online. In collaboration with the BBC, the British Museum has created a *History of the World through 100 Objects* radio show that can also be visited online.

Europeana (www.europeana.eu) is a remarkable site that puts virtually all of Europe's collections at your fingertips. Some allow items to be manipulated—turned or zoomed in on. In fact, via the Internet, one can frequently see things that cannot be seen firsthand—the back of an object, for example, or a close view of a detail not visible behind glass.

2. Webcams That Allow Direct Observation of Phenomena
Africam is an old site that allows the viewer to observe waterholes and the creatures that frequent them in Kruger National Park in South Africa. Since there is a six-hour time difference between the East Coast and Kruger, there is a good chance that an American visitor could see some interesting nocturnal activity. Visitors take photos of interesting moments and share those online.

The Hubble Space Telescope (http://hubblesite.org/) has some spectacular photos on the Internet. We are the first generation of people to have witnessed what Hubble has to offer. The SLOOH Space Camera is equally remarkable. Members can sit in on actual missions where telescopes are turned to see particular objects. Visitors look over upcoming sites, sign up for something of interest, and wait for the countdown. Visitors see the data at the same moment that scientists do. Guests can suggest missions as well. Bob Berman narrates many of the missions.

3. Websites That Provide Data and/or to which Guests Can Contribute Data
The Bermuda Biological Station has such a site. There is no reason why, with professional supervision, students cannot contribute real data to real scientific investigations.

The Human Genome Project articles and data can be accessed via the American Association for the Advancement of Science (AAAS, www.aas .org) or the UCSC Genome Bioinformatics website (which has many other species as well).

4. Sites That Have Historical or Contemporary Film Footage
If you have not seen the Tacoma Narrows Bridge Collapse film, you should. This was available as a film loop as part of the Physical Science Study Committee (PSSC) physics curriculum in 1968 (as an example of resonance vibration). It is now on YouTube. There are many sites like this with spectacular footage. It is possible to pull data from the Tacoma Collapse.

The BBC has a site with many historical films, particularly of World War II vintage. Sites such as these allow the students to follow their own developing interests and get as close to primary sources as they can without traveling to sites.

The Classroom as a Museum

Schools should see themselves as museums—active and engaging museums where students are on the table analyzing cultural artifacts everyday. Gailer had a "cabinet of miracles."

Da Vinci faculties are always on the lookout for artifacts that will help students gain insight into their studies. These include physical reproductions like the crania shown in the cabinet; two-dimensional artistic representations; maps, charts, and graphs; literature; scientific documents and illustrations; historical documents, sculpture, coins, and so on.

So, what can students do with these artifacts? They build inductive towers, and in doing so, learn how to observe closely and think well.

Instructional Technique #2

Seminars and Socratic Method

The unexamined life is not worth living.

—Socrates (born 470 BCE)

Then let's give 'em lots of exams and make their lives worthwhile!

—Anonymous

Socrates, who also famously said that he knew that he knew nothing (and, therefore, was smarter than others who were not aware of their ignorance), is identified with Socratic "questioning," "method," or "dialogue." Socrates is identified in Western culture with the importance of questioning, particularly in an interrogation-like style. His questions were designed to disprove certain ideas and therefore give credence to their opposites. His goal was often to demonstrate the ignorance of his interviewee—not a technique for winning friends (Boorstin 1998). His was a philosophical exercise. It was part of his belief in making life meaningful through examination.

Seminars are a second frequent instructional practice in the Da Vinci classroom. Many secondary school teachers think that they operate their classrooms in a seminar style. Frequently, teachers think that they are running a seminar when, in fact, they have salted a lecture with questions that a small percentage of their students answer (or, perhaps, even engage in mentally). Doing so is not a seminar.

In a seminar, the teacher's role shifts from informing and explaining to questioning and *not informing or explaining*. Once the teacher has established or reestablished herself as the expert, students WILL be reluctant to whole-heartedly risk their opinions—their developing voices will be overwhelmed by the practiced adult voice of authority (and there are plenty of times when this is the right thing to do, but not when the teacher's goal is to promote student voice).

The seminar leader (who may be the teacher or a student) will assign something rich ("educative," in Dewey's usage) for students to examine. This might be a chapter, a painting or sculpture, a scientific investigation, a historical document, a mathematical treatise, a work of literature, or some other cultural artifact. The seminar leader gives students clear direction for their preparatory work. They might be asked questions to direct their attention to aspects of the work. For example, from the history of science, "Describe the expressions of each of the eleven faces depicted in Joseph Wright's painting *An Experiment on a Bird in the Air Pump*" (see chapter 8). From literature, "Based on Harper Lee's (*To Kill a Mockingbird*) descriptions, draw a picture of Boo Radley's house as you see it in your mind's eye." In the first exercise, the student is asked to observe closely and record her observation accurately. In the second, the student is asked to read text and imagine.

There are many ways to lead a seminar. The following provides the teacher and student with clear instructions.

Instructions for Leading a Da Vinci Seminar

You should:

- Prepare in advance.
- Set the stage with a lead question.
- Periodically summarize the conversation (approximately every fifteen minutes, but most importantly, when you see consensus developing or clear differences of opinion). Your summary should model appreciation for different points of view and evidence-based conclusions.
- Direct the classes' attention to particular resources (like a paragraph, aspect of an artifact, set of data, or illustration).
- Redirect from one student to another (but not in a leading way to get to *your* answer): "Sam, what do you think of Josh's claim that Captain Ahab had some similar characteristics to Hamlet? Can you refute or support Josh's idea?"
- Ask provocative questions.
- Solicit background information.

You may not:

- Lecture.
- Use "Direct Instruction."
- Use PowerPoint (unless used to accomplish the above).
- Ask leading questions that are hidden statements. ("Don't you think that Hitler was wrong in killing 6 million people?" "Don't you think that Boo Radley's house would be a little more run down than that?")

You will need to:

1. Present an assignment to the class on the week prior to your seminar.
2. Prepare. Seminar leaders should have plans ready at the beginning of their seminar. This plan should include a large number of questions that the leader will draw upon as her or she proceeds. The plan should give the leader a strong foothold in the beginning of the discussion but should be increasingly flexible as the seminar proceeds. The leader is not taking the class to a predetermined destination; the leader is helping them find *their* conclusion.
3. Engage the class in a seminar for thirty to sixty minutes
4. Take notes during the seminar, capturing key words and phrases and who said them. The leader might want to do so as a diagram that shows branches and differing opinions. Inexperienced seminar leaders may not be able to keep detailed notes and guide the seminar with genuine enthusiasm. Guiding the seminar is more important.
5. At the end of the seminar, present some kind of summary/conclusion of the classes' thinking as it developed in the seminar. This might sound something like the following or might be more diagrammatic.

"When we began our seminar at 10 o'clock on chapter 1 of *To Kill a Mockingbird*, I heard you emphasize at least six different aspects of the work including ___, ___, ___, ___, ___, ___. As I mentioned in my first summary, it seemed to me that by around 10:15 you were settling on ___ and ___ as your primary concerns. I heard Sarah focus the group on ___, whereas Ben felt that ___ was more important for our attention due to _____. You moved between these two threads throughout the rest of the seminar.

By about 10:45, after discussing __ and ___, the group seemed to resolve Sarah's issue by concluding _____ based primarily of ___ on page ___. You then switched back to Ben's issue, which after discussing ___ on page ___ and ___ on page ___ caused you to rethink the conclusion

that you had drawn on Sarah's issue. At the end of the seminar, I heard Michael summarize the group's thinking when he stated '_____
_____.' Although Anna took issue with this stating '_____,' the rest of the group seemed to sign on to Michael's summary. Sam provided a nice synthesis at the very end.

Have I heard the group correctly? In the remaining two minutes, does anyone want to add or correct anything that I have said in my summary? When we discuss chapter 2 tomorrow, do we want to revisit Anna's concerns or simply hold that as a valued minority opinion at this point?"

You may want to consult *The Art of Asking Essential Questions* by Linda Elder and Richard Paul (The Foundation for Critical Thinking, www.criticalthinking.org/).

Chapter 4 Summary

Using the Mind Well—Inductive and Socratic Instructional Practices: Becoming Disciples of Experience

- There are two fundamental ways that humans create inferences—inductive and deductive.
- Inductive thinking, based on evidence, is underplayed in schools but very important in most work.
- Inductive towers are a powerful instructional tool for teaching students to think systematically.
- Practice (elaboration) and theoretical understanding are powerful when paired in this order.
- The Internet and classroom can be museums of cultural and scientific artifacts that can serve as "inductive stimulant."
- The seminar can be a second powerful instructional method.
- Questions are central to good studentship.

~

CHAPTER FIVE

The Da Vinci Teacher—Engaging Teachers, Engaged Students

Nostalgia—it's delicate, but potent. Teddy told me that in Greek, "nostalgia" literally means "the pain from an old wound." It's a twinge in your heart far more powerful than memory alone. This device isn't a spaceship, it's a time machine. It goes backwards, and forwards. . . . It takes us to a place where we ache to go again. It's not called the wheel, it's called the carousel. It lets us travel the way a child travels—around and around, and back home again, to a place where we know we are loved.

—Don Draper, character from *Mad Men*, talking about the Kodak Slide Carousel, 2007 season (www.imdb.com/character/ch0031457/ quotes)

Try to know something about everything and everything about something.

—Thomas Hardy

Chapter 5 examines the intellectual assumption inherent in the Da Vinci teaching role and the intensity of the teaching relationship.

Consider Don Draper from the TV show *Mad Men*. He is an executive in the Eisenhower era. His "girl" makes phone calls for him, writes his letters, and keeps his appointments. She makes excuses for his personal life's failings and serves him drinks in the office. Each of his young executives has a woman who sits outside his office dutifully carrying out his tasks. When the first copier arrives, the secretaries panic—will it take their jobs? Where will they put it?

Draper is a television creation, an entertaining extreme, yet he does illustrate how things have changed in some sectors of our work lives. Draper today might be a woman and her assistant might be a man. Draper (let's call her "Ms. Draper") does the majority of her own correspondence today via e-mail. She certainly does not ask her assistant to manage her private affairs. She has computers, PDAs, smart phones, printers, Web 2.0 (more interactive and mutually participatory than the web of five years ago), and software to help her create, manage, and lead. She might return in the morning to find work done by colleagues working other shifts in India or California. Most dramatically, she leads teams who work together to solve problems. The image of Don Draper blowing smoke to the side and making pronouncements are gone. Ms. Draper is a leader of colleagues, not a commander of an army. Work has changed substantially.

This is less true of secondary school teaching. Teachers still work largely alone. They still create curriculum alone (but with state standards and tests as guides). It still gets a laugh to say that teaching is the second most private act because it remains largely true. Yes, lesson plans are computerized, and some schools use web-based programs such as Curriculum Mapper® or Atlas Rubicon® to document curriculum. Some schools have embraced professional learning communities (PLCs, see chapter 10), but many have not. In most schools, the secondary school teaching job is largely unchanged from the school that Don Draper attended before the Korean War.

Redesigning the Teaching Role

There are new and different teaching jobs. The special educator is a different teaching role. Many states offered their special education endorsements shortly after Congress added Title VI to the Elementary and Secondary Education Act of 1965 creating a Bureau of Education for the Handicapped (this bureau today is called the Office of Special Education Programs, or OSEP). It was another ten years until PL 94-142 when the Education for All Handicapped Children Act (EAHCA) was enacted. Today we know this law as the Individuals with Disabilities Education Act (IDEA). Before 1975, children with disabilities were frequently denied an education. EAHCA, along with some key Supreme Court cases, mandated all school districts to educate students with disabilities. Ultimately, the change in the law led to new teaching roles.

A special education teacher specializes in *how* students learn, particularly those with challenges. The conventional teacher specializes in *content instruction*. Typically the special education teacher has six or more courses in special education in addition to his or her other training. The conventional teacher typically completes a major in their field and a licensure curriculum that requires one three-credit introduction to special education class.

The special educator works in a variety of formats and specialties, depending upon state and local needs. The special education movement created a new teaching role with different priorities, scheduling, training, and accountability.

The conventional secondary school teaching role is not immutable. If we can create new special educational roles, than we can create other teaching roles, such as the "Da Vinci teacher." To change learning to embrace the Common Core, we have to change teaching and to change teaching meant creating a new teacher. In the Da Vinci model, there are two roles, the Da Vinci humanities teacher and the Da Vinci science teacher.

How the Da Vinci Teacher Instructs

What is different about a "Da Vinci teacher" and a conventional secondary school teacher? The conventional teacher's work focuses on a narrow disciplinary specialty for a large group of students. They are "discipline narrow" and "student wide." A Da Vinci teacher is just the opposite; they are discipline wide and student narrow. In other words, the Da Vinci teacher gains a deeper knowledge of their students by engaging in a wider area of content.

For example, the "DV" teacher works with around twenty students for several hours per day but must engage them in a study of the history, literature, archeology, art, ethics, and religious practices of five major early civilizations. This is a tall order, but there are many well-educated professionals able to fill it. The Da Vinci teacher searches have always drawn a large group of qualified applicants. To illustrate the shift in the role of the student and teacher in the Da Vinci Classroom, a metaphor might help. Consider teaching animal tracking.

In a conventional process the teacher begins by delivering content. For example, the tracking teacher might begin by familiarizing students with tracks, spoor, and other animal signs as depicted in books, photos, museum casts, or online sources. Eventually there may be a field trip to illustrate tracking; however, in most teaching, the majority of the work is done in a decontextualized classroom delivering content efficiently by direct instruction. Skilled teachers bring this to life with their rich experiences. In a UbD classroom, the teacher begins by asking him- or herself what is essential about tracking and will build activities and assessments that support these. For example, the teacher may decide that students should be able to distinguish between canine and feline tracks. The teacher then asks, "How will I know when they understand the differences between canine and feline tracks?" From here the teacher builds learning activities.

In a DV classroom the teacher is more likely to do what a skilled French-Canadian tracker did many years ago. He led his students to a place in a hemlock forest. As they kneeled down, he pointed north through the forest and asked the simple question, "What do you see?" Although these students knew this section of woods well, directed to this vantage point, they noticed a low tunnel-like opening through the woods, tufts of deer fur on broken branches, hoof tracks, and deer scat. The tracker asked what all these things meant and his students concluded that they were seeing a virtual super-highway for white-tailed deer. How could they have missed it so many times before?

What exactly had this tracker done? Using his deep understanding of natural history, he brought his students to a particularly fruitful place for observing deer activity. He pointed his students in a particular direction that he knew would be observationally rich and engaging. He had confidence in their ability to see what was before them and in his ability to provide them with a place worthy of observation. He asked his students to observe systematically and then guided them to understand what they had observed. He helped them make sense out of what they had seen; to create insight from sight. Like the tracker, this is what the Da Vinci teacher does—guides the learner toward places with the potential to stimulate enduring understanding. Gailer teachers call these places "hot spots." Dewey said that "not all experiences are equally educative." The teacher's engagement in these richly educative hot spots engages her students.

After their tracking tutorial, these students could see that tufts of fur, broken branches, hoof marks, deer scat, and a tunnel-like opening through the low hemlocks were evidence of a deer run running north-south through the woods. They had evidence for a conclusion that they could test with further observation or experimentation. For example, they could set up a movement-sensitive camera.

Similarly, throughout the Da Vinci Curriculum, students learn to use evidence to create generalizations and to support theses. They then learn to design investigations that generate further data. They learn to see. They learn to *think*. From seventh grade until graduation, every class reinforces their inference-making.

Consider how broad these skills are. Inference-making, both deductive and inductive, is a large part of what we human beings use our minds for, yet inference-making is rarely taught explicitly (that is, metacognitively) in schools.

Gailer Story #5

The Battle of Valcour II—Bold Learning

"Harry, would you mind changing your boat to the *Washington*?" "Sure, put me where you need me."

Little did I know that off Willsboro Point, my little boat, playing the role of the USS *Washington*, would take a relentless barrage of water balloons launched from all sides with lacrosse sticks. Luckily my crew and I had a secret weapon—full suits of foul-weather gear! So, how did we get from the seminar room to a dozen boats on Lake Champlain reenacting the Revolutionary War Battle of Valcour?

I was in class with the first Gailer class, a smart and spunky group. We were discussing our curriculum. The state required us to study American history and, after all, American history is important for us to know. However, we had propelled ourselves through a few thousand years of global history and could not possible do justice to the entire sweep of U.S. history as well. As it was, I was barely keeping a few days ahead of the class. In desperation, I said, "Let's not try to do it all. Let's start with the Revolutionary War. Let's find ourselves an entrée, something we can get close to and use as a way into early American history."

Someone, I think that it was Ethan, said, "You've got a boat—why don't we go out on the lake and see where some of the Revolutionary War battles were fought." Someone else chimed in: "Let's get a bunch of boats and reenact a battle." I recall the educator in me being very excited, and the boat owner in me being equally skeptical: what if one of these guys falls off a boat into 50 degree water and dies? What if the Coast Guard intervenes? There's probably a law against wars on the lake—they must at least require a permit. I could read the headline: *Idiot Headmaster Loses Boatload of Students to Icy Lake Champlain Water—Dream School beyond Resuscitation.* "Come on, Harry, you say you want learning to be *real*." Sure I want them to question authority, but not *my* authority. "If you guys do all the planning, including choreographing the battle, arranging other boats and contacting the coast guard, I'm game—we can use my boat."

A couple of months later with a battle plan in place, Coast Guard approval, and a dozen boats ready, the American fleet was poised just south of Valcour Island waiting for the British ships to attack. On this cool Sunday morning I was sweating with anticipation, eyes focused on Garden Island, a rock off the south shore of Valcour. As our student script required, we sent a boat out to taunt the British as Benedict Arnold had done.

I was surprised to feel the same anticipation that Arnold must have felt over two hundred years ago—we all felt it. We felt deeply anxious about the coming battle!

> We were surprised again later in the day when my boat, stalled off Willsboro Point, was about to be pummeled by British gunboats whose wind kept them sailing—exactly as it had done in the original battle over two hundred years ago. The lessons were particularly vivid.
>
> I still run into the other captains occasionally. Like war veterans, we stop when we pass on the docks and reminisce about the great battle that we were a part of.

Da Vinci Humanities Teaching Position's Structure and Philosophy

Conventional secondary teachers spend approximately 140 hours per year with their students (forty-five minutes per day, five times per week, or the equivalent, in a blocked schedule). This is the equivalent of three to four 40-hour working weeks per year. In contrast, the DV teacher spends over 700 hours per year with his or her students. This is the equivalent of 17.5 working weeks. The conventional teacher spends only 20 percent of the time that DV teachers spend with their students.

This is a substantially deeper intellectual relationship. This means that teachers must be chosen very carefully, supported well with extensive ongoing professional development, supervised, and evaluated carefully. Administrators must be trained in supervision, professional development, professional learning communities, and evaluation. They cannot be hesitant to relieve a teacher who is not right for the school and the students. John Dewey said that "the belief that all genuine education comes about through experience does not mean that all experiences are genuinely or equally educative" (1963). Like the tracker, teachers must be skilled at identifying "genuinely educative" learning experiences. They must be compassionate and have high expectations. They must embrace the mission of the school and understand the Da Vinci Curriculum, instructional practices, and ethic.

Pedagogically, Da Vinci teachers are question-oriented (and inductive) rather than conclusion-oriented (and deductive). They are narrative-based and question-based rather than text-based. They are tuned to the inherent meaningfulness of curriculum, the logic of the flow of history. They are well educated in the liberal arts as well as specialized in their subject area.

Da Vinci teachers know how to facilitate a true seminar in which peers as well as teachers are authorities. They teach their students how to run seminars because to share the act of teaching is to share learning. They see their students' job as being to create knowledge, not simply to amass knowledge. They prize insight and insightful questions. They view each class and student as unique. They realize that, regardless of how many times they have taught *To Kill a Mockingbird*, these students have not encountered that text and its ideas before. They see each class that they teach as a unique event in the history of the universe—the first coming together of particular ideas and their students' minds.

Da Vinci teachers view knowledge as incomplete, tentative, changing, contextual, and qualified. They recognize that much remains unknown and, perhaps, unknowable. The Da Vinci teacher frequently asks, "What is the basis for this claim to knowledge?" They expect their students to do the same. They want their students to be empowered and active, not passive and receptive.

Da Vinci teachers ensure that their students are physically, emotionally, and intellectually safe. They create a culture in their classroom and in the school that expects intellectual excitement and that discourages any kind of intellectual hazing. They create an inclusive culture that is practiced in seeing the value and potential of every member of the school. Da Vinci teachers expect their students to be involved in faculty and administrative hiring, policy making, and classroom decisions. They share leadership with their students while maintaining the authority and responsibility of the teacher.

They are practical visionaries who can put into practice daily lesson plans while cultivating a vision of teaching and learning that is optimistic, enthusiastic, and refreshing. They have healthy and caring relationships with their colleagues. They remain intellectually alive and pursue their own studies, travel, and creativity. They have a strong sense of humor and appreciation for the rocky road of adolescence. Their curriculum is also like the Kodak carousel traveling around and around through history and back home again to relate the lessons of history to the realities of the student's experience today.

Chapter 5 Summary

The Da Vinci Teacher—Engaging Teachers, Engaged Students

- As special education roles have changed, so too can "Da Vinci teachers" become new educational roles.

- Da Vinci teachers skillfully lead their students to places likely to provide rich material for reasoning.
- Da Vinci teachers has a substantially more intense relationship with their students.
- Da Vinci teachers view knowledge as contextual, tentative, and qualified. They acknowledge the unknown and the unknowable.

CHAPTER SIX

~

Recipes from the Da Vinci Curriculum—Chef Leonardo

Those who fail to learn the lessons of history are doomed to repeat them.

—Philosopher George Santayana

And therewithal, whenever I found out anything remarkable, I have thought it my duty to put down my discovery on paper, so that all ingenious people might be informed thereof.

—Anton van Leeuwenhoek, the first person to see live single-celled creatures, June 12, 1716

If you would keep healthy, follow this regiment: Do not eat unless you feel inclined, and sup lightly; chew well, and let what you take be well cooked and simple. . . . Shun wantonness, and pay attention to diet.

I believe that great happiness awaits those men who are born where good wines are to be found.

—Leonardo da Vinci, Editions du Clos Luce, 2008

Chapter 6 compares the Da Vinci teacher to a chef who uses fresh ingredients and knowledge of dietary standards to create healthy and tasty foods.

Preparing Curriculum from Scratch

As students file into the room early in the semester in their graduate curriculum course, they find the professor chopping up vegetables and sautéing them in a skillet over a hot plate borrowed from his colleagues in chemistry. Another pot boils water for pasta. They enter the classroom not quite sure what to think about their professor, who is cooking instead of readying the LCD for a PowerPoint presentation.

He asks each member of the class to come up with a metaphor for making curriculum. As basil and garlic are being added to the simmering tomato sauce, it becomes clear that her metaphor is cooking. As the sauce simmers, the class explores the metaphor: what is the curricular equivalent of fresh vine-ripe tomatoes, of spices and herbs, of a recipe, a menu, a sharp knife, and a hot fire?

A students asks, "Should curriculum always be made from scratch?" As the class considers this, the professor heats up a second pot of water and adds a box of Kraft Macaroni and Cheese. He asks, "Is there ever a place for fast food, comfort food, or convenience food?" "What is your job as a teacher?" "Are you there to serve a nutritional meal?" "What if they're not hungry for what you have to offer?" The conversation continues.

A healthy classroom is one in which the teacher plays the role of a talented chef. Think of what a chef does. He or she does not simply say, "What do you want to eat?" The chef offers a menu of enticing and healthy foods. The diners choose from the menu. The chef then uses his skills and experience to create a meal for his guests. Choice, but not too much choice. Expertise without autocracy. Healthy, yet tasty.

The teacher's job is to create curriculum from scratch; to use his or her expertise much in the way that the chef does, to inform from what is known and to create something new. We are not here to serve up processed products out of boxes.

The following are three examples of curriculum created by Da Vinci faculty. These models underscore the importance of teachers harnessing their intellectual resources to create engaging curriculum "from scratch."

An Example of Robust Curriculum—The Pythagorean Monochord

Nobody studies the monochord in high school. It simply is not a part of the secondary school curriculum. You will not find it in the standards or in the textbooks, but it is a part of the Da Vinci Curriculum. What is the mono-chord and why is it a part of this curriculum?

The monochord is a simple musical instrument. It has a single string stretched over a sound box. In all probability, single string instruments like this were used for thousands of years. However in the sixth century BCE, Pythagoras made a precise scientific instrument out of the monochord by adding a movable bridge and a variable weight that pulled the single string, creating more or less tension. He had, in other words, modified the mono-chord to add two independently controllable variables.

Pythagoras was able to systematically study the effect of bridge position and tension on pitch. Da Vinci teachers decided to study this in the DVC because it was an important moment in the history of science. Variables were being isolated. The effect of the weight pulling the string to alter pitch could be measured and quantified. Alternately, the effect of bridge position on pitch could be measured. Yes, there are lessons in the physics of music, but, more importantly, this was a pivotal step in the scientific enterprise. Another example of Da Vinci science involves the rainbow.

Investigating the Rainbow—Theodoric of Freiberg (c. 1250–c. 1310)

Theodoric was a Dominican monk living in Medieval Europe. Western science was inactive during this time, suppressed by the orthodoxy of the church, whose word was absolute. Yet this monk was responsible for creating our contemporary understanding of a physical phenomenon. How could this be and what was his larger contribution to the scientific enterprise?

Theodoric was a man of the cloth yet a physicist as well. As a Dominican, he was severely restricted in what he could study, yet he could study something godly. He could study the rainbow that was seen as a covenant between God and living creatures—a promise that the world would never be flooded again (Genesis 9:8-17).

How does one study something as distant, transitory, and inaccessible as a rainbow? Theodoric brought the phenomenon down to earth. He modeled a rainbow by using flasks to mimic each individual raindrop in a cloud. He was able to model both single and double rainbows. This Dominican's contribu-tion to science was not so much the specifics of rainbow physics, it was that he created a scientific model. He advanced the techniques of science. Da Vinci teachers look for this kind of lesson.

Bringing History to Life—Anton van Leeuwenhoek

Scientific writing is a genre in its own right and today's journal reporting—the efficient down-to-business style that we read in *Nature*, *Science*, and many other journals, developed over time. Da Vinci teachers are always asking, "Where did this come from?" Contemporary scientific writing came from letters to scientific societies such as the Royal Society of London.

A particularly interesting reporter was the Delft fabric merchant and lens grinder Anton van Leeuwenhoek. Leeuwenhoek, a tradesman who spoke only Dutch, was introduced to the Royal Society through an anatomist friend, Regnier de Graaf (Developmental Biology 9e Online 2011). Leeuwenhoek observed many microscopic living things for the first time, including bacteria, protists, sperm cells, blood cells, nematodes, and rotifers. His observations were highly accurate—even recognizable today—due to the care with which he ground his lenses and what seems to have been exceptional eyesight. He letters to the Royal Society are quaint by today's standards:

> I then most always saw, with great wonder, that in the said matter there were many very little living animalcules, very prettily a-moving. The biggest sort . . . had a very strong and swift motion, and shot through the water (or spittle) like a pike does through the water. The second sort . . . oft-times spun round like a top . . . and these were far more in number.

In the saliva from the mouth of an old man, Leeuwenhoek found

> an unbelievably great company of living animalcules, a-swimming more nimbly than any I had ever seen up to this time. The biggest sort . . . bent their body into curves in going forwards . . . Moreover, the other animalcules were in such enormous numbers, that all the water . . . seemed to be alive. (www .ucmp.berkeley.edu/history/leeuwenhoek.html)

As part of their study of the origin of life, Da Vinci 7 teachers study Anton van Leeuwenhoek. Doing so they gain insight into a key scientific issue of the day; from what does life arise? In addition, students also come to understand the development of scientific writing and scientific societies.

Da Vinci faculties ask students to read van Leeuwenhoek, and then ask them to observe rich protozoan cultures. They are then challenged to write their own eighteenth century letter to the Royal Society in the language of the time. Teachers caution students to be highly precise in their descriptions and drawings—no fabric merchant was going to be taken seriously if he did not present his work with precision, particularly if he were to report on such outrageous findings. Many reports come in on old-looking parchment and appear as period documents. In doing this assignment students inhabit the mind of an early scientist and gain insight into the early European scientific enterprise.

Philosophy of the Da Vinci Curriculum

The job of a Da Vinci teacher is to be a pragmatic intellectual. Intellectual because the Da Vinci teacher, like any extraordinary teacher, sorts through the complex marketplace of ideas and selects that he or she views as the most robust, provocative, stimulating, important, satisfying, or truthful ones. National and state standards, such as the Common Core, inform these decisions. Ideas that have the "ring of truth" and ideas that stimulate further thought and questions are prized.

Da Vinci teachers respect their own intellects, respect their colleagues' intellects, and respect the intellects of their students. "Intellectual" does not imply detachment or dreariness to a Da Vinci teacher or a Da Vinci student. It simply connotes a rich life within the mind. It is not pejorative. It is not bookish. Da Vinci teachers are active and engaged, political, and empowered.

What does it mean to be a "pragmatic" intellectual? It means that the Da Vinci teacher knows how to engage students in intellectual pursuits. Da Vinci teachers successfully relate to students, relate to them intellectually and personally. It is a close bond, not "academic" in the detached sense of the word. Da Vinci teachers find the intersection between what is intellectually important and what will engage the adolescent mind. It is about taking mind-worthy ideas and making them engaging to young people without paternalistically watering down the concepts.

The Da Vinci Curriculum is designed under the premise that seventh–twelfth grade students are capable of learning very sophisticated material, *if taught well*. Note that eighth grade students—ranging from a smart suburban youth with Deerfield and Princeton in his blood, to international students with limited English, to reluctant farm students—successfully read Gilgamesh, the *Aeneid*, the *Ramayana*, Sophocles, and the *Iliad*. With engaging instruction and with differentiation, and with a school climate that supports intellectual engagement, the vast majority of young people can learn intellectually stimulating content.

Travel Vignette #3

The *David*

Recall that the Israelites were fighting the Philistines, whose best warrior—Goliath—repeatedly offered to meet the Israelites' best warrior in man-to-man combat to decide the battle. None of the trained Israelite soldiers was brave enough to fight the giant Goliath, until David—a shepherd boy who was too young to be a soldier—accepted the challenge. Saul, the Israelite leader, offered David armor and weapons, but the boy was untrained and refused them. Instead, he went out with his slingshot and confronted the enemy. He hit Goliath in the head with a stone, knocking the giant down, and then grabbed Goliath's sword and cut off his head. The Philistines honorably retired as agreed, and the Israelites were saved. David's special strength is said to come from God, and the story illustrates the triumph of good over evil.

Michelangelo's *David* is heartbreakingly faithful to human anatomy; Michelangelo had dissected over thirty cadavers. He saw himself "releasing" David from the marble rather than creating him. Michelangelo chose a moment in the David and Goliath story that had not been represented before. The traditional image is of David moments after slaying the giant Goliath. David often stands triumphant with one foot on Goliath's giant head. For example, examine Donatello's bronze statue of David created in approximately 1440. David the shepherd boy stands victorious, foot on the giant's severed head. Compare that to Michelangelo's *David* (1501–1504). David stands moments before the confrontation, slingshot over the shoulder, stone in hand, his gaze fearsomely focused.

Just sixty years after Donatello's *David*, we see that artists can have ideas of their own and have freedom to express those ideas rather than simply carry out their tradesman contract. They are *interpreters* of the Bible, not just chroniclers. As David had a choice—free will—so does the artist. And their works were, in many cases, public works. In other words, average citizens saw that people could have ideas, could interpret, and could create. If artists could think for themselves, then why couldn't ordinary people? And today, why can't teachers create using their medium, curriculum?

Digital Curriculum Mapping

Once a curriculum is developed, how do faculty preserve it as a dynamic process? There is no perfect way to represent a curriculum. Heidi Hayes Jacobs presents the ins and outs of curriculum mapping (Hayes Jacobs 2004). Electronic web-based curriculum mapping programs—like Curriculum Mapper (part of Collaborative Learning, http://login.clihome.com) or Atlas Rubicon (www.rubicon.com)—are a significant improvement over paper-based maps.

Most teachers have seen the scramble that schools go through just prior to a visiting approval team arrival. "Quick, time to update the curriculum!" After the visiting team leaves the school, those fat notebooks return to the principal's or curriculum director's office where they gather dust for another decade until the next visit. One pair of curriculum directors (M. Benn and N. Cornel 2008) summarizes their preferences for curriculum mapping as follows:

- electronic mapping makes curriculum public
- encourages professional learning communities (PLC) or critical friends groups (CFG)-like conversations
- has changed how teachers view curriculum (encouraged the use of power standards and backward design)
- gives them an opportunity to locate overlap and gaps
- opens up vertical and horizontal discussions among faculty about curriculum

Different teachers wrote the Da Vinci Curriculum documented in this text over several years. It is a handpicked representation of the Da Vinci Curriculum. It offers an overview of units, a narrative description of each year's curriculum, a table for each year that shows units in each major subject area embraced by Da Vinci, and a book list. It is a hybrid of many years' work by many faculty. The school today is smaller than it was and, for several reasons, differs somewhat from what you see here. The introduction of the Common Core calls for an updating of the Da Vinci readings and standards.

The 85 Percent Rule

Part of the philosophy of the Da Vinci Curriculum is that the large majority of the curriculum—approximately 85 percent—remains relatively stable over time. This allows twelfth grade students to have common experience upon which they can build. It means that there is a continuous curriculum experience—a logic and flow that makes sense and is predictable. Curriculum is not left to the whim of each faculty member—it's bigger than that. Curriculum is a community endeavor. A tenth grade teacher can weigh in on considerations to adopt a new text for seventh grade. A student may as well. Curriculum is ours, not mine.

Travel Vignette #4

Genius

It seems to me that human intelligence—even genius—can be cultivated, and it is the job of schools to do so.

Before we can consider how a school might foster genius, we have to identify what genius is. Lewis Terman (http://en.wikipedia.org/wiki/Lewis_Terman) and Leta Hollingworth (http://en.wikipedia.org/wiki/Leta_Hollingworth) classify genius as simply someone who crosses a certain IQ threshold. This seems simplistic. It is not clear that IQ can be measured in any reliable way; and if measurable, IQ does not take into account will, motivation, drive, cross-disciplinary patterns of thinking, the ability to connect knowledge that others view as disparate, or sheer insight and creativity—the Steve Jobs type of genius. IQ does not require accomplishment or effectiveness. Stephen Hawking said, "People who boast about their IQs are losers."

Most people would agree that "a genius has a unique and novel way of approaching situations and the world, retooling ideas and potentially creating something so monumental that it changes the way other people think" (www.wisegeek.com/what-is-a-genius.htm), in other words, *divergent* thinking. Margaret Mead's work, for example, was central to the field of anthropology. Charles Darwin gave us a unifying theory in biology. Leonardo's polymath accomplishments bridged the sciences and the humanities. Albert Einstein was able to create an equation with just five symbols that equated matter and energy. Isadora Duncan pioneered modern dance. Were each of these people "geniuses"? Can schooling cultivate range and depth of genius? Are there countless others who could flourish in different environments?

I believe so, but not in schools as we know them. The educational system in America (and others maybe more so) is fundamentally convergent. Students learn according to prescribed standards in order to perform well on standards-based exams. Most teachers approach the standards using "direct instruction," meaning some modification of lecture. This has been even more so in Asia, although Yong Zhao (*Catching Up or Leading the Way*, 2009) questions whether this should be the case. Schools can teach divergently while ensuring that students acquire the skills and knowledge identified in the standards.

To do so, students need to acquire knowledge and skills for some higher purpose rather than as ends in themselves. This may sound daunting, but there is good news in this proposition. Higher purpose is motivating. Motivated students learn efficiently (but not necessarily identically).

Human beings engage well and are motivated by higher purpose. Meaningful learning is memorable. As human beings, we are wired for meaning making; for purposeful pursuit. In an effort to scaffold learning, schools so often disarticulate understanding by removing context and make the simplest learning tasks far more difficult than they need be. The pursuit of genius is the pursuit of meaningful understanding in and across disciplines. We foster genius by fostering independent thinking.

Yet there is another dimension to genius—the ability to see connections that others do not see. Not all geniuses can do this—some are highly focused on narrow skills (great chess players are famously narrow and tend to be unable to extend their chess expertise to other fields). Perhaps Michelangelo is an example of this single-minded focus. Beyond elementary school (and more and more within elementary school) educators systematically teach within ever more narrow disciplinary regimes. In other words, we are taught to think the way that we do—disciplinarily. There are other possibilities. Schools can foster project-based learning (the MET school comes to mind) or interdisciplinary study (the Da Vinci Curriculum, for example).

Does each category of intelligence have its own geniuses? I suspect so. I suspect that if there are at least seven ways to be intelligent, there are at least seven ways to be a genius—perhaps an infinite number of ways of being genius, if genius means reaching between intelligences.

The curriculum tables in chapter 7 do not include state or national standards, although Gailer developed standards that crossed disciplines in the late eighties, long before the standards movement gained traction. They did so by modifying educational outcomes that the Vermont Business Roundtable drafted. The school evaluated students in all fields against these cross-disciplinary standards. The Common Core gives urgency and consistency to the standards movement.

Chapter 6 Summary

Recipes from the Da Vinci Curriculum—Chef Leonardo
- Teacher: be a chef.
- Teacher: be a researcher.
- Teacher: be a performer.
- Consider digitally mapping your curriculum.
- Genius can be cultivated.

CHAPTER SEVEN

~

Details of the Da Vinci Curriculum and Alignment with the Common Core State Standards

Better to have tried something bold and have failed than never to have ventured from the classroom.

—Gailer head upon utter failure of the
Great Pyramid of Khufu Project

Chapter 7 presents an example of an engaging Da Vinci inquiry and then examines the Da Vinci Curriculum in depth along with its relationship to the Common Core.

How does a school engage students in passionate study while meeting educational standards like the Common Core? Let us begin with a story that addresses that question.

It was an autumn day. The class had worked for weeks trying to capture the sheer scale of the Great Pyramid of Khufu. This building, the only intact structure of the original Seven Wonders of the World, covered thirteen acres and was 450 feet tall! The structure is both immense and remarkably precise. It represents an engineering feat that is hard for us to imagine today. To complete the pyramid in twenty years, 800 tons of stone had to be placed every day, or twelve enormous blocks every hour, twenty-four hours per day. The class was dazzled by the size of this wondrous thing. So, they decided to replicate it.

But not in stone. They decided to survey the base (thirteen acre flat fields are not as easy to find as you might think), mark the four base edges with fluorescent surveyor's tape, and then lift the four edges (also using surveyor's tape) to their requisite height using a weather balloon. It seemed like a good plan. All they needed was the tape, an eight-foot weather balloon, a canister of helium, and the surveyor's equipment.

With the help of a local surveyor and his equipment, they laid out the base and attached the surveyor's tape. Everything was set—all they had to do was fill the balloon and guide it with tethers to its measured height and position. Students would guide each tape, and, they hoped, for a few minutes at least, they would have the great pyramid represented in full scale in Vermont. Local television was there to capture the event.

Just before launch, the balloon was almost fully inflated. Eight students surrounded the balloon, some carefully keeping the balloon off the ground, others with their palms gently holding it in place. What could go wrong? Their only concern was wind—would the light breeze keep them from guiding the balloon to its correct position and height?

Suddenly, there was a dull popping sound and where there had been a giant balloon with students on all sides, there were students facing each other, their palms held up as if in some ancient Egyptian prayer. Where there had been red rubber, there was now a person, a fellow student, looking across an eight-foot void. A small red object lay on the ground below, deflated and defeated.

That was the precise moment that the television reporter thrust his microphone in my face, his cameraman not far behind and asked, "What do you think, Dr. Chaucer?" Bewildered, not quite taking it in yet, I spoke the quote above—better to have tried and failed than not to have tried at all. At the time, it sounded Churchillian. Now it just seems honest.

I do not think that there is likely to be question as to whether this event was engaging; enthusiasm and motivation were strong. This was, after all, *their* project driven by *their* enthusiasm. But were the standards addressed? Was this fluff, a PR stunt, or was it substantive? What did they really learn from this?

The Math Common Core—What Students Really Learned

When speaking of four distinct math pathways (traditional and integrated; either compacted or not), the Common core states, "Ultimately, all of these pathways are intended to significantly increase the coherence of high school mathematics." What is coherence? Coherence implies sticking together, cohesive, being harmonious. We can assume that the Common Core writer's call for coherence is ultimately a call for coherence *in the mind of the student*. Otherwise, it is an abstraction of no use to the learner.

A project like the Great Pyramid Project is inherently coherent because the need to know is generated from the problem that was identified by students. Specific math skills required arise directly from this need. Since curiosity drives the study, there is no disharmony between application in the real world and preparation.

Specifically, these students learned how to calculate the length of a side of the great pyramid knowing the height and width using the Pythagorean theorem. Without knowing this, they were unable to measure out their surveyor's tape. For many, this may have been the first time that they used the theorem for a practical purpose—the first time it meant something to them—the first time they could see its power. This is a fundamental principle referred to as Common Core Unit 2: Similarity, Proof, and Trigonometry:

> Students apply their earlier experience with dilations and proportional reasoning to build a formal understanding of similarity. They identify criteria for similarity of triangles, use similarity to solve problems, and apply similarity in right triangles to understand right triangle trigonometry, with particular attention to special right triangles and the Pythagorean theorem.

They also had to learn the basics of surveying, another real world skill. I recall conversations among students and the local surveyor about the difference between surveys that follow a contour and those that do not. They were intrigued by the notion that an acre can be defined differently depending upon the assumptions. In addition, they had to work with landowners, the press, the local airport (an earlier attempt resulted in UFO reports), and weather balloon and survey companies.

Can all of math be taught like this? Schools like the MET school and its protégés make this kind of individualization work. In the Da Vinci curriculum, the applied side of math is taught parallel to systematic skill development in traditional math courses.

Curriculum Tables

This section provides charts that display the Da Vinci Curriculum in different forms. The first chart shows a six-year overview of the Da Vinci Curriculum. Each year is broken down into six units of study. Gailer calls these "macro units" because of their interdisciplinary nature (they are more than disciplinary units). The right-hand column shows associated Common

Core Reading Standards. The Common Core calls for a progression of skill development. The Common Core guides teachers in this process by giving examples of readings and both qualitative and quantitative measures of reading. The Da Vinci Teacher's job is to find the intersection between the skills identified by the Common Core and the historical Da Vinci Curriculum.

Note also that the Common Core describes three types of writing (argument, informational/explanatory, and narrative): "While all three text types are important, the Standards put particular emphasis on students' ability to write sound arguments on substantive topics and issues, as this ability is critical to college and career readiness." This is true of the Da Vinci model as well. Thesis, argument, and evidence are the currency of inductive learning in the Da Vinci classroom.

The second section gives a synopsis of each year in paragraph form. It adds some flesh to the bone and identifies some key readings.

The second chart (table 7.2) lists key readings for the eighth grade in the Da Vinci classroom and as recommended by the Common Core. Note the increasing reliance on the information text in the Common Core illustration. See the Common Core website for more details and sample writings.

The last section includes a sample table for part of one year of the curriculum. These tables identify key content—themes, topics, and readings—for each unit and discipline. Note that the last curriculum entry for each chart identifies transitional content that connects one year's study with the next. This represents vertical continuity. These charts also estimate time devoted to each unit and discipline, which can be converted to Carnegie Units. This allows the world of Da Vinci to "talk to" the conventional academic world without resorting to extensive written narrative.

Da Vinci Yearly Synopses

Da Vinci 7: Truth and Universe

In Da Vinci 7, students explore themes such as truth, creation, the universe, and evolution. The themes integrate writing, literature, religions, art, and history. The year begins with students choosing "truth tellers" to invite to class to interview about their perception of the nature of truth and human knowing. Students invite interesting people from a variety of walks of life—law, advertising, used car sales, law enforcement, government, religion, science, public service, and writers, for example.

Students ask questions concerning the guest's perception of truth within his or her field. They can be shocked to hear a lawyer claim that the law "does not care about truth—it wants resolution of conflict" or a newspaper

Table 7.1. Overview of the Da Vinci Curriculum and Corresponding Common Core Reading Standards

Da Vinci Unit Overview (content)	Common Core Reading Standards (skills)
Da Vinci 7: Truth and Universe 20 BYA–10,000 YA • Truth and Metamorphosis • Origin of the Universe • Origin of Life • Fundamentals of Life • Origin of Species, Evolution • Primates, *Homo sapiens*, Early Humans	By the end of the year, read and comprehend literature [informational texts, history/ social studies texts, science/ technical texts] in the grades 6–8 text complexity band proficiently, with scaffolding as needed at the high end of the range.
Da Vinci 8: Into Civilization 6,000 BCE–200 CE • Mesopotamia: Neolithic First Cities: Sumerian, Assyrian, Babylonian, and Persian • Egypt: Neolithic to New Kingdom including Nubia • China: Early Yellow River Valley Settlements to Han Dynasty • Greece: Bronze Age to Alexander the Great • India: Early Indus River Valley Settlements, Vedic Age, Mauryan Empire • Rome: Etruscan to Roman Empire	By the end of the year, read and comprehend literature [informational texts, history/ social studies texts, science/ technical texts] at the high end of the grades 6–8 text complexity band independently and proficiently.
Da Vinci 9: Age of Faith 200 CE–1400 CE • India: Gupta Empire to Moslem Invasion • China: 200 CE to Mongol Takeover (T'ang and Sung Ages) • Europe: "Middle Ages" 400 CE–1400 CE • Islam: Rise of and Spread of Islam; Arabian Peninsula to Europe, Africa, and Western Asia • Byzantine Empire • Meso and South America: Mayans, Aztecs, and Incas	By the end of grade 9, read and comprehend literature [informational texts, history/ social studies texts, science/ technical texts] in the grades 9–10 text complexity band proficiently, with scaffolding as needed at the high end of the range.
Da Vinci 10: Discovery and Invasion 1400 CE–1700 CE • Europe: Renaissance, Reformation, Discovery Voyages • Europe: Scientific Revolution • America: Native, French, English, and Spanish Intervention • India: Mogul Dynasty, Hindu and Moslem Conflict • China: Ming and Manchu Dynasties • Russia: Peter the Great (absolutism) and Catherine the Great (despotism)	By the end of grade 10, read and comprehend literature [informational texts, history/ social studies texts, science/ technical texts] at the high end of the grades 9–10 text complexity band independently and proficiently.
Da Vinci 11: The Reach of Europe 1700 CE–1917 CE • Europe: Enlightenment, Industrial Revolution, Liberalism, Nation States, WWI • America: Colonial, Revolution, Civil War, WWI • Russia: Tsarism, 1905, 1917 Revolutions • India: British Empire, Resistance • China: Manchu Empire, Opening • Africa: Boer, Ashanti, Impact of Slave Trade	By the end of grade 11, read and comprehend literature [informational texts, history/ social studies texts, science/ technical texts] in the grades 11–CCR text complexity band proficiently, with scaffolding as needed at the high end of the range.
Da Vinci 12: The Global Community 1917 CE–Future • American Civil War Part II • Between the World Wars • The World in Crisis: World War II • The Post-War Era • The Rise and Fall of Empires—The "American Century"? • The Future: Utopia or Dystopia?	By the end of grade 12, read and comprehend literature [informational texts, history/ social studies texts, science/ technical texts] at the high end of the grades 11–CCR text complexity band independently and proficiently.

reporter claim that she "buys and sells truth." After several interviews, students consider what they have heard. Is truth a universal? Is it contextual? Do different fields have the same criteria for claims to truth? This theme—the Human Search for Truth—continues throughout the six-year study. This examination of human knowing jump-starts the intellectual process that Perry (1999) and Knefelkamp (personal communication, 1999) at Columbia Teachers College describe in their claim that students become more contextual and sophisticated in their understanding as they progress through college. The Da Vinci Curriculum accelerates this intellectual process in the middle school years. This habit of mind is perhaps the most important single factor in students successfully transitioning to college.

Major works of literature include *To Kill a Mockingbird*, *Lord of the Flies*, *Their Eyes Are Watching God*, and *The Giver*. Other literature includes nonfiction, poetry, creation stories, and primary documents. Class instruction revolves around hands-on activities, inductive towers, Socratic seminars, discussions, presentations, and lectures. The seventh grade year focuses on teaching students how to have a productive and respectful dialogue where listening is as prized as talking and changing one's point of view is valued. Students are encouraged to ask their own questions about truth, creation, the universe, and evolution. Students' work also includes oral presentations, creative and analytical writing, nightly readings, student-led discussions, seminars and group projects.

Da Vinci 8: Into Civilization

The Da Vinci 8 curriculum comprises the study of six ancient cultures: Mesopotamia, Egypt, China, India, Greece, and Rome. Students explore each of these cultures through historical, literary, scientific, and artistic perspectives. Students ask: What is civilization? How does the land affect the course of development? How do cultural aspects such as family life and organization of society and religion differ from one civilization to another?

Several epics are read throughout the year—the *Epic of Gilgamesh*, the *Iliad*, the *Ramayana*, and the *Aeneid*—as is other literature such as *Fahrenheit 451* and *A Single Pebble*. Writing essays and narratives, creating art pieces, and designing projects for presentations are several ways in which writing and verbal skills are integrated and practiced.

Da Vinci 9: The Age of Faith

In Da Vinci 9, students explore the global issues and themes of the "Age of Faith" (200–1400 CE). The study reaches back to the time of Moses,

Hinduism, Buddhism, Taoism, Islam, and Confucianism. Primary sources include the *Tao Te Ch'ing*, the Koran, the Old and New Testament, and the *Bhagavad-Gita*. Literature from this time period includes such works as *The Canterbury Tales*, *The Arabian Nights*, *Beowulf*, and *Sir Gawain and the Green Knight*. Later literature read to shed light on this time period includes *Grendel* and *Siddhartha*.

Religion, art, art history, science, and government are brought together into this historical study. Student work includes written essays, art projects, oral presentations, nightly readings, and written reflections.

Da Vinci 10: Encounter and Change

Da Vinci 10 examines the themes of encounter and change. Weekly assignments include short essays, journals, seminars, presentations, graphical representation of knowledge, and artistic explorations. Primary source historical readings include selections from the Renaissance, the Scientific Revolution, and the Reformation. Geographical studies highlighted in the European encounter with the new world, examine changes in the natural and political landscapes brought on by historical events. China, Russia, and India are case studies of the evolution of world religions as social and political infrastructures.

Da Vinci 10 students weigh Chinese, Viking, and European claims to first contact with the Americas. Literature studies, including works by Dante and Pushkin and the Chinese folk novel *Monkey*, allow students to analyze works as cultural artifacts. The "Age of Discovery" was an age of scientific discovery, most notably in the areas of geology and biology. Darwin's theory of evolution resulted from his collections made during the famous *Beagle* mapping expedition. The scientific focus on biology ("natural philosophy" at the time) encourages students to learn and practice contemporary experimental methods while understanding the importance of unifying theory within a scientific discipline. Evolution leads students to plate tectonics and continental drift, unifying theory from geology.

Da Vinci 11: The Rise of Liberalism, Industrialism, and Globalization

Da Vinci 11 focuses its study on the cultures of North America, Europe, and China. DV 11 examines these cultures between the end of the seventeenth century and the beginning of the twentieth century. During this time, the philosophies of the Enlightenment fostered a shift in people's perception of their relationship with nature as well as their relationships with other people. Thus, the rise of liberalism changed the social, political, and economic face of Europe. With an understanding of the ideas of John Locke and

Jean-Jacques Rousseau, developments such as the American Revolution, the French Revolution, and the Industrial Revolution are seen in a larger, more understandable context.

After laying a largely Eurocentric foundation, DV 11 students turn their attention to the Far East where the Manchurian Qing dynasty came to power in the mid-seventeenth century. Students find that while the West espoused mankind's individual "natural" rights such as life, liberty, and the pursuit of happiness, Eastern cultures valued adherence to strict social conventions and the collective good. Such a comparison helps students understand the myriad of cultural differences that exist on our tiny planet as well as the influence the past has had on the complexity of international relations today.

To complement these historical inquiries, students delve deeply into literary works such as the *Adventures of Huckleberry Finn*, *Black Elk Speaks*, *Frankenstein*, *Heart of Darkness*, and *A Daughter of Han*. During Da Vinci 11's study of Europe, students take part in an intense investigation of the art history of the nineteenth century; field trips to museums are common.

The study of Russian scientist Mendeleev's Periodic Table gives a natural entrée into the study of chemistry. Within this chemistry course, students study integrated units such as the chemical composition of gunpowder, which coincides with westward expansion, the chemistry of the photographic process to complement our unit of art history and warfare documentation, and the neurochemistry of drugs in the nervous system to enhance our understanding of the Opium Wars.

Da Vinci 12: The Twentieth and Twenty-First Centuries

Da Vinci 12 students construct meaning of global history, art, science, and literature of the twentieth and twenty-first centuries and project their understanding into the foreseeable future. We ask the following: How has technology changed the way wars are fought and lives are lived? What strategies for survival have emerged in the modern and postmodern world? How will the clash between extreme religious ideals be reconciled in a world of diminishing resources, increasing global warming, exponentially increasing human population, and increasing Balkanization? Simply put, how will we survive as a species in a biologically and culturally diverse world?

DV 12 emphasizes primary source historical narratives such as *Hiroshima*, *Night*, and *Life and Death in Shanghai*. Literature includes historical fiction such as *All Quiet on the Western Front*, *Catch-22*, *Slaughterhouse Five*, *Cat's Cradle*, and *The Sun Also Rises* as well as novels such as *Jazz*, *The Great Gatsby*, and *Tobacco Road*. Art, art history, science, and philosophy of the twentieth century are brought into this historical context. The primary method of instruction is student-led Socratic seminar. Student work includes weekly essays, oral reports, research papers, art projects, lab reports, and primary source-based histories.

The development and use of the atomic bomb provides a poignant entrée point for a thorough study of contemporary physics stressing twentieth century developments.

Table 7.2. Comparison between Eighth Grade Da Vinci Core Texts and Representative Sixth–Eighth Grade Common Core Language Arts Texts

Core Da Vinci eighth grade texts:

Title	Author
Epic of Gilgamesh	N. K. Sander
Fahrenheit 451	Ray Bradbury
A Single Pebble	John Hersey
Things Fall Apart	Chinua Achebe
The Iliad	Homer/Fagles
Black Ships before Troy: The Story of the Iliad	Rosemary Sutcliff
Sophocles I, Three Greek Tragedies	Grene and Lattimore
The Ramayana	R. K. Narayan
The Roller Birds of Rampur	Indi Rana
The Usborne Book of the Ancient World	J. Crisolm
Twelfth Song of Thunder	Navajo Traditional
A Short Walk through the Pyramids and through the World of Art	Phillip Isaacson
In the Time of the Butterflies	Julia Alvarez

Sixth through eighth grade Common Core English language arts texts "illustrating complexity, quality, and range of reading":

Title (Literature, Stories, Drama, Poetry)	Author
Little Women	Louisa May Alcott
The Adventures of Tom Sawyer	Mark Twain
"The Road Not Taken"	Robert Frost
The Dark is Rising	Susan Cooper
Dragonwings	Laurence Yep
Roll of Thunder, Hear My Cry	Mildred Taylor

Title (Informational Texts: Literary Nonfiction and Historical, Scientific, and Technical Texts)	
"Letter on Thomas Jefferson"	John Adams
Narrative of the Life of Frederick Douglass, an American Slave	Frederick Douglass
"Blood, Toil, Tears, and Sweat: Address to Parliament on May 13th, 1949"	Winston Churchill
Harriet Tubman: Conductor on the Underground Railroad	Ann Petry
Travels with Charley: In Search of America	John Steinbeck

Note: The Common Core describes these readings as "representative of a range of topics and genres." Appendix B of the Common Core presents a longer list with sample excerpts.
Note: See HarryChaucer.com for a complete listing of Da Vinci texts.

English Language Arts Texts and the Common Core

The Common Core lists fictional literature (stories, drama, and poetry) and nonfictional (informational texts including literary nonfiction and historical, scientific, and technical texts). See the Common Core website for samples of literature and informational texts illustrating the increasing complexity intended by the Common Core (and included below). See appendix B of the Common Core for text exemplars and sample performance tasks. The Common Core measures text complexity using three measures including quantitative and qualitative measures. Da Vinci teachers are faced with evaluating the new Common Core readings in light of the historical curriculum.

The 85 Percent Rule

As referred to earlier, in the DVC 85 percent of the core curriculum (like the book list) is prescribed and agreed to by the faculty. This is to maintain continuity and provide an opportunity for a vertical conversation through the student's years at Gailer, between family members, and to make sure that "enduring" works endure. The other 15 percent is open to student and faculty discussion. This allows for spontaneity, creativity, experimentation, and personalization of the curriculum.

A text may relate to a historical period in many different ways. Texts such as *Cat's Cradle, Black Elk Speaks,* or the *Iliad,* serve as primary sources written during the period of study. The Works Progress Administration (WPA) slave narratives or the *Narrative of the Life of Frederick Douglas* are examples of the insights that may be gained from primary source texts.

Literature is often written in retrospect about an era. *Siddhartha, Passage to India,* and *All Quiet on the Western Front* represent this type of literature. Other works neither come from the era nor represent it directly but can be related to the time period. For example, *To Kill a Mockingbird* is a story from the early part of the twentieth century but is taught in the seventh grade when the origin of the universe, life, and our species is under study. *Mockingbird* is taught then because it raises questions about truth, an underlying theme in seventh grade. Likewise, *Lord of the Flies* is taught during that same year. It is taught then because it raises questions about our species and about good and evil. Are we civilized? What is civilization? How deep is our civilized nature? What Golding imagines happening when a group of civil boys are left to their own devices on an island raises questions about the human species. Some books fast forward to our era, making connections to the past.

Table 7.3. Sample Da Vinci Curriculum—Da Vinci 7: Truth, Origins, and Evolution, 13.7 BYA—10,000 YA

Unit	Historical or Scientific Texts	Science Investigations	Writing	Literature	Geography	Religions	Performing Arts	Visual and Musical Arts	Mathematics
Yearly Overview	Truth, Origins, and Evolution	Quant. and qual. evidence, sci. enterprise and method	Creative, expository, and analytical writing	Themes: truth, metamorphosis, evolution, and human nature	Universe, Beagle voyage, Galapagos	Creation stories, struggle for truth	Inherit the Wind/ Scopes Trial reenactments	Literature quilts and mobiles, settings (Mockingbird)	Exponents: large and small numbers, Powers of Ten (film and text)
Unit 1: Truth and Metamorphosis	The Year of the Butterfly, Ordish; "Our Deepest Fear," Williamson; Novum Organum, Bacon	Monarch metamorphosis, controlled experiment truth-teller interviews	Field observ., lab reports, truth-teller analysis, creative writing, play writing	Mockingbird, Lee; Their Eyes Were Watching God, Hurston; Time of Butterflies, Alvarez	Migration routes of monarchs and painted ladies	Truth-teller qualitative interviews; Evolution's Captain, Nichols; Seekers, Boorstin	Performance from stage writing, 12 Angry Men	Artistic representations of required and independent readings	Mathematics of migration and proliferation, Malthus
Unit 2 Origin of the Universe	Red Giants and White Dwarfs, Jastrow; Leeuwenhoek; Brief History of Time and Grand Design, Hawking	Powers of Ten, vacuum investigation, universe research paper	Nature and universe poetry, lab reports, Royal Soc. letters	In the Beginning (Hamilton and Moser), selected poems	Large-scale structure of the universe, expanding universe	Creation stories, Genesis	Performing creation myths	Representing creation stories, myth and science, music: "The Planets" by Holst	The scale of the known universe and its exploration
Unit 3: Origin of Life	Darwin's writings, MLK Writings, Biology Coloring Book	Leeuwenhoek protozoan lab, organelle lab, cell models	MLK "Dream" speeches, personal narratives	Creation of life myths; Flowers for Algernon, Keyes	Mapping stromatolites and early life on earth	Origin of human life, politics, and biology of abortion	Origins theatre	Life representations	TED—Truth and Beauty Bolinski Biovisions Prob. of life
Unit 4: Origin of Species and Evolution	In the Shadow of Man, Dian Fossey readings	DNA lab, Mendelian Genetics, Darwin's finches—natural selection, adaptation	Short stories	Lord of the Flies, Golding; In the Shadow of Man, Goodall	The early earth, Pangaea to today, continental drift	NOVA: Judgment Day: Intelligent Design on Trial (2.08)	Dian Fossey: Gorillas in the Mist and Nat. Geo. representations	Images of life on other planets	Human Population / Exponential growth
Unit 5: Primates, Hominids, H. sapiens	Ascent to Civilization, Nat. Geo.: research and films	Cranium Lab; Nova, Becoming Human, parts 1 and 2	Pre-historical fiction—imaging early human life	The Giver, Lowry	Africa, primate evolution, migration	What is it to be human?	Primate film series	Cave paintings—creation of a prehistoric cave	The origin of mathematical thinking—McLeish, ch.1
Continuity—transition to DV 8	Evolution of humans to development of civilizations	From sci. method to river civilizations and technologies	Lab reports and five paragraph essays to defending theses	From stories to epics	From humans to civilizations	Creation stories and the world's religions	Origin of music and theatre in early civilizations	Design and architecture in early civilizations	Earliest innumeracy to geometry, algebra, and trigonometry

Flowers for Algernon is one example. We might see Charlie's rise and fall of intellect as a metaphor for the evolutionary rise of our species and the fall of civilization connecting prehistoric times with our twenty-first century.

This is all to say that there are many ways to connect text to historical study and that not all connections have to be literal. But connections must be overt. Students must understand what they are studying and why they are studying it—that is the nature of the Da Vinci Curriculum.

Grade-Level Curriculum Maps

The sample curriculum map (table 7.3) documents the Da Vinci Curriculum across nine disciplines (history, science, writing, literature, geography, religions, performing arts, visual and musical arts, and mathematics). Note that each year is broken down into five units. Each year has a title for each discipline. Note also that the previous Da Vinci foundation and the next year of the Da Vinci Curriculum are anticipated on each year's study. This is to encourage continuity between the years as well as between the disciplines. Continuity and context are central to the Da Vinci Curriculum. See website for curriculum maps for each of the six years of the Da Vinci Curriculum.

Schools cannot live isolated in the world of Da Vinci without being able to translate their work into understandable standards and units of study. Therefore the Da Vinci Curriculum can be linked to standards (see above) and translated into familiar time-based Carnegie Units of study when necessary.

Chapter 7 Summary

Details of the Da Vinci Curriculum and Alignment with the Common Core State Standards

- The Da Vinci Curriculum is presented in a six-year table format.
- The relationship between the Common Core and Da Vinci Curriculum is discussed.
- The six years of the Da Vinci Curriculum are presented in a synopsis for each year.
- Core texts are presented.
- The 85 percent rule states that 15 percent of the curriculum remains open to customization by each Da Vinci class while 85 percent is prescribed and remains consistent year to year.
- Grade-level curriculum maps are presented in table format.

~

CHAPTER EIGHT

Selected Examples of Rich Inductive Content from the Seventh to Ninth Grade Da Vinci Curriculum

All our knowledge has its origin in our perceptions.

—Leonardo da Vinci (Les Pensees, p. 23)

Wisdom is the daughter of experience.

—Leonardo da Vinci (Les Pensees, p. 28)

Chapter 4 described two powerful Da Vinci Curriculum teaching methods: Inductive Teaching (based on John Clarke's Inductive Towers) and the Da Vinci Seminar (based on Socratic seminar). Chapters 8 and 9 present examples of intellectually rich content ripe for the inductive inference-making process. This chapter describes examples from the seventh through ninth grade curriculum, while chapter 9 presents examples from the tenth through twelfth grade curriculum. Following this are ten examples of elaborate inductive techniques that lead students beyond the basic inference-making process to more sophisticated learning.

In each case, the examples may be adopted or adapted into existing programs or may serve as a model for curricular and instructional development. For example, in the seventh grade human cranium exercise, students are given some knowledge (the age of the crania they are examining) and challenged to propose the relationship between species represented by the crania. This could also be done with a series of science investigations, examples of art that represent different periods, or writing styles that are related. The point is to leave the most important intellectual work to the student, while ensuring that students meet the Common Core Standards.

Seventh Grade

Creation (Origin of the Universe–10,000 BCE)

Creating a Viable Hypothesis—Examination of Human Crania

Chapter 1 describes the seventh grade Da Vinci classroom's use of human crania. Louis Leakey asked the underlying questions "Who am I and where did I come from?" In pursuit of these questions, students systematically make observations of human crania (*cranium* refers to the part of the skull that covers the brain, whereas *skull* includes the jaws; some of the artifacts we have used in this study are technically skulls). Several distributors carry high quality replicas of human skulls and crania.

The teacher poses a question to her class: "Which species are directly on the human line and which are not?" In other words, the top of the inductive tower is a conclusion regarding ancestry. The skulls are arranged in a sequence that represents a hypothesis regarding human ancestry.

In figure 8.1, the gray rectangles represent a group of tables put together covered with rolled paper. In preparation for the class, the Da Vinci teacher creates a time line from the earliest crania that the class has observed to the present. The teacher then puts the crania in place temporally (horizontally, in the top drawing of figure 8.1). The student's job is to determine the other dimension—the dimension of relationship, lineage, and ancestry (the vertical dimension). Based on his or her analysis of the data, each student proposes a lineage. We see a simple form of this in the bottom drawing of figure 8.1. The class then discusses the pros and cons of each proposition. After the students have done their work, the experts are consulted.

The Cro-Magnon and Neanderthal are interesting to compare in their own right, since these two *Homo sapiens* species coexisted. A possible relationship between the two species is presented in the novel *Dance of the Tiger* (Kurtén 1995) and in a 2011 *New Yorker* article ("Sleeping with the Enemy" by Elizabeth Kolbert, August 15, 2011). The novel may be used as a stimulus for inductive thinking in its own right.

Replicating a Key Scientific Investigation—Pasteur's Swan-Necked Flasks

Students can create artifacts or replicas of artifacts. For example, Da Vinci students created swan-necked flasks to mimic the crucial medical investiga-

(Students are given one dimension (age of the crania) of the two-dimensional problem)

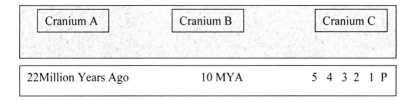

(Students hypothesize the second dimension – the relationships between species - of the two-dimensional puzzle)

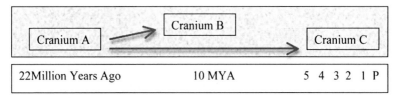

Figure 8.1.   Human Crania Investigation Set-Up and Results

tion done by Louis Pasteur in 1862. The question concerned the origin of life. Could life spontaneously arise, as seemed to be the case when maggots developed on meat or fruit flies on fruit?

The Italian scientist Spallenzani boiled media (and the air above it) and demonstrated that no organisms spontaneously developed, but critics suggested that boiling may have eliminated some vital force in the air that was necessary for life. Pasteur performed the definitive experiment by creating s-shaped necked flasks that could be sterilized but that would allow air (with "vital factors") to enter and leave the vessel while trapping small particles that we now call bacteria. The flasks that seventh grade students prepared remained clear for over a decade. Pasteur's flasks remain clear of bacteria 150 years after his investigation.

There are many other seminal scientific investigations worthy of replication. For example, Johannes Baptista van Helmont performed a crucial experiment in 1649. He was curious about where the wood that makes up large trees came from. He grew a willow cutting into a 162 pound tree. He added nothing but water. Having weighed the soil before and after the experiment, he noted that only 2 ounces of soil were used to produce 162 pounds of material. Where did the new plant come from? This experiment raised crucial questions about atmospheric gases, photosynthesis, and plant growth. It is easily replicable, but may take more than one year to perform. Therefore one class can produce an experiment that will be completed by another, or the investigation can be carried out over several years and "harvested" by the larger school community.

Physical Phenomena—Observations from Nature

Dorothy Wallace-Senft (http://cvermontsnowflakes.com/posters.shtml) created an illustration from snowflake images make by Vermont's "Snowflake Bentley." It shows a physical phenomenon related to temperature (there is a vertical temperature scale in the center of the picture). Students can analyze the pictures and propose relationships between temperature and snowflake shape. Once a pattern has been established, students might ask why that pattern exists in nature. This might lead them to investigate Clarence Birdseye, an innovator who learned that foods "flashfrozen" retain their texture and flavor, thereby beginning the frozen food industry.

Using Sensory Stimuli as Entrée into a New Field

On the first day of school, Carl wanted his students to be present—*really* present. He did not want them to leave their emotional selves at home, sanitize their minds of all that was important to them, and reduce their schoolwork to a series of detached intellectual tasks. A student recalls opening day:

> I remember the first day of 11th grade extremely well—what I remember most was an introductory activity that our teacher led. He had a small, unlabeled kitchen jar that he brought around to each person at the table. We were instructed to stick our noses in the jar and write about the first memory that the smell evoked. This was a simple, but brilliant first day activity. The smell that hit me hard when I dipped my nose was cinnamon. The smell evoked a strong memory of being with my family in Mexico, where they put cinnamon in their hot chocolate (the best I've ever had). But beyond that, the smell brought me back to the feeling of safety I had as a child; the knowledge that everything would be all right as long as my parents were there. I had recently acquired my driver's license and was discovering that driving was a tenuous and dangerous activity. The feeling of safety, almost invulnerability, that I had felt riding with my parents, even in stormy weather, was ripped away as I saw the truth about driving: one wrong move and trouble would hit you at 50 mph. This recollection, combined with my reflections on childhood and adult perspectives, had been conjured up with a strong smell and a well-introduced process. The use of personal, even emotional, experiences to draw connections to the world was always an important part of the Da Vinci experience.

We want to graduate whole people whose minds, bodies, and hearts are inseparable. To do so we must invite the whole person into the classroom. Dartmouth Professor Chris Jernstedt says that we must address the emotional

deconstruct Sir Leonard Woolley's interpretation. Oftentimes they discover that their interpretations are more closely tied to the physical object than the expert's interpretation. The student asks of the expert, "How closely do your conclusions reflect your evidence?" See figure 8.3 for a visual representation.

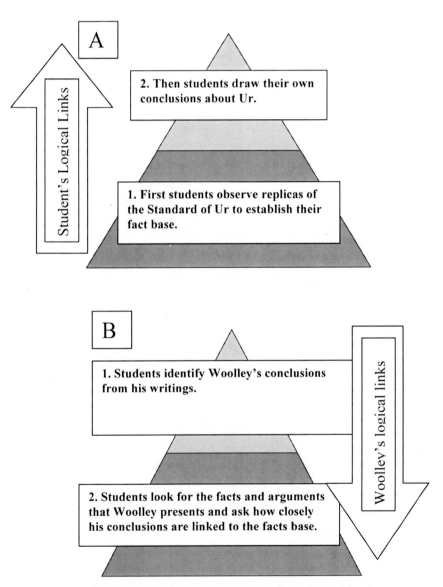

Figure 8.3.   Student-Constructed Tower (A) Compared to a Tower That Deconstructs Expert Opinion (B)

In step A, students draw their own conclusions based on their observations of the *Standard of Ur*. In step B, students deconstruct the expert's claims by identifying the evidence that Sir Leonard Woolley refers to in his original interpretation of the artifact.

Deconstructing a conclusion is a sophisticated intellectual task, yet eighth-grade students can do it easily with guidance, and structures guide them. It is important that Da Vinci students first carry out their own inductive work *before* reading the experts'. Otherwise expert opinion will "jam their radar," making it nearly impossible to make observations and inferences with an open mind. There's always room for expert opinion *after* students have exercised their own minds. Remember that Aristotle's views went largely unquestioned for over a thousand years. We don't want to repeat that, now do we?

Imaginative Assessment—The Comprehensive Exam
There is a summative evaluation at the end of the eighth grade study of ancient civilizations. This is part of their "comprehensives." Comprehensives are like midterms and finals, but the emphasis is on a comprehensive synthe-

Figure 8.4. Giles and Randy Smelt Copper

Gailer Story #6

Copper Smelting

It was early morning. Students were waking from their tents. However, two students were completing their shift of stomping on bellows to keep the fires going. Two others were sitting in lawn chairs with blankets wrapped around them. The fires were two feet down in our handmade hearths. The bellows that they rode directed air deep into the hearths. Our eighth grade class was smelting copper.

It was their idea. In class, as they read about the Bronze Age, they were struck by the technical advance of adding impurities to copper to make a stronger metal, and how simple the idea was. At the same time, they became intrigued with the moment when humans first made metal from ore—when we first smelted copper. This was a BIG IDEA, they said.

They also said if people could smelt copper thousands of years ago with primitive tools, they could do it today.

At this moment, the teacher's role shifted. So often, as teachers, we light fires to get intellectual fires burning. We bring fuel to the fire. But here, in seminar, a spark had hit a tiny bit of tinder. The teacher's role shifted from fire lighter, or firewood provider, to a person who pumps a bellows to give as much oxygen as he can to the intellectual spark that he saw take form. His job was to feed this fire and to help his class accomplish their tentative goal. "Do you think that you could do that?" "What would you need?" "How would you find out how copper is smelted?" The fire raged.

The class divided up into groups with tasks—one group looked for information on copper smelting from ancient Egyptian, Greek, and Meso-American texts. Another contacted the U.S. Bureau of Mines, a mine in Indonesia, and another mine out west. One group worked on the apparatus they would need. They were encouraged when they discovered a photo of an Egyptian painting that depicted copper smelting.

It took three trials, but they finally extracted copper from copper ore.

I recall a couple of conversations between those students sitting in the lawn chairs. One said, "We really needed Matt—without him, we couldn't have built the bellows and certainly would not have thought of the one-way valves." Another thought aloud about the people who made this metal—where they low-level tradesmen or highly respected priests? He imagined the fires burning—breathing really, with the bellows pulses—and could see a desert filled with this mysterious alchemy. Later, another student began to speculate on the wood and charcoal needed to keep the fires burning—"Did they ship wood or charcoal?" he asked. "Did they return with goods?" "Where did they find the wood?" "With whom did they trade?" Their inquiry had sparked more than a charcoal fire. In Debra Meier's words, their intellectual fire represents the Power of Their Ideas.

sis rather than a reiteration of information and ideas learned throughout the year. "Comps" are another chance to elaborate learning but this time with a larger data set available—a half year or full year of material.

In this eighth grade comprehensive exam, students were challenged to create a plausible conversation between artifacts from different times and cultures. A Thai Buddha, Homer, a Japanese dragon, a Greek vase, and a Roman warrior were on display. Students were asked to construct their dialogue so that they showed the knowledge that they had learned about the civilizations and about the nature of civilization in general.

In another year, eighth grade students were challenged with a different comprehensive problem. These students were asked to write a short play that plausibly brought together as many of the civilizations that they had studied as possible in time and place. They were asked to create an interaction that exemplified the traits of these people, their cultures, and times. One class chose the Silk Road and was able to plausibly bring all but Meso-Americas together in a creative and instructive play that gave them a vehicle to "conserve, transmit and expand" what they had learned (Dewey 1934).

Early Documents: The *Code of Hammurabi*

The *Code of Hammurabi* is an eight-foot stele (carved public posting) making clear to the people the laws of ancient Babylonia. Partial replicas are available from museum stores. The sixth Babylonian king, Hammurabi, in approximately 1760 BCE, enacted this code. It is one of the earliest codes of law. It serves as a rich source of inductive work for Da Vinci students.

Students might begin with the bas-relief image at the top of the stele. Given knowledge of the date, place, and the fact that the stele was a public posting, they can use an inductive tower to puzzle out the two figures shown in the image at the top of the stele. Having attempted to do so, the teacher might review the first line of the text that states, "Anu and Bel called by name me, Hammurabi, the exalted prince, who feared God, to bring about the rule of righteousness in the land." Students are coaxed toward an understanding of the image as one of Hammurabi presenting his rules of law to his god. The right hand raised was considered to be a sign of respect to the god.

Students then examine a translation of the actual laws. For example,

If a judge try a case, reach a decision, and present his judgment in writing; if later error shall appear in his decision, and it be through his own fault, then he shall pay twelve times the fine set by him in the case, and he shall be publicly removed from the judge's bench, and never again shall he sit there to render judgment. (http://eawc.evansville.edu/anthology/hammurabi.htm)

We too have judges, cases, and legal decisions, although we do not penalize our judges for their errors in judgment. However, consider this Hammurabi law:

> If any one brings an accusation against a man, and the accused go to the river and leap into the river, if he sink in the river his accuser shall take possession of his house. But if the river prove that the accused is not guilty, and he escape unhurt, then he who had brought the accusation shall be put to death, while he who leaped into the river shall take possession of the house that had belonged to his accuser.

This is quite unfamiliar to us, but perhaps not unfamiliar to our colonial ancestors. We do not expect our rivers to arbitrate our disputes. From this ancient document we can see both traces of our own legal systems and some very unfamiliar cultural artifacts as well. Historical artifacts like *Hammurabi's Code* are relevant because records like this are part of the development of the human story. Striving for justice is an important aspect of our story.

Ninth Grade

The Age of Faith (200 CE–1,400 CE)

Primary Source Texts as Cultural Artifacts

Texts believed to be sacred are used as the basis for inductive work in the ninth grade. Sections of the Bible, Quran, Bhagavad-Gita, Siddhartha, Confucian Analects, and other texts such as the *Tao of Pooh* serve as primary sources for the study of the world's religions. These texts form the foundation of inductive towers that lead to the fundamental questions "What does each religion strive for?" "Are the world's religions fundamentally similar or dissimilar in their beliefs about human beings, ethics, and god(s)?"

One student, after reading many sacred texts, concluded that Buddhists strive for enlightenment; Christians, for redemption; and Native Americans, for transcendence. If this is true, does this reflect an underlying similarity, or are religious beliefs symbols of human differences? She then asked if there were universal values beyond these divergent religious views.

Replicating Engineering and Architecture—The Arch and the Column

Da Vinci said that "an arch is nothing other than a strength caused by two weaknesses; for the arch in building is made up of two segments of a circle, and each of these segments being in itself very weak desires to fall, and as the one withstands the downfall of the other the two weaknesses are converted into a single strength" (MacCurdy 2003). The arch and the column were important advances in architecture. Replicating these elements gives students a feel for the forces involved and an appreciation for the historical development.

Several YouTube clips show students assembling arches much like Da Vinci students have done. Watching groups of students at work, one can see the two weaknesses of the two segments and the strength that is created by uniting them into one continuous arch. The BBC has a demonstration online that can help students understand the process and forces involved (www.bbc.co.uk/history/interactive/animations/arch/index_embed.shtml). The experience of building an arch (column, dome, cantilever, etc.) provides students with an opportunity to see and feel the forces at work so that they can reach a deeper understanding and appreciation of architectural elements.

Chapter 8 Summary

Selected Examples of Rich Inductive Content from the Seventh to Ninth Grade Da Vinci Curriculum

- A viable hypothesis can serve as the nucleus of a unit (seventh grade, examination of human crania).
- Replicating historical investigations can trigger a unit of study (seventh grade, Pasteur's swan-necked flasks).
- Direct observations from nature can drive a study (seventh grade, snowflake observation from either nature or Snowflake Bentley graphic).
- Sensory stimuli can ignite a study (seventh grade, cinnamon).
- Giant models can make learning vivid (seventh grade, chromosome models).
- Deconstructing expert opinion following a structured inference-making process can be a powerful teaching tool (eighth grade, the *Standard of Ur*).
- Imaginative assessment that demands creative and comprehensive synthesis can provide students with a second opportunity to engage in rich content (eighth grade, the comprehensive exam).
- Primary source artifacts can engage students by bringing them close to the action as scientists (eighth grade, the *Code of Hammurabi*).
- Primary source documents can draw students into an engaging study (ninth grade, religious texts).
- The arch and column are an example of how students can experience the forces at work in key architectural elements.

~

Selected Examples of Rich Inductive Content from the Tenth to Twelfth Grade Da Vinci Curriculum

Beware of the teaching of these speculators, because their reasoning is not confirmed by experience.

—Leonardo da Vinci (Les Pensees, p. 14)

Although nature commences with reason and ends in experience, it is necessary for us to do the opposite, that is to commence with experience and from this proceed to investigate the reason.

—Leonardo (Atalay and Wamsley 2008, 95)

Chapter 9 gives examples of rich inductive content from the tenth to twelfth grade.

Tenth Grade

Encounter and Change (1,400–1,700 CE)

Comparing Historical Accounts and Images—Columbus's Encounter with the New World

"In fourteen hundred ninety-two, Columbus sailed the ocean blue." Every schoolchild knows this little poem, but what was the nature of Columbus's exploration? Was he a courageous explorer doing the noble work of spreading the good word of the Christian God? Or was he a barbaric and egotistical self-promoter who was interested in colonizing the new world without regard for the human beings who lived there previously? Was Columbus, in fact, even the first from another continent to visit the Americas?

Paintings from the 1500s depict two very different stories. Some (see www.friendsofart.net/en/art/john-vanderlyn/columbus-landing-at-guanahani -1492) depict a glorious landing in the new world with flags unfurled and Columbus's sword touching the ground as if to claim it. Others show a very different story—hands being cut off native people who failed to produce their quota of gold. This image comes from Theodorus de Bry (1528–1598), who depicted atrocities recounted by Bartolomé de las Casas in *Narratio Regionum indicarum per Hispanos Quosdam devastatarum verissima* (Bry and Alexander 1976).Wherein lays the truth?

An inductive approach to teaching Columbus begins with a stimulating and provocative question or artifacts. The Da Vinci teacher challenges students to determine the truth of the matter: Was Columbus the first to discover the new world? What was the nature of his interaction with native peoples?

Students will then read Father Bartolomé de las Casas, a priest who documented in *Historia de las Indias* (Casas and Sanderlin 1992) the treatment of native people whom Columbus encountered. Today, how do we react when a religious leader gives "a speech in Brazil that claimed that natives were 'silently longing' for Christianity before it was presented to them—and that this was in no way 'imposition of a foreign culture'" (Widmer 2007)? Da Vinci students' investigations often lead them to the present as they examine the past. These connections are what have become known as "Da Vinci Moments."

Astonishing Primary Sources—The Waldseemüller Map

The Waldseemüller Map has been called "America's Birth Certificate" because it is the first time that the name "America" shows up on a map. One can just see it in the far left side of the map within Brazil.

Ted Widmer writes about this important map in his article titled "Navigating the Age of Exploration: And Restoring Our Capacity for Astonishment" in *American Educator* (Winter 2007–2008). What a great subtitle: "Restoring Our Capacity for Astonishment." We want to place astonishing things in front of our students. We want to see them awestruck to find that so little of the Americas had been explored just four hundred years ago. We want them amazed to discover that the author of this map, Martin Waldseemüller, chose the name "America" mistakenly thinking that Amerigo Vespucci, a gatherer of map data, had discovered the new world. Every Da Vinci class class should "restore our capacity for astonishment."

It is interesting for students to compare this Waldseemüller Map with others shown on the "1421" website (www.1421.tv/maps.asp). See below.

Pursuing a Provocative Hypothesis—The "1421" Thesis

Alternatively, students may be interested in the question of when and by whom the first contact with the new world occurred. They might research the Helge Ingstad discoveries at L'Anse aux Meadows in Newfoundland in 1960 that suggest that the Vikings traveled to American five hundred years before Columbus (www.mnh.si.edu/vikings/voyage/subset/vinland/archeo .html). They might explore the text and website by Gavin Menzies titled "1421." Menzies states:

On the 8th of March, 1421, the largest fleet the world had ever seen sailed from its base in China. The ships, huge junks nearly five hundred feet long and built from the finest teak, were under the command of Emperor Zhu Di's loyal eunuch admirals. Their mission was to "proceed all the way to the end of the earth to collect tribute from the barbarians beyond the seas" and unite the whole earth in Confucian harmony. The journey would last over two years and circle the globe.

When they returned, Zhu Di lost control and China was beginning its long self-imposed isolation from the world it had so recently embraced. The great ships rotted in their moorings and the records of their journeys were destroyed. Lost was the knowledge that Chinese ships had reached America seventy years before Columbus and circumnavigated the globe a century before Magellan. They had also discovered Antarctica, reached Australia three hundred and fifty years before Cook and solved the problem of longitude three hundred years before the Europeans.

From a Da Vinci teacher's perspective, the point is not to amass a discrete body of facts nor is it to definitively solve the mystery of American discovery. The point is to interact intelligently with time, people, culture, the arts, science, and geography. The point is to engage and learn how to think about history, which, from the Da Vinci teacher's vantage point, is the only game in town. All ideas and understandings have historical antecedents and context. These narratives are powerful teaching tools. Provocative theses stimulate thinking.

Science is a discrete discipline, but it also has a history and can be accessed via that history. Why approach a field like science through the humanities? Because to many students, the humanities—the story of humankind—is inherently accessible. Through the humanities a student can access quantitative science and other fields. Once engaged, students accumulate a vast fact base because the teacher has generated a need to know. Once the need to know is present, learning is virtually limitless.

Provocative Thesis II—Hockney and the Great Masters

Not every student has a driving desire to study art history. However, art history can become engaging when students are asked to consider a provocative thesis like this one: the old Masters cheated!

This is a bit of an exaggeration of David Hockney's suggestion that many painters used a variety of visual devices to trace with precision fleeting smiles, accurate proportions and spatial relationships. *Secret Knowledge: Rediscovering the Lost Techniques of the Old Masters* (Hockney 2001) and *Vermeer's Camera: Uncovering the Truth behind the Masterpieces* (2001) by Philip Steadman develop this thesis in some depth. The thesis may or may not be true; that is not the point. The thesis is provocative and will engage students—it is worthy of thought. Da Vinci students have built a camera lucida, a simple device that appears to project an image onto paper.

Eleventh Grade

Rise of Liberalism, Industrialism, and Globalism (1700–1900 CE)

Rich Visual Display of Data—Napoleon's March to Moscow

Figure 9.1 is an example of a type of illustration that the Da Vinci teacher cherishes. Da Vinci teachers collect interesting visual displays of informa-

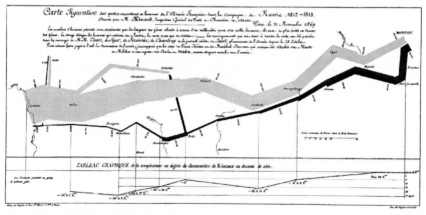

Figure 9.1.   Charles Joseph Minard's "Napoleon's March to Moscow" 1869. © Graphics Press, LLC. Supplied by Edward Tufte. Source: www.edwardtufte.com/tufte/minard

Gailer Story #7

Sandy and Dean

Sandy and Dean were two very bright students. Calling them nerds wouldn't be going too far. Sandy was a brilliant math student and singer; Dean excelled in the sciences. Both were well rounded and could master most anything they set their minds to. In their sophomore year, they set their minds to each other.

In school, their performance dropped. One teacher, John, began each of their evaluations with, "In case we miss the elephant standing before us in the living room..." He then talked about how wonderful a thing it was that they had fallen in love, and how concerned he was that they seem to have fallen out of love with Shakespeare. They each grinned at the thought. John considered a joint conference.

Later that week, a teacher came to me during fitness and said, "Sandy and Dean are missing." "Missing?" I replied. "You have a fitness class of eight students in a school of eighty; they can't be missing." We found out later that they were at one of their houses, apparently engaged in an alternate fitness activity. I suspended them for two days. After the first blush of their first romance, they returned to their studies and both did quite well.

Two years later, they were each applying for college. Sandy applied to and attended a prestigious college. Dean's application, however, created a moral dilemma for me. "Has this student ever been suspended or expelled?" the Ivy League reference form asked. Yes, in fact he had, but it was none of their business. This was an internal matter—between the school, the parents, and the students. I chose to deal with it that way. I think that it was the right thing to do.

Dean completed his degree from that prestigious school. In fact, he won their most demanding academic award as an athlete. He went on to another Ivy League master's program.

Dean and Sandy are happily married, living with their three children in northern New England.

tion. This map of Napoleon's march to Moscow and subsequent retreat displays quantitative historical information showing the relationship between the number of troops (width of the line as troops march from left to right and as troops retreat from right to left) and geography (note the river crossings) and temperature (in Celsius on the retreat). Students "read" this map inductively and draw conclusions about Napoleon's attack on Moscow.

Edward R. Tufte has four books collecting this kind of imagery: *The Visual Display of Quantitative Information, Envisioning Information, Visual Explanations,* and his most recent, *Beautiful Evidence.* Each is remarkable in its own way and can serve as a rich source of inductive stimulate. Another outstanding source is the *Atlas of Science: Visualizing What We Know* by Katy Börner (2010).

Entrée into a Field of Knowledge—Mendeleev's Periodic Table

In the Da Vinci Curriculum, as in most conventional school curricula, students study chemistry in their junior year. However in the Da Vinci classroom, there is reason for placing chemistry in that year. The study has a natural entrée in the nineteenth century study via the Russian scientist Dmitri Mendeleev. It was Mendeleev who saw and captured in a table the periodicity of the elements, which gave him insight into the atomic structure of the elements. His 1869 table is printed on the associated website.

From this table, one of Mendeleev's early versions, students ask questions about chemistry that are just as relevant today as they were in the nineteenth century. What accounts for the regularity of the elements? What elements were known in 1869? Did Mendeleev predict other elements to fill in the gaps in his table? Could there be other elements that we have not found (or manufactured)? Are there other characteristics that display periodicity aside from mass? What does periodicity tell us about the structure of atoms and their bonding to create compounds?

Mendeleev's period table is a rich entrée into the world of chemistry and provides insight into the development of the scientific enterprise in the nineteenth century. It also gives Da Vinci students an opportunity to look back through history at the development of human concepts of elemental structure—of atoms. The early Greeks identified earth, air, fire, water, and ether. We identify ninety-two naturally occurring elements. The manipulation of these elements pharmacologically and industrially is largely responsible for the world that we experience today. Even a minimally educated person today understands the concept of "carbon footprint." Writing these words, I am aware that I am manipulating electrons, a concept inconceivable to Dmitri Mendeleev or Aristotle.

Combining Conclusions to Build a Larger Insight—Thinking Systemically: Human Circulation

In conventional biology classrooms, students study anatomy and physiology as part of "systems" such as the muscular-skeletal system. Yet students rarely understand that the concept of "system" is relatively new and that the conceptualization of circulation as a "circulatory system" of interrelated parts is a recent thought with three key breakthroughs that made it possible. Our thinking is so systemic that it is difficult to imagine thinking in other ways.

It took three concepts—the heart as a pump, the capillary connection between arteries and veins, and one-way valves in veins—to build the concept of a circulatory system. Three experiments can be done, each of which lead to a conclusion. The three conclusions form the base of another tower, at the top of which is the concept of circulatory system.

Until around 1500, the human heart was considered to be a heater rather than a pump. You might find that hard to believe—students do—until the teacher places a large mass of wet fibrous tissue—a cow pluck (heart, lungs, and trachea) on an enamel tray in front of them and says, "Make sense out of this—it's a cow heart and related organs." An hour later, they can barely tell up from down and front from back, not to speak of identifying structures and their interrelated functions. Even after close examination, there is no reason to believe that the heart has anything to do with pumping blood. Yes, there is blood present, but that's true with any internal organ. The heart valves ("these look like mozzarella cheese," said one student) are stringy insubstantial things, unlike any manufactured value.

In struggling with this, students learn how hard-fought our biological understanding is. Open a freshly killed deer and you find a warm central organ—a heart—a heater by all accounts. It was not until the 1500s that the heart was viewed as being a pump for the circulation of blood.

The second two elements of circulation were equally preposterous. Arteries and veins were easy to see with the naked eye either through the skin or in a freshly butchered animal, but the capillaries could not be seen easily prior to the invention of the microscope (although Leonardo observed them far earlier, a testament to his exceptional eyesight). Students can easily see capillaries by examining the tail of a live fish put on a glass slide. Thousands of donut-shaped pillows (corpuscles) squeeze through the capillaries, looking like taxis in a city seen from the upper floors of a hotel. Consider this abstract from "Malpighi and the Discovery of Capillaries" by J.M.S. Pearce in *European Neurology* (http://content.karger.com/produktedb/produkte .asp?doi=107974):

> Leonardo da Vinci clearly observed and described capillaries. Using the microscope, Marcello Malpighi examined the brain and major organs to demonstrate their finer anatomical features. This led to his discovery in 1661, of capillaries that proved fundamental to our understanding of the vascular system in the brain and cord. He hypothesized that capillaries were the connection between

arteries and veins that allowed blood to flow back to the heart in the circulation of the blood, as first asserted by William Harvey.

The third element is fun to demonstrate. The teacher can gather students around or demonstrate this on an Elmo or other projection device. It takes distinct veins to see this well. The early Egyptians could have done this experiment—any humans anywhere—all they needed for equipment were two hands. Historically,

> therefore, our investigations revealed that Estienne and Canano discovered the venous valves in the 1530s. Fabricius ab Aquapendente's achievement was their full recognition sixty-four years later. However, it was not until 1628 that their function was fully understood, with the discovery of blood circulation by William Harvey.

It took some time for the existence of venous valves to be accepted and understood and even longer to see values as being part of blood circulation. To demonstrate venous values, you simply place the index finger from your right hand between your index and middle finger knuckles on the back of your left hand. This stops the blood from flowing back to the heart (up your arm). Then, with moderate pressure, leaving your index finger in place, slide your thumb about one inch toward your elbow. You will see the vein between your index finger and thumb collapse. As you remove your thumb (leaving your middle finger in place), note that the vein remains deflated. This means that you have pushed the blood back toward the heart past a one-way valve (that keeps the blood from returning toward the fingers). Then, dramatically, remove your index finger and the vein will fill with blood. If you watch carefully, you can see the vein fill from the fingers toward the heart, demonstrating both the presence of a valve and the direction of blood flow in veins.

Putting the three concepts together, the heart as a pump, capillaries, and the one-way nature of venous valves, and you have the concept of circulatory system. Dissection and experimentation can illustrate other refinements such as renal or pulmonary circulation. This work can easily be connected to studies that Leonardo did comparing a dissection of an old man's arteries with that of a boy. He documented the degeneration of the arteries over time and attributed the "death so sweet" of an old man to declining blood supply. Leonardo identified the heart as the key organ of the vascular system, rejecting the medieval concept of the liver being central (Nicholl 2004, 419).

When all is said and done, learning this way students not only understand the idea but they understand the development of the idea. Elaboration is both educationally and scientifically meaningful. Meaning, for Da Vinci teachers, is the Holy Grail.

Primary Sources and Audience—WPA Slave Narratives (Slave Narratives: An Introduction to the WPA Slave Narratives, 2011)
This lesson uses a unique combination of primary sources to produce a powerful lesson. During FDR's New Deal WPA program, many people, including writers, were employed in government projects. In this project writers were asked to capture the experience of the few former slaves who were still alive (this was about sixty-five years after slavery ended). A student reads the first narrative aloud, being careful to respectfully read the dialect verbatim as written. Embellishment could easily lead to stereotypic speech. (See below for an edited version.)

The class is then asked to extract key words that capture the first person's experience. They usually choose words such as "good," "laugh," "kind," and "fair." They are then asked to generalize about that person's experience. They conclude that slavery for this person was not all that bad.

They then read a second narrative (below) and are asked to again identify key words and draw conclusions from those words. The identify words such as "whipped," "slave," "screaming," and "separated." They are then asked to generalize and usually state that life was pretty bad for this person. They are then asked to speculate as to why these reports might be so different. They often suggest that one might have been a field slave and the other a house slave, that they lived in different states, or that they had different masters.

After the hypothesis-creating process, the teacher introduces one simple new fact: the two narratives captured the experience of the *same* former slave. Da Vinci teachers then ask their students to hypothesize why the narratives were different knowing that the same person's experience was being captured. Students come up with many suggestions: the person may have been different age, may have been sold to a different owner, may have been subject to punishment between the two interviews, and so forth.

If students do not come up with it on their own, the teacher adds the last fact: one writer/researcher was white, the other black. With this in mind, students are asked to write about and discuss why the former slave described her experience so differently to a black and a white researcher. They are asked how the concepts of "voice" and "audience" have been enriched from their experience in this class. They are asked how their own listening has been altered as a result of the two readings.

#1 Interview with Former Slave (edited)

"I kin remember some things like it was yesterday, but I is 104 years old now and age is starting to get me, I can't remember everything like I use to. I getting old, old. You know I is old when I been a grown woman when the Civil War broke out. I was hired out then, to a Mr. McDonald who lived on Atlantic Street, and I remembers when de first shot was fired, and the shells went right over de city. I got seven dollars a month for looking after children, not taking them out, you understand, just minding them. I did not get the money, Mausa got it."

"Don't you think that was fair?" I asked. "If you were fed and clothed by him, shouldn't he be paid for your work?"

"Course it been fair," she answered. "I belong to him and he got to get something to take care of me."

"We lived on St. Philip Street. The house still there, good as ever. I go 'round there to see it all de time; the cistern still there too, where we used to sit 'round and drink the cold water, and eat, and talk and laugh. Mr. Fuller have lots of servants and the ones he didn't need hisself he hired out. The slaves had rooms in the back, the ones with children had one room, not to cook in but to sleep in. They all cooked and ate downstairs in the hall that they had for the colored people. I don't know about slavery but I know all the slavery I know about, the people was good to me. Mr. Fuller was a good man and his wife's people been grand people, all good to their slavers. Seem like Mr. Fuller just git his slaves so he could be good to dem. He made all the little colored children love him. If you don't believe they loved him what they all cry, and scream, and holler for when dey hear he dead? 'Oh Mausa dead, my Mausa dead, what I going to do, my Mausa dead.' Dey tell dem t'aint no use to cry, dat can't bring him back, but de chillen keep on crying. We used to call him Mausa Eddie but he named Mr. Edward Fuller, and he sure was a good man.

"Mr. Fuller was a good man, he was sure good to me and all his people, dey all like him. God bless him, he in de ground now but I ain't going to let nobody lie on him. You know he good when even the little chillen cry and holler when he dead. I tell you dey couldn't just fix us up any kind of way when we going to Sunday School. We had to be dressed nice, if you pass him and you ain't dress to suit him he send you right back and say tell your ma to see dat you dress right. Dey couldn't send you out in de cold barefoot neither. I 'member one day my ma want to send me wid some milk for her sister-in-law what live 'round de corner. I fuss cause it cold and say 'how you going to send me out wid no shoe, and it cold?' Mausa hear how I talkin' and turn he back and laught, den he call to my ma to gone in de house and find shoe to put on my feet and don't let him see me barefoot again in cold weather."

"Were most of the masters kind?" I asked.

"Well, you know," she answered, "times den was just like dey is now, some was kind and some was mean; heaps of wickedness want on just de same as now. All my people was good people. I see some wickedness and I hear 'bout all kinds of t'ings but you don't know whether it was lie or not. Mr. Fuller been a Christian man."

#2 Interview with Former Slave (edited)

"I'm a hund'ed an one years old now, son. De only one livin' in my crowd frum de days I wuz a slave. . . . My master . . . owned the family of us except my father. There was eight men an' women with five girls an' six boys workin' for him. Most o' them wus hired out. De house in which we stayed is still dere with de sisterns an' slave quarters. I always walk to see de old home which is on St. Phillip Street. . . .

"People den use to do de same t'ings dey do now. Some marry an' some live together jus' like now. One t'ing, no minister nebber say in readin de matrimony 'let no man put asounder' cause a couple would be married tonight an' tomorrow one would be taken away en be sold. All slaves wus married in dere master house, in de livin' room where slaves an' dere missus an' massa wus to witness de ceremony. Brides use to wear some of de finest dress an' if dey could afford it, have de best kind of furniture. Your massa nor your missus objected to good t'ings.

"W'en any slaves wus whipped all de other slaves wus made to watch. I see women hung frum de ceilin' of buildings an' whipped with only supin tied 'round her lower part of de body, until w'en dey wus taken down dere wusn't breath in de body. I had some terrible bad experiences.

"De white race is so brazen. Dey come here an' run de Indians frum dere own lan', but dey couldn't make dem slave 'cause dey wouldn't stan' for it. Indians use to git up in trees an' shoot dem with poison arrow. W'en dey couldn't make dem slaves den dey gone to Africa an' brind dere black brother an' sister. Dey say 'mong themselves, 'we gwine mix dem up en make ourselves king. Dats d only way we'd get even with de Indians.'

"All time, night an' day, you could hear men an' women screamin' to de tip of dere voices as either ma, pa, sister or brother wus take without any warning an' sell. Some time mother who had only one chile wus separated fur life. People wus always dyin' frum a broken heart.

"One night a couple married an' de next mornin' de boss sell de wife. De gal ma got in de street an' cursed de white women fur all she could find. She said: 'dat white, pale-faced bastard sell my daughter who jus' married las' night' an' other t'ings. The white man tressen' her to call de police if she didn't stop but de collud women said: 'hit me or call de police. I redder die dan to stan' dis any longer.' De police took her to de Work House by de white women orders an' what became of 'er, I never hear.

"W'en de war began we wus taken to Aiken, South Ca'lina w'ere we stay until de Yankees come t'rough. We could see balls sailin' t'rough de air w'en Sherman wus comin'. Bombs hit trees in our yard. W'en de freedom gun was fired, I was on my nees scrubbin'. Dey tell me I wus free but I didn't believe it."

Both narratives were documented as part of the New Deal WPA Writer's Project in the thirties. The narratives are edited to avoid similar references like addresses.

Using Art to Illustrate Science—An Experiment with an Air Pump

Art can be used to gain insight into times, cultures, disciplines and places. For example, in the painting *An Experiment on a Bird in an Air Pump* (Joseph

Figure 9.2. *An Experiment on a Bird in an Air Pump* 1786, by Joseph Wright "of Derby," oil on canvas, 183 x 244 cm, © The National Gallery, London.

Wright, 1768, Derby, England) students can see depicted every possible reaction to the Scientific Revolution in the ten faces.

The ecological story of succession from old growth forest to cleared fields and reverting back to forest through several stages can be seen through American art that was intended for other purposes.

Travel Vignette #5

The Spoils of Conquest

Our train leaves in a few minutes from Saint Pancras, U.K., to Paris Nord. In Windsor we examined approximately 150 da Vinci drawings. In the British Museum we enjoyed many collections, most notably the Renaissance work. Several works are said to have been inspired or composed, but not painted, by Leonardo. There are no paintings attributed to Leonardo's hand in the British Museum, which is odd given the breadth of their collection. Perhaps this is a reflection of the fact that England never, to my knowledge, colonized Italy (although the reverse is true at the time of the Roman Empire).

There are several works by Michelangelo, most notably the portrait of Pope Julius II, the "warrior pope" who commissioned Michelangelo to paint the Sistine Chapel. Although "churchy" and Christian in its allegory, I am beginning to understand the imagery and history of the time, and am developing an appreciation of these works. Seeing Christian work in Syria with our guide, Rhyad, helped me understand the importance of this work. *Michelangelo and the Pope's Ceiling* relates the politics of art and the patronizing nature of patronage. The author, Ross King, is less kind to Leonardo than Leonardo's biographers.

The British Museum displays the spoils of colonialism, of which there are many. Most striking, perhaps, is the museum's explanation of the friezes taken from the Acropolis in Athens. Contrasting with the rest of the recorded narrative, the Parthenon friezes were introduced by the director of the British Museum. He was, in a word, defensive. Although not directly mentioning the controversy over ownership and Greece's repeated requests for Britain to return the art, he argued the following:

1. This work would have been destroyed, if Britain had not saved it.
2. Greece wasn't really Greece when they took the temple illustrations.
3. You really couldn't see them that high up on the Pantheon anyway.

It was a transparent argument for colonial spoils. Having said that, I believe that there is an argument for leaving some works, say half, in the context of the place to which they are relevant and spreading the other half through the world's museums to increase understanding of culture by those who cannot afford to visit foreign sites. And I see no reason why foreign sites should not pay an annual fee to the country to which the work belongs.

We dutifully marched through the collection examining the ancient world and impressionists most carefully. The *Standard of Ur* was, sadly, on loan; however I was surprised to find Joseph Wright's *An Experiment on a Bird in an Air Pump*. Given the reproductions that I admired at university back in the early 1970s, I have always imagined the piece to be small—two by three feet or less. The actual work is quite large. The colors are vivid, the light extraordinary. There is no more detail to be seen in the mysterious substance in the central jar, but there are items on the table such as Magdeburg Hemispheres and other symbols of contemporary science. It is a remarkable piece, far more so in the original.

Twelfth Grade

Twentieth and Twenty-First Century (1900–Future)

The Power of Modeling—Hiroshima Models

As part of their study of the twentieth century, Da Vinci students study the wars that occurred in that century. Students examine World War II in detail through historical readings and novels such as *Catch-22*, *Slaughterhouse Five*, and *Hiroshima Pilot*. Their study of physics parallels their historical work. They study the physics of nuclear fission, the manufacturing of the atomic bomb, and the ethics of Harry Truman's decision to drop the bomb on Hiroshima and Nagasaki.

In order to understand the impact of the bomb on Hiroshima, one class decided to create a detailed model of the city before and after the bombing as well as the reconstructed city today. These models were on display when a survivor of Hiroshima, Kazue Campbell Edamatsu, visited class to tell her story. Kazue wept as she told of hundreds of people exiting the city with skin flowing off their bodies. As she spoke, she used the accurate student models to describe her home, school, and her uncle's home.

After returning to her work at Tufts University, Kazue wrote the class and asked if they would be willing to send their models to the Peace Museum in Hiroshima to be put on permanent display. The students declined—they wanted to personally bring the models themselves.

Figure 9.3. Hiroshima Newspaper Account of Students Presenting their Models of Hiroshima Before and After the Bombing as well as Models of the Contemporary City (*Asahi Shinbun* Newspaper, August 6, 2000).

After several months of fund-raising, the students—and their models—traveled to Hiroshima. The photo below showing some of the students was published in a Hiroshima newspaper on August 6, the anniversary of the first atomic bombing.

There's another part to this story that bears telling. One student, Michael, was a brilliant mathematician with a developed interest in engineering. In fact, Michael built a small rocket that broke the sound barrier in ninth grade.

Michael had a great deal of promise as a math student but had not taken the time to develop himself to the same degree in the humanities. During the trip to Hiroshima, Michael was interviewed on Japanese television and wept as he spoke of the importance of engineers understanding the implications of their work. The study broadened Michael as a human being as well as a student.

Comparing Art across Time or Culture—Nineteenth and Twentieth Century Paintings

Debra Michlewitz published a delightful article on the use of paintings in her classroom (2001). Michlewitz told of four paintings that she uses to encourage students to understand the transition between the nineteenth and the twentieth centuries. Building on her work, Da Vinci teachers use the paintings as inductive stimulant. First, they present the four paintings, asking

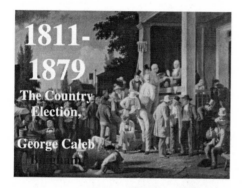

Figure 9.4.   Four American Paintings with Titles, Artists, and Dates; Comparison Taken from Debra Michlewitz (2001). *The County Election,* 1852, by George Caleb Bingham, oil on canvas, 38″ x 52″, Saint Louis Art Museum; *Election Night,* 1954, by Jack Levine, oil on canvas, 63 1/8″ x 6′ ½″ © Susanna Levine Fisher/Licensed by VAGA, New York; *Washington Crossing the Delaware,* 1851, by Emmanual Gottlieb Leutze © The Metropolitan Museum of Art. Image source: Art Resource, New York; *Washington Crossing the Delaware,* 1953, by Larry Rivers, oil on canvas, 149″ x 255″ © Estate of Larry Rivers/Licensed by VAGA, New York.

simply, "What do you see?" Students describe the predominant colors, the figures, the tone, the lighting, the degree of realism, and so on.

Each painting results in its own inductive tower. After creating four towers capturing inferences that students have made, they are asked to compare and contrast the paintings in pairs.

Students often describe the two paintings on the left side of figure 9.4 as "realistic" but readily concede that standing up in an open boat in midwinter is a highly unrealistic action. Then they examine the other pair shown on the right side of figure 9.4.

Students often describe this pair as drab, "out of focus," dark, and caricature-like. The Da Vinci teacher then shows the last slide (figure 9.4) with the dates and titles of the four paintings and ask students to talk about artists' depictions of roughly the same topics in the nineteenth and twentieth centuries. Students create interesting insights into human perception, representation, and art in the nineteenth and twentieth centuries. They often compare these insights with developments in other fields such as science or literature.

Seminal Writings—Francis Bacon's "Phantoms" or "Idols"

In *Novum Organum*, Bacon warned of four "idols" or "phantoms" that "beset the human mind" and keep a person from making fair and honest inferences. We call these "preconceptions" or "prejudges" today. He categorized them as the phantoms of the tribe, den, market, and theater. Da Vinci students read *Novum Organum* and understand that the four phantoms are as alive and well in twenty-first century minds as they were in seventeenth century minds.

The first phantom of which Bacon warns us is the bias that we carry as human beings. He calls this the idol of the tribe. As humans, he warns us, we reflect the world as "uneven mirrors" and "distort and disfigure" the objects that we view. On the dawn of science, Bacon warns us that we will tend to impart our "own properties to different objects."

Bacon also cautions us against our own individual phantoms. Referring to Plato's allegory of the cave, he warns that we each have a "den or cavern, which intercepts and corrupts the light of nature." He mentions several corrupting influences: our dispositions, our education, our readings, the authorities whom we revere, as well as our temperaments.

He calls the third phantom the "idol of the market" because he focuses here on the biases that we adopt from our being part of human society. He describes words, the fundamental tool that we have for understanding and communication, as "a wonderful obstruction to the mind." Bacon cautions us to be wary of the confusion, vanity, controversies, and fallacies that words can foster.

Lastly, Bacon warns us of the systems of philosophy to which we ascribe. He cautions that philosophies create "fictitious and theatrical worlds," so he calls this phantom the idol of the theater. He explicitly warns us of the traditions and axioms of science itself.

As Da Vinci students learn to make inferences, they must also learn to guard themselves against the phantoms that Francis Bacon warns us of. Our biases—human, personal, societal, and philosophical—are as active today as they were four hundred years ago. This classical writing can be matched with contemporary thoughts about scientific method such as Thomas Kuhn's *The Structure of Scientific Revolutions* (1962) or a *New Yorker* article titled "The Truth Wears Off" (Lehrer 2010). Kuhn speaks of paradigm shifts in science and Lehrer suggests that scientific "truths" may inevitably degrade over time. Understanding the power and limits of science is crucial to citizenship today.

Induction on STEROIDS

Taking Inductive Towers Up a Notch

Da Vinci teachers have come up with several refinements of the inductive towers. For example:

Prior Experience Towers

Sometimes Da Vinci students create two related towers, one from an artifact, and a second that represents prior knowledge. For example, when analyzing an experimental result concerning oxidation, one farm student said, "I don't know what this means, but I think it has something to do with the fact that when welding a gas tank, my Dad first pumps exhaust into the tank, then begins welding." His observation became a new piece of information that students were able to make sense of through the inductive process. They figured out that this young man's father was pushing out the oxygen by replacing it with carbon dioxide. This decreased the chance of an explosion, which is a nothing more than rapid oxidation. In *How People Learn*, Bransford (2000, p. 119) and his colleagues at the National Academies state that "teachers must draw out and work with the pre-existing understanding that student bring with them." That is what these students were doing—working with their preexisting understanding.

Linkages to Other Disciplines and Years

Da Vinci teachers value and make explicit connections to prior knowledge. Towers are an efficient way to capture prior knowledge. For example, when considering the recent "Arab Spring" and the possibility for civil wars, students might gather together what they know about the American Civil

War and then compare circumstances between the two times and regions. Prior learning often sheds light on more recent learning.

Art as a Creation at the Top of the Tower

Marshall McLuhan said, "The artist is always thought of as being way ahead of his time because he lives in the present." Leonardo said, "Art is the queen of all sciences communicating knowledge to all generations of the world."

Da Vinci teachers view art in several ways; art may be a historical reflection of a time period as with any other field such as science, music, or politics. Art can be viewed as a human enterprise that developed over time with unique cultural attributes. Art can be studied by those who want to develop their artistic skills in various media. Lastly, art can also be used to express what is learned in the Da Vinci classroom. In other words, art can be at the top of the inductive tower as a creative expression of what has been learned. See "The Role of Art" in an earlier chapter. One student recalls the following:

> This college-like atmosphere was neat for struggling teenagers because Marc gave us a lot of freedom along with a lot of responsibility. He allowed us to design our course of study from time to time and for us to be creative in our exploration of the humanities. He was a strong believer in the dramatic arts and in music. We read a lot of plays and we did a lot of improvisation and scripted, rehearsed acting. We wrote short plays.
>
> How many tenth graders perform *Waiting for Godot*? How many teachers would assign a tenth grader with no experience (me) to direct it, then abandon them to discover what it was about? When you leave tenth graders alone for a period of time to work on projects like this, there is time lost to goofing around; it may also be the only way to get high school students to realize that they are there to benefit one person, themselves. And if you spend all of your *Waiting for Godot* time goofing off, then (a) you'll embarrass yourself at the performance and (b) you really will have wasted an opportunity. Besides, *Waiting for Godot* is a hoot, in addition to being an incredible existentialist drama.

Refinement of Knowledge as the Student's Abstract Knowledge Grows

Complexity of thinking grows as students learn. Models become more sophisticated, more complex, and more representative of the real world. For example, a chemistry teacher may speak of atoms "wanting another electron" or being "fulfilled" as a way to introduce electron dot diagrams and bonding. As students' conceptualization develops, more complex views of orbitals, hybrid orbitals, and electron clouds develop.

Conceptually, it is as if one simple inductive tower is replaced by another with more data and a more sophisticated generalization.

Bransford (2000) tells us that experts

- notice features and meaningful patterns of information,
- organize their content knowledge in ways that reflect deep understanding,
- understand the importance of context and interpretation according to circumstance,
- retrieve information with little effort,
- have varying levels of flexibility in their approach to novel situation, and
- do not necessarily teach their discipline well despite their knowledge.

This is important for us to understand because even though our students are generally novices, they are in the process of increasing their expertise. They benefit from our understanding the nature of expertise. For example, we can guide them toward expertise by asking them to think about the contextual nature of their knowledge.

Comparing Student's or Group's Conceptualization (and Fact Identification)

This is powerful! The most important thing that teachers work with in schools—thinking—is invisible. However, inductive towers can take what is in the mind and commit it to paper. Peers and teachers can see what facts a group of students have identified and how they transform those facts into meaningful groups. Then the teacher (and peers) can see exactly what generalizations students have made and what logical links they make to the fact base. This is to thinking what graphs are to math and science—a way to add visibility to the concepts. Making thinking visual makes thinking collective.

Deconstructing Expert Knowledge

See previous description of the *Standard of Ur*.

Using the Internet as a Source of Primary Sources, Knowledge, and Testable Hypotheses

Think of the Internet as a magnificent source of cultural artifacts. Students search for artifacts that represent a given culture and era. For example, "Greek artifact*" (with the * indicating a wild card) gets 1,530,000 hits on

Google in .29 seconds! Of course, not all of these are worthy of your students' time. Searching and determining what is of value is a lesson in itself.

Using the Internet to Discuss Findings with Other Classes in Other Towns or Countries

Classrooms can so easily be linked via the Internet. Imagine two classes, one in Beijing and another in Los Angeles, working on a similar artifact and question. The classes could exchange images of their towers and have a conversation about their thinking. Wouldn't it be interesting to see how different cultures view the same stimulus? The same exchange could be done between students in Boston and students in Yazoo City, Mississippi; between black, Latino, Asian, and white students; or between rural and urban students. The intellectual understanding of content becomes a vehicle for intercultural understanding. Similarly, students can photograph artifacts and exchange the images with others from different walks of life.

Using the Internet to Jigsaw Inductive Towers

Different towns along the same river can collect data for inductive analysis. Or different schools on different rivers in different countries can compare notes. Different schools in different countries can collect data on similar economic, political, cultural, or environmental systems. The inductive towers can be jigsawed together to create a larger understanding impossible for any one school working alone.

Asking about Implications

It is great that students will harvest facts, make transformations, and draw conclusions, but isn't it even more important that students ask, "What are the implications of this conclusion?" or, "What does it mean?" or, "Where do we go from here?" As Dewey said, this represents "expanding" and "rectifying" knowledge. Like artistic expression, this represents the top of the tower. What we do with our knowledge is as important as what knowledge we accumulate.

Induction and the Elements of Human Thinking

Richard Paul and Linda Elder (2009 or www.criticalthinking.org/index.cfm), describe eight "elements of thought." Inferences and conclusions are one of these elements of thought. Table 9.1 shows their elements of thought, questions derived from the elements of thought (from Paul and Elder at the Foundation for Critical Thinking), and two columns showing responsibil-

Table 9.1. Questions and the Elements of Thinking as Defined by Richard Paul and Linda Elder (2009) in Conventional and Da Vinci Classrooms

Element of Thought (FCT)	Questions (Foundation for Critical Thinking)	Conventional Classroom	Da Vinci Classroom's Relationship to Questions Asked by the Foundation for Critical Thinking (column 2)
Purpose	What am I trying to accomplish? What is my central aim? My purpose?	Purpose usually resides in the domain of the teacher. Students follow the teacher's lead. "Purpose" is determined by curriculum.	The very broadest purposes are determined by the school and Common Core: metacognition (thinking about thinking), practicing democratic principles, and culturing compassion, for example. Broad curricular purpose (like engaging with the Renaissance) is determined by the teacher and curriculum. Once determined, students help design the study by asking the three questions asked in column 2.
Question	What questions am I raising? What question am I addressing? Am I considering the complexities in the question?	The most conventional teachers do not focus on questions at all—topics drive the curriculum. Less conventional teachers ask the questions and give most of the answers. Even less conventional teachers ask the questions and choreograph instruction so that students provide their own answers.	Da Vinci Teachers engage students in shaping questions that will drive their inquiry. They think progressively, that is, they expect their students to ask initial questions, seek information, and then (having progressed to a new understanding) will have new and richer questions to ask.
Information	What information am I using in coming to that conclusion? What experience have I had to support this claim? What information do I need to settle the question?	Conventional teachers control the information flow. That is their job. Occasionally, students are assigned research reports of papers that provide some leeway for student to ask questions and seek information.	These are key questions for Da Vinci students. What do I need to shape my thinking? What experiences will enrich my knowledge and skills?

Inferences/ Conclusions	How did I reach this conclusion? Is there another way to interpret the information?	Inference making is rarely explicit. When it is, it is often after the fact, as a way to demonstrate the truth of expert opinion.	Using inductive towers, the inference-making process is visual, shared, and open to discussion.
Concepts	What is the main idea here? Can I explain this idea?	Instead of asking, "What is the main idea here?," the conventional teacher says, "This is the main idea here." Good conventional teachers ask their students to articulate in their own words or show in some artistic way the ideas that they have been asked to learn.	This is the heart and soul of the Da Vinci classrooms. The curriculum is about seeking ideas and insights. Artistic representation or having an impact in society is at the top of the inductive tower.
Assumptions	What am I taking for granted? What assumption has led me to that Conclusion?	These questions are not consistently addressed in the conventional classroom. There is little time for self-reflective learning.	This is the essence of combating prejudice whether of the egocentric or sociocentric variety. This is central to the Da Vinci classroom's larger purpose of democratic citizenry.
Implications/ Consequences	If someone accepted my position, what would be the implications? What am I implying?	Implications imply application. Application varies from classroom to classroom. Technical centers excel at this.	This moves the somewhat theoretical inductive tower work into the realm of the practical.
Points of View	From what point of view am I looking at this issue? Is there another point of view I should consider?	Conventional classrooms rarely have time for multiple points of view—there are other standards and chapters to cover.	This is the basis of empathy and intercultural understanding. The cross-cultural Da Vinci study fosters these kinds of questions. Da Vinci students keep Francis Bacon's "phantoms" in mind as they learn. This encourages metacognition and awareness of biases and point of view.

ity for these questions in the conventional classroom and in the Da Vinci classroom.

Each of the eight elements has opportunities to enrich student thinking skills and ability to think about thinking (metacognition). Da Vinci teachers view thinking as the Holy Grail and content as the path. Often conventional teachers fail to explicitly and systematically develop thinking in their quest for content, and yet thinking skills are widely transferable whereas content is subject to revision.

Many teachers might read a chart such as this and think that they are the exception. However I have asked thousands of teachers if they value and encourage students' questions. Virtually all raise their hands in affirmation. Yet when I then ask how many teachers record or credit the questions that students ask, a handful of hands remain raised. Many of our classroom and school systems do not reinforce our deeply held beliefs about learning and teaching or even our perception of our own teaching.

Chapter 9 Summary

Selected Examples of Rich Inductive Content from the Tenth to Twelfth Grade Da Vinci Curriculum

- When primary sources are compared with modern interpretations, students are faced with a fruitful cognitive dissonance that fosters learning (tenth grade, Columbus's encounter with the new world).
- Spectacular primary sources can draw students into a study (tenth grade, the Waldessmüller Map).
- A provocative thesis such as the 1421 thesis can motivate students to want to learn more about a subject (tenth grade, the 1421 thesis suggests that China visited the new world seventy-two years before Columbus).
- A provocative thesis such as the camera lucida thesis can motivate students to learn a subject like art history (tenth grade, *Secret Knowledge* by David Hockney develops this idea).
- The visual display of data, used inductively, can be a powerful teaching tool (eleventh grade, Napoleon's march to Moscow).
- Primary sources can serve as entrees into new fields of study (eleventh grade, Mendeleev's Periodic Table and chemistry).
- A number of inductively established conclusions can serve as the base for a second level of inductive tower synthesis (eleventh grade, the study of human circulation).

- Considering audience can move students to deeper understanding (eleventh grade WPA Slave Narratives).
- Insights can be gained when art is used to study history (eleventh to twelfth grade, The Philosopher by ___).
- Models can be powerful teaching tools (twelfth grade, Hiroshima models).
- Comparing art across time or cultures can lead to new views of cultural change (twelfth grade, Michlewitz article, 2001).
- Key writings, however difficult, if interpreted well, can help students understand how human ideas evolve and change over time (tenth grade through twelfth grade, Francis Bacon's phantoms).
- Inductive towers can be made richer and more complex. Prior non-school experience and earlier schooling can be introduced as part of the fact base. Artistic creation—the representation of knowledge—can be the capstone for an inductive tower. Earlier towers can be revisited as students' theoretical framework becomes more sophisticated. Expert knowledge can be deconstructed and compared to novice knowledge. The Internet can be used as a source of hypotheses, artifacts, and collaborators. Induction can be understood as part of our human capacity to explore our world.

~

CHAPTER TEN

Leonardo da Vinci—His Life and His Relevance to Our Lives Today

Biographical curricula invite us to relate a life that we admire to the world and time in which we live. This chapter captures Leonardo's life and its relevance to our lives. Leonardo's life serves as an example of a life well lived and worthy of emulation through curriculum. Around whose life might you build a curriculum? What are the lessons of that person's life?

It has taken five hundred years for the world to plumb the depths of the man Leonardo da Vinci. He is complex, enigmatic, and brilliant. His unbridled mind and his creativity inspire this curriculum. The time in which he lived—the Renaissance—demonstrates that fundamental societal change can occur rapidly, if the right forces are in place. Can understanding Leonardo's life—a life that has become synonymous with renaissance—guide us as we create a renaissance in our public schools?

For much of the time during the generations proceeding, during, and following Leonardo, Florence was a cultural factory town run by one family. When the painter Botticelli created the *Adoration of the Magi*, he painted Florence's patrons, the Medici, into the center of the composition. The Medici were godfather-like in their control and their ability to give favors to the citizenry. Although Leonardo was born in Tuscany and apprenticed in Florence, he did not always live there.

Leonardo's life falls into several distinct eras. He lived in what we now know as "Italy" until the last three years of his life when he retired to Amboise, France. Italy was not unified into one country until one hundred and fifty years ago (1861). In Leonardo's time, the region was made up of rival city-states. Florence, for example, was a political entity run largely by the Medici family, and Milan, a rival city-state run by the Sforza family. Leonardo moved between cities as the fortunes of his patrons, and therefore his, rose and fell.

The following chart will give the reader an overview of Leonardo's intellectually complex and full life with many patrons, colleagues, works of art and engineering, and scientific investigations. Leonardo's life took place during an unsettled era when Medieval Europe was changing rapidly. Popes were involved in Papal intrigues, city-states and countries were at war, wealthy families—patrons—were falling in and out of power, the Black Plague periodically reached pandemic proportions (killing one-third of the Italian population in 1348, one hundred years before Leonardo's birth), and figures such as Machiavelli (an advocate for ruthless leadership) and Savonarola (an equally ruthless priest who fought Renaissance Humanism) were keeping the caldron at a fast boil. There are simplifications here as there are in any overview. For more detail, see Nicholl (2004), D'Epiro and Pinkowish (2001), Atalay and Wamsley (2008), and Pedretti (2004).

Leonardo had become an industry before the *Da Vinci Code*, and has become a multi-national behemoth after. Not all that is published, however, is accurate. The Internet is riddled with quotes that have no basis in Leonardo's journals or other documentation but have taken on a life of their own. To get to know Leonardo, I found myself asking, "Who is the man behind the hype?"

Vinci and Anchiano

Vinci is the likely town of Leonardo's birth. "Likely" because Leonardo was born in either the town of Vinci (hence "da" or "from" Vinci) or in the village of Anchiano, which is close by. There is a home in Anchiano that is said to be the home in which Leonardo was born and lived in his youth. That this was truly Leonardo's birth home is questionable because the home was not in the family until about thirty years after his birth. The roughshod home today sports a winged lion, the Vinci family crest. The home sits among old olive trees (there is one on Crete that has grown around a Roman column and was calculated to be sixteen hundred years old!) and vineyards. Some of these olive trees might well have been alive in Leonardo's time.

Vinci is quintessentially pastoral. The warm Tuscan sun ripens the grapes and the olive oil is kept like gold (or perhaps crude oil) in locked rooms. Although roughly the latitude of Toronto, the warmth of the Mediterranean modulates the temperature—rarely does the winter drop below 48 degrees Fahrenheit. It is rural, but has been cultivated for centuries, ordered with rows of trees and vines to the horizon. Leonardo's first dated drawing ("Study of a Tuscan Landscape") gives us a sense of his Tuscan environment.

Vinci sits upon a rise allowing the sun and breeze to reach into the narrow medieval streets. It is easy to imagine the boy Leonardo feeling safe here, free to walk the cobblestone lanes, streams, groves, and upland pine, oak, and chestnut forest. The chestnuts provided flour for bread. Surely young Leonardo played along the Vincio River, "Vincio" meaning Osier, the river being the place where Osier willows grow and from which his town and therefore family name is taken. The willow shoots were used to make wicker baskets. Nicholl (2004, p. 40) muses:

> To pursue the etymology for a moment, the Latin *vincus* is connected to the old Norse word for an osier, *viker*, from which comes the English "wicker," as in wickerwork and also "weak" which has a root meaning of pliability.

It is a softly beautiful landscape, "easy on the eye" as some would say. The light, so important to Leonardo as artist and scientific observer, is strong and clear, the summer evenings long. The roof tiles are made from the earth—as anyone with a crayon box knows, the color is "burnt sienna."

Santa Croce Church, although recently updated, was present when Leonardo was born. It sits on the highest rise in the town.

The only real certainty of Leonardo's youth is that he was baptized in the baptismal font that still sits in the church of Santa Croce. The records show that the baptism was a large celebration, not less so due to his illegitimacy, which was more accepted in his time. In fact, his grandfather recorded the date and time of his birth in a ledger: "1452. There was born to me a grandson, the son of Ser Piero my son, on the 15th day of April, a Saturday, at the 3rd hour of the night. He bears the name Lionardo." The third hour of night was about 10:30 p.m. (Nicholl 2004, p. 20). In mid-April, the fragrant, cream-colored olive flowers would have been in bloom. Vinci today lives on the fame of Leonardo as well as its grapes and olives. The small castle that defended Vinci is now a museum.

Vinci had been a possession of the Florentine Republic since 1254, a kind of medieval suburb of the city of Florence. Yet in Vinci, you have no sense of its relationship to Florence visually—no view of the city lights in the distance. The connection is practical. A few miles from Vinci, the Arno River, and a road that follows it, leads upstream to Florence and downstream to Pisa and the Tyrrhenian and Mediterranean Seas.

Table 10.1. Leonardo's Life and Extant Paintings

Place	Dates	Age	Patron(s)	Key Works and Focus	Location (bold visited 2010)
1. Vinci and Anchiano	1452–c. 1466	0–c. 14	None	Birth town, church, baptismal font	**Tuscany, Italy**
2. Florence, Italy Apprenticeship	1466–1477	14–25	Andrea del Verrocchio, whose main patrons were the Medici	1. Gilded ball erected on Florence's Duomo (Leo. is 19)	**1. Florence Duomo**
				2. *The Baptism of Christ* (angel, landscape—1472–1475)	**2. Uffizi, Florence**
				3. *The Annunciation* (earliest extant work by Leonardo—c. 1472–1475)	**3. Uffizi, Florence**
				4. *Tobias and the Angel* (1470–1480) Verrocchio with some work by Leonardo (fish and dog?)	**4. National Gallery, London**
				5. *Madonna and Child with St. Joseph* (recent attribution to Leonardo based on a fingerprint)	**5. Galleria Borghese, Rome**
3. Florence Studio (bottega)	1477–1482	25–30	The Medici, especially Lorenzo the Magnificent	6. *Portrait of Ginevra de'Benci* (c. 1476)	6. National Gallery, DC
				7. *Benois Madonna* (1478)	7. Hermitage, Saint Petersburg
				8. *The Madonna of the Carnation* (1478–1480)	8. Munich
				9. *St. Jerome in the Wilderness* (c. 1480)	**9. Vatican Museums**
				10. *Adoration of the Magi* (1481)	**10. Uffizi, Florence**
4. Milan I New Horizons	1482–1490	30–38	The Sforza	11. *Virgin of the Rocks* (1483–1486 version)	11. Louvre, Paris
				12. *Lady with an Ermine* (1485)	12. Krakow, Poland

Period / Location	Years	Patron	Works	Current Location
5. Milan II At Court (Note that in 1494, Florence restored the republic and expelled the Medici family. The Medici returned to power in Florence in 1512)	1490–1499	The Sforza	13. *Madonna Litta* (disputed – Marco d'Oggiono, c. 1490?)	13. Hermitage
			14. *Portrait of a Musician* (1490) Also "The Duchess"	**14. Pinacoteca Ambrosiana, Milan**
			15. *La Belle Ferronniere* (disputed 1490)	**15. Louvre**
			16. *The Last Supper* (1495–1498)	**16. Santa Maria delle Grazie, Milan**
			17. *Virgin of the Rocks* (1495–1508 version)	**17. National Gallery, London**
			18. Sala delle Asse ceiling frescoes (c. 1498–1499)	**18. Castello Sforzesco, Milan**
			19. *The Virgin and Child with St. Anne and St. John the Baptist* (c. 1499–1500)	**19. National Gallery, London**
			20. *Madonna of the Yardwinder* (two versions, c. 1500)	20. Private collections (one stolen in 2004, recovered 2007)
6. Itinerant years (Mantua, Venice, Romagna, Florence, Rome, Florence, Imola)	1500–1506	Cesare Borgia	21. *Mona Lisa* or *La Gioconda* (c. 1503–1506)	**21. Louvre** (stolen 1911, recovered 1913)
			21B newly attributed *Salvator Mundi* (circa 1500)	21B National Gallery, London
7. Milan III (short return to Florence)	1506–1513	The Sforza	22. *The Virgin and Child with St. Anne* (c. 1510)	**22. Louvre**
			23. *Bacchus* (1510–1515)	**23. Louvre**
			24. *St. John the Baptist* (1513–1516)	**24. Louvre**
8. Rome, Italy	1513–1517	Giuliano de Medici–Pope Leo X		
9. Amboise, France	1517–1519	King Francis I, France		
Copies of Lost Works			25. Peter Paul Rubens, *The Battle of Anghiari*	**25. Louvre**
			26. *Leda and the Swan*, Anonymous	**26. Galleria Borghese, Rome**

Note: This table was assembled from Atalay and Wamsley 2008, Nicholl 2004, Pedretti 2004, and Reynal 1956.

Leonardo lived the formative first three decades of his life in and around this great city of Florence, ground zero of the Italian Renaissance. There is no reason to believe that he traveled to Florence until leaving the town of his youth, but his father, a worldly notary—like a lawyer-accountant today— from a long line of respected notaries, surely had dealings with important people in Florence.

Little is known of Leonardo's early life. He described himself as "omo sanza lettere," an unlettered man (Nicholl 2004, p. 54). Nicholl takes this to mean that although schooled, to some degree, he was not prepared in the seven liberal arts and therefore, not prepared for university. "Unschooled" in those days meant unable to read Latin (hence the "Latin Quarter" of many cities such as Paris). Leonardo's education took place in his master's workshop where he learned the skills of a tradesman rather than the more liberal pursuits—grammar, logic, rhetoric, arithmetic, geometry, music, and astronomy. Ironically, the last four arts became life-long areas of study for Leonardo.

In his childhood, we don't know if Leonardo lived with his biological father, Ser Piero di Antonio da Vinci, or his unmarried mother, Caterina. Ser Piero seems to have been a largely absent father. He was of a respected class, whereas Caterina was one or more rungs below on the social ladder, depending upon which source you trust. At age thirteen or fourteen, Leonardo and his father left Vinci and walked or rode twenty-eight miles following the Arno River upstream to the grand city-state of Florence with its green, white, and pink marble Duomo and all of its Renaissance splendor. His father brought him to the studio of Andrea del Verrocchio in Florence, just around the corner from his own offices. Ser Piero brought some of Leonardo's drawings to Verrocchio, who was impressed enough to offer Leonardo an apprenticeship in his studio. Here Leonardo lived for five years under his master's care. As a strapping young apprentice, he surely helped place the golden globe atop the Duomo whose roof was built by Filippo Brunelleschi. There are self-portraits from this era and master works as well. Perhaps his portrait of Genevra de' Benci is one of his best. Nicholl calls this Leonardo's "first masterwork" (p. 108). It is the only painting of Leonardo's that resides outside of Europe (in the National Gallery of Art in Washington, DC).

Brunelleschi was a key early Renaissance figure. He, along with Donatello, visited Rome's Pantheon, the beginning of the search for Roman and Greek inspiration. Brunelleschi invented—some would say reinvented—linear perspective, a central Renaissance artistic concept that Leonardo exploited. Brunelleschi's and Leonardo's lives did not overlap—Leonardo was born six years after Filippo died—but their work did. One might say that in placing the gold dome atop Brunelleschi's dome, Leonardo inherited the Renaissance from his creative father.

In 1476, while an apprentice, Leonardo was accused of being a "consort or customer" of a young man who was accused of "immoral activities" and "sinful acts" (Nicholl 2004), in other words, homosexuality. Florentines could accuse anyone of acts such as these by leaving a message in a "hole of truth," drums that were placed around the city like suggestion boxes. These suggestions, however, had serious ramifications. Although Leonardo was absolved of the charges, there is reason to believe that he spent a short time in jail. The charge could have led to execution. Although most biographers today view Leonardo as homosexual, these charges may have been inspired by another studio jealous of Leonardo's work.

Leonardo struck out on his own in the year 1477. He developed his own studio—"bottega" by the language of the day. Lorenzo de Medici, Lorenzo the Magnificent, supported much of his work. The Medici family, originally doctors ("Medici" reflects their work in medicine—their shield is decorated with pills), was made up of bankers, ruthless moneylenders in a time when money lending was prohibited by church law. They used Jewish lenders as intermediaries, thus circumventing church doctrine. Historians tell us that their interest rates were as high as 200 percent.

They had wealth enough to design Florence to their needs. The Medici could, for example, pass through Florence in a raised passageway isolated from the commoners below. With their astonishing wealth they collected and they supported the arts. It is not too much to say that the Medici family bankrolled the Renaissance. In fact, it would be hard to believe that the Renaissance would have occurred as it did without the wealth, however ruthlessly gained and self-serving, of Lorenzo and his family.

Leonardo's most generative years, from age thirty to forty-seven, were spent in Milan. After this, as his patrons' fortunes rose and fell, he lived an itinerant life for seven years until age fifty-four. He settled back in Milan from ages fifty-four to sixty-one. Although we associate Leonardo so closely with Florence, in fact his adult life was spent largely in Milan, his adopted home. After Milan, he lived under the patronage of another Medici generation in Rome—the son of Lorenzo the Magnificent, Pope Leo X. After Rome, he "retired" to Amboise, France, to live out his last years as a friend of the young French king, Francis I.

Not far from the town of Vinci is a villa that was built as a hunting lodge by Caterina de' Medici (1519–1589), Lorenzo's great granddaughter. Her father was Lorenzo II de' Medici (to whom Machiavelli dedicated *The Prince*). Caterina married Henry II, Francis I's son. Henry would become King Francis

II of France. It was his father, Francis I, who offered Leonardo a home at Clos Luce in Amboise, France. After her husband died, she became regent (the actual power behind the throne) and mother of three French kings as well as queen. Due to her ruthless schemes and bloody slaughter of Protestants, she was known as "Madame La Serpent." Remarkably, visitors can stay at her villa.

The Villa Dianella Fucini sits atop a vineyard surrounded by olive groves. Dianella reflects the hunting goddess, Diana. In late September, the grapes are ready to be picked. There is a sense of anticipation—a readiness in the air, a luscious fullness to the grapes. When the harvest came, it would be all hands on deck—bookkeepers, everyone associated with the Villa would help, regardless of their usual job.

The Dianella Fucini cellars are a history of Tuscan winemaking, particularly Chiantis. The early Medici tanks were glasslined, an innovation in its time. Two crops, olives and grapes, united the Medici family to all Tuscans, regardless of station. Today, one can sit in the late day sunlight drinking Tuscan Chianti from the Medici wine cellars.

Florence

A vast quantity of paintings, architecture, and sculpture has been preserved in Florence. Yet after a week of being enmeshed in the galleries, museums, and churches, one inevitably wonders why there was so little contemporary art. Why has this city, the quintessential city of art, not drawn contemporary artists to build their own artistic traditions drawing from the past? Young artists are occupied copying the masters in chalk on city streets. In contrast, Paris seemed alive with new art, the Louvre's glass pyramid for example. Even the Eiffel Tower stands as testament to the new as does the Musée de l'Orangerie, built to display Claude Monet's work. In Paris, one senses that art did not end with the Renaissance. Paris seemed unafraid to put glass and steel next to stone and mortar. Florence, by contrast, seemed a museum-city—breathtakingly lovely, but frozen like its statuary in another time.

After visiting medieval cities of Europe, one is drawn to ask how the Renaissance penetrated the previously unchanging Medieval European world. What was this period we call "Renaissance," and how did it supplant the period that preceded it? Can a people call forth a renaissance, when broad sweeping change is needed, as with secondary schools (Senge, Evans)?

The Renaissance brought a rebirth of classical (particularly Greek) cultural thinking to fourteenth through seventeenth century Medieval Europe. Florence was the epicenter of this movement from which the shockwave spread. Although there the fourteenth century movement was primarily cultural (and was followed by the Scientific Revolution). (Earlier waves of cultural cross-pollination have occurred over time, such as the reforms that Julius Caesar brought back from his exploits with Cleopatra in Alexandria in the first century BC.)

The Greek and Roman ideas stimulated late medieval artists and architects to reposition the human being, rather than God, at the center of their attention and to create realistic works using newly rediscovered techniques of perspective and realism. Hence we have da Vinci's famous "Vitruvian Man," a representation of the ideas of the Roman architect Marcus Vitruvius Pollio, who wrote *De architectura* (a treatise on architecture) in the first century BCE. As was true of many Greek and Roman writings and art, Vitruvius's text was rediscovered in the Renaissance (in the 1400s). Leonardo's Vitruvian man captures Vitruvius's notion of man being "the measure of all things," a sentiment passed down from the fifth century Greek Protagorus. We find an interesting set of examples of man and architecture in an Internet article titled "Architecture and Proportion" (http://leonardodavinci .stanford.edu/submissions/clabaugh/history/architecture.html):

> Renaissance architects seem to have truly believed that "Man is the measure of all things." As Wittkower emphasizes, this is not evidence of an anthropocentric world view. Since man was made in the image of God, so it was believed the proportions exemplified in the human form would reflect a divine and cosmic order. (Steadman, p. 17)

Drawings by Francesco di Giorgio illustrate such proportional concepts directly and vividly (from *Trattato di architettura di Francesco di Giorgio Martini* as referenced by Toby Lester). We see in these drawings and writing a link between God, man, and architecture. Man's work, his buildings, reflects his image, which is the image of God.

The transition from Medieval Europe to Renaissance Europe was rapid. It was more like a light switch being thrown than a dimmer being slowly turned up. Why did the Italian Renaissance occur and why so rapidly? Can rapid changes such as this be planned or anticipated? Could such a rapid and widespread change occur in our secondary educational system in the next decade?

As mentioned earlier, three artists—Brunelleschi in architecture, Donatello in sculpture, and the painter Masaccio—traveled to the ruins of ancient Rome to rediscover Rome's architecture and art (which reflected earlier Greek, Byzantine, and Etruscan works). Having examined the

Pantheon in Rome, Brunelleschi solved the problem of capping the enormous Duomo in Florence (D'Epiro and Pinkowish 2001). These three artists were perhaps the most influential early Renaissance artists—three sparks that ignited dry tinder in their respective disciplines. In contrast to introducing an entirely new idea, in Roman and Greece there was a wealth of artistic and architectural models available to stimulate change. They were not starting from scratch—they were emulating and building upon existing aesthetic ideas. Others consulted ancient texts, many of which had been preserved and improved in the Islamic world.

These three men formed the nucleus of a wider group of artists who came together synergistically in Florence as a like-minded but competitive brain trust. They were financed by the Medici family, one of two most prominent families of bankers in Florence. The Medici family, the wool guild (which was wealthy and influential then), the banks, and the papacy were related by blood and self-interest, creating a concentration of power in few families. Renaissance artists, while challenging the *way* that we view Catholic imagery, did not question the authority or values of Catholicism per se. In fact, their topics remained sacred and their patrons were often popes or families that produced popes.

The recently authenticated painting "Salvator Mundi" (Saviour of the World), circa 1500, is an example (*The Telegraph*, November 7, 2011). One author claims that China influenced Renaissance thinkers (Menzies 2008). This thesis claims that a wealth of Renaissance ideas came to Florence via trade with China.

At the same time, the Papacy was becoming increasingly corrupt and distrusted (critics were concerned about papal indulgences—the ability to pay for sins without jeopardizing God's judgment), papal intrigue including murder, papal excesses such as "obsession with wealth, land, tithes, titles, and all the other trappings of the worldly institution it had become during the later Middle Ages" (D'Epiro and Pinkowish 2001). These excesses stimulated the Reformation, a movement to cleanse the Church and return to its core values. In today's terms, the Church needed some good press and dazzling new art provided the necessary public relations.

With the combination of funding, stimulus from ancient cultures, a brain trust of brilliant artists, and a growing distrust of the status quo as represented by the Church, change occurred rapidly. The way was cleared for Leonardo, Michelangelo, Raphael, and scores of other Renaissance artists.

Can such a change occur in American secondary education? Are the forces in place? Or will we see the opportunity for Renaissance eclipsed once more by the mild adjustments of reform? The human tendency to resist change (Evans 1996) is great. It's far easier to keep "kicking the can down the road" than to pick it up and do something significant with it.

Milan—*The Last Supper* and Codices

The Clark reproduction of Leonardo's study of Judas for *The Last Supper* (available online) is a pale and colorless image when compared to the original. In the original (red chalk on red paper), lines are few. Much of the depth and shadow is shown with smudged chalk. The red of the paper strengthens the drawing. A single line, for example, defines the shirt neckline over much of its length. The throat is defined by lines in some places but by shadow in others. The shadowing reveals no structure except toward the back of the neck where shadow lines are visible. The hair at the back of the head only suggests the rear of the head.

Leonardo's studies help us understand process. This is analogous to seeing drafts of student work. What was he thinking? Working on? In an early study of *The Last Supper*, we see Judas shown at the table front leaning toward Jesus. Leonardo had not yet freed himself from the traditional view of Judas across from Jesus and his fellow apostles. *The Last Supper* shows otherwise. In the study, we are witness to his thinking, his puzzling out of the final presentation. Students benefit from being shown drafts of famous works in progress so that they can understand that brilliance does not just occur—it also takes hard work and trial and error.

In *Coition of a Hemisected Man and Woman*, Leonardo captures a man and a woman's detailed anatomy while having intercourse (The Royal Collection 2010, Her Majesty Queen Elizabeth II). That Leonardo captured the anatomy of intercourse is remarkable both as a person of the 1400s and, we presume, a homosexual. His drawing is anatomically accurate, yet passionless. The female face is not shown and the male is without expression, certainly not an ecstatic figure. Does this reflect the times that he could not show the emotion of sexuality but could get away with the anatomical connection?

The Last Supper

It does not seem possible to capture personal impressions of *The Last Supper* without comparing personal reactions to other revered works of art. *David*, for example, leaves visitors spellbound. To feel the impact of *David*, visitors must migrate toward the right side of the sculpture (*David*'s left)—to where his gaze falls on Goliath before battle. It is *before* battle, because he has a stone in hand and his sling over his shoulder. Move as far from the sculpture as possible to subject one self to his unnervingly stony stare. It feels that, like his sculpture, the flesh and blood David would have held the gaze for five hundred years. Relentless. Concentrated. Assured. Certain. Anticipatory. These are the words that come to mind as this young marble giant focused his stony eyes on the visitor, sitting in for the ogre Goliath.

The piece is moving. One can feel blood in those marble veins. One can understand that Michelangelo felt that he had found David alive in the marble block and freed him to fight. Look away and he seems to move, breathe, give up his pose for a moment. But his eyes never leave their target. They hold their ground.

In contrast, some find Michelangelo's Sistine Chapel ceiling unnerving. The ceiling itself is spectacular—a grand spectacle of story, allegory, and beauty. It is the dark blue nightmare of the altar wall that, some feel, damages the chapel and all too successfully competes for the visitor's attention. It can feel as though one is hearing a persistent phone ring during an intimate moment. It was not the nakedness—it was the obscenity of the allegory—the judgementalness of the last judgment, the apocalyptic nature of his apocalypse, the sheer darkness of the imagery that disturbs.

St. Bartholomew, a self-portrait, is particularly upsetting. It shows the saint displaying his flayed skin. The Michelangelo altar shatters the symmetry and plan of the original walls. It is brutish and holds none of the grace and beauty of the *David*. It seemed to express his anger rather than to channel it. It seems to reflect his identification with radical Dominican friar Savonarola, moralistic book-burner of bonfires of the vanities fame.

One approaches *The Last Supper* as our ancestors probably did their inner cave sanctums. A small group moves quietly from chamber to chamber as the guide prepares you for the encounter. Anticipation and silence build as visitors prepare for the reverent moment when they will be with this masterwork. They will see the moment when Christ tells his twelve disciples that one of them has betrayed him. They will see each person wrestle with this awful truth as we each wrestle with the undeniable truths that there are people carrying out immoral acts in our presence each day, and we must admit that not all of our acts are what they could be.

Visitors arrive and move slowly into the final chamber. The painting is grand—even bigger than imagined. Its colors are strong, muted, but strong. What one has read about Leonardo's failed experiment and the subsequent damage seems not to be true as one witnesses—absorbs perhaps describes it better—this image. The restoration and preservation seem to have worked—the colors seem right—these were simple people, not kings with finery. They are having a simple meal, their last together. It is a work of extraordinary beauty.

Unlike the *David* sculpture that only implies Goliath, here the antagonist is present. His hand clutches the reward of his betrayal. His fellow apostles sit at the dining table with him. Leonardo has moved him to Christ's side of the table, a new view of this old narrative. It is pure Leonardo—experimental, innovative, and excruciatingly beautiful.

Itinerant Years

In this stage, Leonardo was protected and supported by one of the most ruthless rulers in Renaissance Europe, Cesare Borgia. Cesare was the illegitimate son of the Borgia Pope, Alexander VI. Cesare murdered his brother and brother-in-law and attempted to create his own papal state in northern Italy. As long as his father was pope, he was able to expand his power. Four years after his father's death, Cesare was killed in battle.

Niccolò Machiavelli, author of *The Prince*, witnessed Cesare Borgia's rise to power. From this, Machiavelli concluded that a new prince (meaning a non-hereditary ruler who takes power rather than one who inherits the throne) must use power and trickery while appearing to be honest and trustworthy. Some believe that his writing is satirical. Leonardo's knew well both Cesare and Niccolò. Machiavelli and Leonardo were fellow functionaries of the same ambitious and ruthless leaders.

Over these six years, Leonardo's wanderings took him to Mantua, Venice, Romagna, Florence, Rome, and to Imola. One wonders what Leonardo saw in Rome, what he thought about drinking from the well of the ancients. This was late in his life, around age fifty. If it were another person, we might assume that his path was chosen and his destiny was set, but, with Leonardo, we have to assume that he moved by his exposure to the remains of the glory of Rome. Yet, surprisingly, in searching his notebooks for the word "pantheon," there is only one reference, a brief reference to a building with a hole in the ceiling like the Pantheon in Rome. The search engine does not find a reference for "Coliseum." Of course, we only have a fragment of his work, but one would expect his time in Rome to have been an important part of this life story—a kind of pilgrimage.

Amboise, France

"When I thought I was learning to live, I was also learning to die" (da Vinci, *Codex Atlanticus*). In 1516, Leonardo arrived at his final earthly destination, Amboise, France. It is here that the man from Vinci lived his last three years. He left Rome for France in the late summer or early fall of his sixty-fourth year. He arrived and settled into the young French king's manor house, Clos Luce, on the Loire River, at Amboise before the first of the year. He lived here just over three years. He died on May 2, 1519, two weeks after his sixty-seventh birthday. It seems fitting that he would die in the spring—fitting that his life would end at a time of renewal, of rebirth—a time of nature's annual renaissance. The olives were again in bloom. Here he breaks off one of his last writings by saying, "The soup is getting cold."

What kind of man was he? If we strip away the legend and folklore, if we overlook his recent popularity and the image that he cultivated for the sake of his ongoing patronage, who was this man from whom we have thousands of pages of writing and drawings, some of the world's most recognized, valued, and loved paintings, and yet about whom we know so little, personally?

His journals are not what we think of today—they are not diaries or daily logs of events and feelings. They are investigations—investigations into the workings of the world and his mind's ability to understand that world. They are solutions to problems—problems of perspective, of composition, and of turbulence. His subjects are light and water, military machines and defenses, beauty and the grotesque, politics and allegory. And horses—he had a particular love for the muscle, form, and movement of horses.

The man can be hard to find in this wash of thoughts and images. Was he secretive because this was the way that people were at the time? Why the mirrored writing? Or was he an outsider—an illegitimate son, most likely a homosexual, and unlettered—needing to protect himself from society's judgment? Did the sodomy trial when he was a young man teach him to protect his inner thoughts? Where do we look to find the man Leonardo?

One finds him in the hills of Tuscany, in his life's work, and in his soothing home at Amboise. It was here that he had the utter appreciation—we might say, love of the young French king, Francis I. Here the gardens are restful; the home is warm and sunlit. He had the attention of his housekeeper and that of Melzi, his longtime friend. There is a tunnel that leads from Chateau Amboise, Francis I's home, to Clos Luce. Through this channel, the young king is said to have visited Leonardo almost daily. Clos Luce, as it is shown today, is restful, contemplative, and worthy of Leonardo's last years. One senses that this home was peaceful, a place for an old man to consider life, death, soul, and afterlife, a last vantage point to witness the sun's light, which would soon turn dark. This home that may have reminded him of his bittersweet Tuscan childhood, in which his father rejected him but nature embraced him.

In the park at Clos Luce, his paintings and drawings hang on giant translucent prints in the forest with the sun's light penetrating them, creating from these familiar icons art to be seen anew. As families walk through the trails of Clos Luce, they encounter his machines. Kids fire cannons, paddle boats, turn Archimedes screws, and climb on bridges. They see flying machines and parachutes overhead. Although having no children of his own, one senses that Leonardo would have liked this, liked to see gentle creatures at play—perhaps using them as models for angels. At Clos Luce, there is a particularly beautiful dovecote, a small building with an eight-sided interior housing a thousand doves. Their eggs were likely a source of protein for Leonardo, who was, at least in his older years, a vegetarian. With his love of flight and early memories of birds, it is easy to imagine him strolling to the dovecote and enjoying the flights and sounds of birds.

After reviewing his work, the scholar finds himself to be ever more amazed at the breadth of Leonardo's intelligence. He was even more far-reaching, inquisitive, unbounded, even uncontainable, than his popular image. He would have been a giant in any one of the fields in which he worked—painting, music, architecture, military machines and defenses, philosophy, science. The Bramante Sacristy in Milan has an entire show of pages from the *Codex Atlanticus* devoted only to Leonardo's thoughts about politics and allegory. He broke ground in so many fields that, in most cases, would not be turned again for hundreds of years. In some cases, he served as a documenter of other's ideas; in other cases his work was original. Few people work at the level that he did in both art and science. Observation united these fields for Leonardo—they were not disparate. Art taught him to see and science taught him to reflect upon what he saw. It may be that he had a particularly acute ability to see—almost a stop-action ability. He records the flights of birds as if his eye had a shutter speed faster than most. There was, for Leonardo, no division between the thirty or more bodies that he dissected and the paintings and drawings that he made. Under the garments, we can sense the muscle and bone, tendons, and organs. One senses, from his drawings particularly, and from the record of his incomplete contracts, that much of his works were studies rather than products—that he was more interested in working out the problem than in finalizing the product.

Seeing his work and the places in which he lived, Leonardo presents what seems to be an enigma. He was simultaneously (a) a gentle soul who lived a good life as an artist-scientist and (b) a central figure in the fifteenth and sixteenth century military-architecture-engineering complex. Oddly, there seems to have been no internal conflict about this paradox, although we have precious little personal writing. Similarly, he moved easily from patron to patron, many of whom were archenemies. The Medici family, the Sforzas, the various popes, and Francis I—somehow he charmed them all, even when he failed to complete his contracts. He depended upon patronage as so many people in our time depend upon grants and fellowships.

Although a peaceful man personally, his work was often of a military nature—defenses, machine guns, mobile tanks, redirecting rivers to either flood or withhold water from towns under siege. Perhaps his mind was too intrigued by these problems to resist them and that his need for patronage was too great for him to resist the payment. Perhaps his patrons were surrogate fathers whom he wanted to please, feeling that he had failed to do so with his own father.

Leonardo was "unlettered." We have no reason to believe that he was readied for university. He did not know Latin, the language of scholars (hence Paris and other cities' "Latin Quarters"—areas of cities where the common language was Latin). Leonardo was an outsider. We see this in his mirror script. As well as to guard his professional secrets, Nicholl (2004, p. 58) tells us that he wrote in mirror fashion simply because he was left-handed and no schoolteachers forced him to do otherwise. As educators, the fact that he was unschooled is important. How is it that Leonardo, and many other learned geniuses, paradoxically developed his genius outside of the institutions that we have developed for the express purpose of learning? Can the unschooled advantage be schooled? His example causes us to ask about the potential of vocational-technical education—that is, after all, what Leonardo's apprenticeship with Verrocchio was.

The Gailer school attracted many homeschoolers. Homeschooled kids, at least those without a religious orthodoxy, are fresh, focused, open-minded, attentive, and hard working. They often watched little or no television. They do not project a sense of attention deficit—instead, they can listen well and attend for prolonged periods of time. They have a sense of what is important to them, never at a loss for a project to begin or a book to read. They are, in some ways, like Leonardo, "unschooled." Can we foster this within the broad confines of the institutions that we call schools? Many alternative educationa: settings and technical center programs accomplish this sense of "unschooling."

Years ago, Howard Gardner spoke about children's early perceptions of musical notation. He had slides showing how students progressively came to be able to use conventional notation. One preschooler depicted musical notes as little fluffy sheep bouncing at different levels, the level reflecting the tone of the note. It was heartbreaking to see this little person had learned in school how to write notation correctly, that is, conventionally. It seems that humankind extinguished a creative spark when that occurred. One student used to find himself angry when a teacher introduced his class to a new Robert Frost poem—that was no longer a poem that he could write. School, he felt, had taken something from him rather than had given him something.

Leonardo's temperament was pleasant and outgoing, particularly when compared to Michelangelo, who was angry, impolitic, isolated, possessed by his work, and influenced by the ultra-conservative monk Savonarola. Yet Leonardo had a jealous streak that can be seen in relation to Michelangelo.

In all probability, Leonardo saw works by Donatello or his apprentices before leaving his birth home of Vinci. Area churches, including Santa Croce, had works from Donatello's studio (a "fine polychrome wood sculpture of Mary Magdalene," according to Nicholl 2004, p. 56). These were likely Leonardo's first contacts with the Renaissance. Donatello was old at this time, as were his contemporaries such as Ghiberti (who created Florence's *Baptismal Gates of Paradise*) and Brunelleschi (of Duomo dome fame). Donatello represented the early Renaissance, whereas Leonardo was a generation later (and Michelangelo almost a generation after Leonardo). The mantel of the Renaissance was easily passed from Donatello's generation to Leonardo's, but not so easily to Michelangelo's.

David was intended for a niche high up on the Duomo, one of many fine works. However, when completed, it was clear that *David* was no ordinary sculpture to be hidden away in a niche a hundred feet off the ground. All who saw it knew immediately that they were in the presence of a work of unique brilliance. Rather than hide it in a niche, the Duomo works department called together thirty of the most prominent artists of Renaissance Florence to consider the placement of *David*. Leonardo was among the group. He suggested that the piece be sequestered away in the Loggia (near the Palazzo Vecchio, behind a low wall).

Michelangelo and Leonardo had a history. They were rivals—Michelangelo the young upstart and Leonardo the Renaissance torchbearer. Michelangelo had been asked to produce a giant fresco battle scene that would face Leonardo's battle of Angier planned for the Florentine Council Hall. Furthermore, the young Leonardo had probably served as the model for his master's *David* that Michelangelo's was now in danger of eclipsing. This was a rivalry proportional to the genius of the rivals themselves. Despite Leonardo's resistance, *David* was placed prominently in the Palazzo Vecchio, where a replica now stands. This antagonism seems not to be a usual part of Leonardo's character—it seemed to have been focused on his rival, Michelangelo.

Where they both geniuses? Clearly. Was their genius the result of extraordinary love of their subject(s) or was it native talent (2010)?

Michelangelo, having grown up in a stonemason's home at a marble quarry, may have developed an extraordinary love and feel for marble, yet not all boys who grow up in stonemasons' homes create works like *David*. He was also driven with a religious fervor. His claim to "release" the sculptures from the bounds of their marble is almost revelatory—he sees himself as an instrument of God rather than a human sculptor. His drive allowed him to begin the Sistine Chapel with minimal background in fresco and little interest in painting, and complete the work as an expert. Fresco, applying paints on wet plaster before it dries, is particularly challenging. Without question, this fresco novice created one of the greatest works of art of all time.

Leonardo's genius was far broader yet no less deep. As said earlier, he grew up outside of the confines of school. Was this lack of schooling a stimulus to freethinking genius? There are lots of unschooled children in the world today, yet few make extraordinary breakthroughs in art and science. He too was driven, but not from a religious zeal. Did both Leonardo and Michelangelo benefit from the synergy of resources and talent that concentrated in Renaissance Florence? Was the Renaissance self-generating? Was their rivalry a source of stimulus? Was there some inborn genetic component to each of their geniuses, some inimitable aspect of nature working in concert with nurture?

In Milan, where the *Atlantic Code* will be on display in its entirety over many years, Leonardo's aphorisms are as important a contribution to his body of work as his art, science, mathematics, and his engineering. For example, consider his thoughts on the soul and killing:

> And you, O Man, who will discern in this work of mine the wonderful works of Nature, if you think it would be a criminal thing to destroy it, reflect how much more criminal it is to take the life of a man; and if this, his external form, appears to thee marvelously constructed, remember that it is nothing as compared with the soul that dwells in that structure; for that indeed, be it what it may, is a thing divine. Leave it then to dwell in His work at His good will and pleasure, and let not your rage or malice destroy a life—for indeed, he who does not value it, does not himself deserve it.

Or on vanity: "The mirror conducts itself haughtily holding mirrored in itself the Queen. When she departs the mirror remains there." He can be sarcastic: "You grow in reputation like bread in the hands of a child." He was philosophical:

> That is not riches, which may be lost; virtue is our true good and the true reward of its possessor. That cannot be lost; that never deserts us, but when life

leaves us. As to property and external riches, hold them with trembling; they often leave their possessor in contempt, and mocked at for having lost them.

Leonardo cultivated his extraordinary powers of observation. He was a "disciple of experience." He developed the skills to be able to capture what he saw in paint, charcoal, and sculpture. In addition to his vision, he was a visionary. He saw what could be—machines and Madonnas—because he could see so clearly what was.

When all is said and done, Leonardo is an enigma, a brilliant, once-in-history figure, but one from whom we can learn and one from whom we can teach. His life is worth thinking about as we consider schools and learning.

The "Vitruvian Man"

The Euro dollar that celebrates Italy has an image of Leonardo's "Vitruvian Man" on its face. In fact, Vitruvius did not initially draw the "Vitruvian Man."

> Marcus Vitruvius was a Roman architect in 1 BCE and authored the famous treatise on architecture entitled *De Architectura*. . . . His book was the authority on these subjects up through the Renaissance, and still has influences in modern architecture today.

It is in the beginning of Book III, in his discussion on the building of temples, where the concept of "Vitruvian Man" emerges:

> Similarly, in the members of a temple there ought to be the greatest harmony in the symmetrical relations of the different parts to the general magnitude of the whole. Then again, in the human body the central point is naturally the navel. For if a man can be placed flat on his back, with his hands and feet extended, and a pair of compasses centered at his navel, the fingers and toes of his two hands and feet will touch the circumference of a circle described therefrom. And just as the human body yields a circular outline, so too a square figure may be found from it. For if we measure the distance from the soles of the feet to the top of the head, and then apply that measure to the outstretched arms, the breadth will be found to be the same as the height, as in the case of plane surfaces which are completely square.(Marcus Vitruvius, *De Architectura*, Book III, chapter 1, p. 3)

Scores of Vitruvian-like representations have been drawn. It is remarkable to see how deeply imbedded into our popular culture this image of Leonardo's has become. It is even found in recent versions of *Frankenstein*.

As Victor Frankenstein puts the finishing touches on his creation in the 1994 film *Mary Shelley's Frankenstein*, he glances at a reproduction of the Vitruvian Man. On this diagram, several key points have been marked, which Frankenstein proceeds to reproduce on the body of his figure. His quest is the creation of the perfect man and a new life, and in this quest he imitates the "Universal Man." (*Mary Shelley's Frankenstein*, dir. Kenneth Branagh, 1994).

Chapter 10 Summary

Leonardo da Vinci—His Life and His Relevance to Our Lives Today
- Leonardo's genius is worthy of emulation.
- Leonardo epitomizes the era that we call the "High Renaissance."
- He was a man, but a genius of a man.
- His powers of observation and ability to capture what he saw were extraordinary—he was truly a "disciple of experience."
- His "Vitruvian Man" image has become iconic.

~

CHAPTER ELEVEN

Rounding Out the Program—Satellite Programs and Common Questions

Let no one who is not a geometer enter my house. That is, 'Let no one who is unjust come in here,' for geometry is equality and justice.

—Sign over the door of Plato's Academy (Boorstin 1998)

Chapter 11 examines the satellite programs that are required to build a full and rich program for students. This chapter also examines a number of frequently asked questions.

A core curriculum is not a complete curriculum. Developing young people have complex needs. Along with the history of mathematics, students need to learn computation and the processes of mathematics. They need to learn another language. They need to learn how to serve their community, to inquire on their own, to learn to govern, and to enjoy sports. These are the satellite programs that revolve around the Da Vinci core. Yet they are not cut off and separate from the core program. In fact, using standards, assessments should be done across programs.

Assessment across Programs

Each program teacher writes and talks about the student's developing literacy, for example. In Spanish the student might be at the top of the class, having been energized by the trip to the Dominican Republic last year. Similarly, in the literary aspect of Da Vinci, the student may be doing exceptional work. Math, another form of literacy, may not have taken hold with the same enthusiasm. The work of the assessment team is to talk about the student's strong areas of literacy development and to encourage the student to see math as one more aspect of literacy, another power to embrace.

Entire books could be written about each of these programs, but that is not the purpose of this book. Suffice it to say that each program demands the same kind of thoughtful consideration that the core program does.

All-School Meetings and Governance

The presence of students improves decisions. Students rarely fail to bring a unique perspective and valuable insights to the policy table. Another benefit to institutionalizing student involvement in governance is that students tend to resist decision less if they have been a part of the process (as long as they really are a part and are not there to be co-opted). Virtually all policies and faculty hiring should involve students. The exception is issues of faculty discipline or nonrenewal. It is simply inappropriate for students to be involved in those personnel issues.

In a school with a strong community, there are lively discussions between teachers, students, and administrators in the governing body. Early in the development of the Da Vinci program, the forum added an interesting twist to the decision-making process. Two students noticed a pattern in the forum's decision making. Proposals would come before the forum for discussion. As part of that discussion, oftentimes proposals would be modified and improved. The forum would consider other implications that may not have been spoken to in the initial proposal. The forum would come to a consensus (defined as having been reached when even those who dissent acknowledge that the will of the group is clear) and a representative would then report back to their Da Vinci class the next morning. What the two students noticed was that the final product often bore little resemblance to the initial proposal—the spirit of the reform had often been lost.

They proposed a simple remedy: a two-step decision-making process. Instead of a final product going back to Da Vinci classes, the final proposal went back for discussion. This final proposal was warned to be voted on at the next forum meeting. If no changes were suggested (or only what the forum agreed were minor ones), the proposal would be voted on in the next forum meeting. If major changes were proposed, then the proposal would return to a draft status for further work. Although some changes might take weeks to accomplish, once the school had a decision, it generally had overwhelming support.

When the school began, there were only eight students. The only rule was this: "You can swing your fist, but only within an inch of my nose." That simple rule said it all. In later days, students were tired of what had evolved into many negatively worded rules—lots of "do nots." A student group proposed, and the forum accepted, a document called "The Gailer Code of Conduct." This was a positively worded document that encouraged students to work cooperatively. It helped shape the culture of the school for many years.

Creation and Discovery Days

Daniel Boorstin, librarian of the United States Congress from 1975 until 1987, wrote a trio of books titled *The Discoverers* (1983), *The Creators* (1992), and *The Seekers* (1998). The first was about the world of science, the second was about art, and the third concerned spirituality. The school named a program after Boorstin's first two books in the series. We called a few special days each year "Creation and Discovery Days."

During Creation and Discovery (C&O) Days, the regular program comes to a halt. A series of workshops replace the regular program for a day or two. The workshops were about either artistic creation or scientific discovery—or ideally, both. For example, a parent with experience teaching mountain climbing might rig up a climbing apparatus in the open chimney-like space running between three floors of the former building. For a day, he taught climbing. What was different about his approach, and what made it an ideal C&D activity, was that at each step of the process, he had Newton meters hooked to the ropes measuring the various forces that he was teaching students how to handle. C&D activities ran the gamut. They were a good way to see another side of both students and teachers—a good break from business as usual, no matter how unusual business at Gailer was.

Mathematics

In Da Vinci, students gain an understanding of mathematics as a human enterprise. They see how, where, and by whom key mathematical concepts developed. They develop a greater appreciation for other cultures. They gain a sense of the larger picture. The school used *The Story of Numbers* by McLeish (1994) and *Innumeracy: Mathematical Illiteracy and Its Consequences* (1988) by John Allen Paulos as guides in this process. McLeish presents an overview and does not attempt to explain the processes of mathematics while presenting the history of mathematic concepts. It is readable by almost any student, whereas many math histories require a high level of math study.

Keep in mind that the Common Core is "focused in the areas of mathematics, reading, writing, speaking and listening." See appendix A of the Common Core for "standard" and "compacted" math pathways.

The math classroom complements the Da Vinci classroom. Here math is learned as a series of skills that are practiced in order to become part of the student's skill repertoire. The math classroom uses manipulatives, textbooks, and problem solving. Math teachers often make reference to math history as a way of reinforcing the Da Vinci approach to integrated studies.

Based on placement exams and prior performance, math students are placed in classes that present the topics that the student needs and does so at a pace that will satisfy and not overwhelm the student. Some follow a "standard" curriculum and others a "compacted" one.

Spanish

A second language is a central skill today. A recent *Journal Sentinel* article reinforces this (Schmid 2010). The author notes that budget cuts are axing languages disproportionally. "From 1997 to 2008, the share of all U.S. elementary schools offering language classes fell from 31 percent to 25 percent, while middle schools dropped from 75 percent to 58 percent." Schmid then asks, "How can Americans expect to carve new trade routes into nations where they cannot understand the TV shows, websites or train conductors?" He notes that many European and Asian countries require a second and third language and begin language instruction early in grade school. He then mentions the predominance of Mandarin in the world (Chinese speakers outnumber English speakers worldwide by a two to one ratio). Research indicates that "there is a significant side benefit to learning the Chinese language: the cognitive skill that comes from mastering a complex, graphic, non-alphabetical writing system" (Schmid 2010). And yet, we are cutting back.

Service Learning

In order to contribute to the world, students must learn how to use and develop their talents. Doing so makes life worthwhile, efficacious, and meaningful. From the earlier days of the school, Wednesday has been spent in service learning and in a program of independent study called "Inquiry."

Inquiry

At the broadest levels, the Da Vinci program prescribes the curriculum. Although there is a great deal of freedom for students to fundamentally individualize the study, it is not an option to avoid a study of the Russian Revolution or Manifest Destiny. The broad historical topics are nonnegotiable. Inquiry, however, turns the tables on conventional curriculum. Here the student determines his or her learning agenda and how to pursue that agenda. Here the school supports the student as he or she set priorities and learns how to satisfy those priorities. There is no hiding from learning—no opportunity to blame the teacher or the school—in Inquiry, the student is in charge and has the responsibility for his or her own education.

For example, Sarah wanted to pursue her interest in medical anthropology. She found a course offered at a local college and took the course as her Inquiry. The school supported her by giving her the time to take the course, by requiring her to reflect on her learning, and by crediting the course. Recently, Sarah graduated from the Boston University School of Health with an MS in International Health.

Ben wanted to learn about small engines. He found an aircraft mechanic who worked with him as he disassembled a lawn mower engine and learned the basics of internal combustion. Ben has completed a pre-med degree and is applying to medical schools.

Michael wanted to learn about photographic composition. His photographic work with his father resulted in a show of his photos. Michael is now at the University of Vermont studying film.

Anna, now a farm manager, wanted to learn more about veterinarian practices. She devoted her Inquiry to aiding a veterinarian one day per week for two years. Inquiry allowed her to build her résumé as she saw fit for her future. It is striking how many inquiries have developed into life work.

Inquiry and community service take place on Wednesdays when the faculty collaborate on curriculum and the forum (including student representatives) meets to consider policy. These two programs require guidance and support. Some students are just waiting for us to cut the cords that restrain them, whereas others have no idea what to do or how to do it when given the freedom. They have to be taught and guided.

Fitness and Sports

For much of the school's history, fitness was required of every student every day. It was part of being a student at Gailer. The idea was daily exercise, rather than a minimal credit requirement, be met before beginning the long, slow slide to middle age. Sports were popular—basketball, soccer, Ultimate Frisbee, and broomball were the favorites. Some years the school had competitive teams (particularly during the years when we had many excellent Indonesian students), and some years we just had fun. Broomball took on

Gailer Story #8

Matt: The Go-Cart from Hell

Matt was a reluctant writer, but he sure could weld. At first he didn't yet understand that to assemble a tractor was no different from assembling a paragraph—that each part served to make the thing work. He made me a bird sculpture from old tractor parts and metal he found around the farm. When it came to Inquiry, Matt knew exactly what he wanted to do—he wanted to build a go-cart.

Inquiry was his program. If he wanted to build a go-cart, that was fine with me. His dad was willing to sign on to oversee the project—to keep Matt safe as he worked with gasoline, welding tools, and what turned out to be a very fast go-cart. His uncle had an old run-down go-cart that Matt could rebuild. The project was moving.

Matt's advisor asked one thing of him—to document the project with pictures. She asked him to take pictures at each step as he took apart the old go-cart, cleaned and replaced parts, built some new parts, and souped up the engine. When he was well along on the project, the advisor asked him to mount the pictures on a piece of cardboard and bring it in to show her. He did and she asked questions: What's this? Are these the brakes? How did you do that? She told him that for her to understand what he had done, the pictures needed captions. He took the display home and added captions.

The next time they met, she asked him to tell her more about each stage of the process, each picture. He did so and she took notes. When they were finished, she asked if he could write up a paragraph for each photo using her notes. He did and returned the next week. Feigning ignorance, she told him that she still did not fully understand the process that he went through—could he elaborate a bit here, add a sentence or two there, flesh out an idea over here. He did and returned the next week. Together, they assembled his digital pictures and text into a booklet—quite an accomplishment for a reluctant writer.

There are two closing notes on this story. First, Matt brought his go-cart in and test-drove it for the entire student body. We didn't clock it, but I'll bet it hit 45 mph judging by the lawn that it tore up. And second, Matt wrote a piece about a unique rotational scheme that his farm used. He had it accepted for publication in a national farm journal. This reluctant writer became the school's first published author!

Gailer Story #9

Our First Soccer Game

An established independent school was willing to play us. This was an exciting moment for my little school. Not being a team-sport player myself, but knowing how important sports can be for kids, I was anxious to get us a game. We had one slight problem. We were one player shy of fielding a soccer team.

But there was Ethan. He was a good sport, although without a bit of interest or experience in any sports. He was more of a dancer and performer. He was light on his feet, but when I asked him if he would play, he asked if those things at the ends of the field were called "goals." I told him they were and others would teach him the rest of the game on the bus. He agreed to play.

Shortly after the game began, we knocked the ball out of bounds. Their player threw the ball in by doing a head-over-heels flip. I recall watching their team drive the ball toward our goal as our team stood in place, shocked, immobilized with their mouths hanging open. They had never seen such a move.

When the time was over, the score was tied. Their skills were up against our spirit. They won in overtime. We went home victorious.

---

a life of its own. Duct-taped brooms, secret screws in the bottom on boots, and broomball as a metaphor for life were all parts of the spirit of the sport.

Common Questions

Here are a few common concerns:

- Does the Da Vinci Curriculum and associated instructional practices work in the real world? *Yes, I know that having taught scores of students this way.*
- Will it work in public schools? *Absolutely. There is nothing that we were able to do in a small, low-cost, diverse, independent school that could not be as effective in a larger public school. In fact, some public schools have done so.*
- Would the Da Vinci Curriculum have to be a school's only curriculum? *No. There is no reason why a school-within-a-school cannot offer multiple*

stimulating curricula, but Da Vinci should not be used as a way to disintegrate schools by race, socioeconomic status, aspiration level, and so on. I saw the Da Vinci Curriculum work for rural farm kids, special education students, international students, and privileged suburban kids.

- Is there no disadvantage to learning this way? Yes, there is. *The primary disadvantage is that when the core program is committed to the Da Vinci Curriculum, students might not feel that they have as much choice as they have in a typical comprehensive high school's curriculum. American kids have become accustomed to choice—they often have a thousand songs on their iPod playlist. The way to address this is to be sure that students have a lot of choice in all of their other programs, and a lot of choice within Da Vinci. Ideally, students will be involved in determining what the essential questions and authentic assignments should be for a given study. If possible, in larger schools, students could choose between Da Vinci and other curricula.*
- How about hiring faculty who become "Da Vinci teachers"? Where do you find them and how do you train them? *We hired three kinds of teachers, Da Vinci humanities teachers, Da Vinci science teachers, and conventional teachers. Conventional teachers taught math, Spanish, an independent study program called "Inquiry," and various humanities options, and advised community service. We looked for exceptional teachers with conventional résumés, and a desire to teach in a school that valued deep-rooted inquiry. For Da Vinci humanity teachers, we looked for exceptional preparation within the historical period that they were responsible for (Ancient Civilizations or the Age of Discovery, for example) as well as breadth of study across the disciplines. Although we did not expect teachers to be equally well prepared in all disciplines, but a phobia in any one discipline was a deal-breaker. We did not want to have our teachers pass on a negative attitude to their students. We needed something different in Da Vinci Science teachers. We looked for the right combination of science skills (but without the rigidity that Highly Qualified Teacher regulations impose), with a developed interest in the humanities. We wanted our science and humanities teachers to want to learn from each other, to model co-teaching and co-learning.*
- How about materials? My school is diverse. Can you find materials for all readers that accomplish the high intellectual goals that you write about? *I was worried about this when I designed the school. As it turns out, plenty of exceptional books, artifacts, prints, poems, histories, geographies, and so forth, exist at all levels of literacy. Some do occasionally go out of print, but we were easily able to work around that. Many nontraditional*

learners are visual and kinesthetic learners—artifacts and inductive learning are ideal for these students.

- Does it take special training to convert conventional teachers into Da Vinci teachers? *Absolutely. Lots of it. Constantly. Teachers must have a great deal of time in the summer and during the school year to collaborate, teach each other, learn to be comfortable working in new disciplines, and be a part of school governance. My goal was to be able to leave school for a day at any moment and turn the place over to any member of the faculty with complete confidence that the school would run without interruption. Leadership must be cultivated.*

- Is the Da Vinci Curriculum the only thing that makes the Gailer School unique? *No. Gailer was designed to be a constellation of programs that in total provided the student with a well-rounded education with each of the programs reinforcing each other.*

- Is the Da Vinci Curriculum the only way to organize a school? *Of course not!* Is it the best way? *Probably not.* Is it a substantial move toward a meaningful and integrated interdisciplinary curriculum well suited for today's students? *Yes.* It is possible to engage the large majority of students in an intellectually satisfying curriculum that asks students to understand and affect our species "heritage of values"? *Yes, it is. I've seen it happen over and over.*

The American Secondary School Curriculum fails to meet the intellectual needs of today's students. Millennials understand that the problems that

---

Travel Vignette #6

Venetian Harbor, Crete

My oldest son, Ben, and I stand a half-mile out on the breakwater of the old Venetian Harbor at Heraklion, Crete. Ben was just six years old when I started my school. He is twenty-five now, a pre-med student. He attended Gailer from seventh through twelfth grade. I had the great pleasure of having him in class and handing him his high school diploma. And now we stand side by side thinking about the long stretch of human history, the far longer time lost in prehistory, the rise and fall of peoples, and the short time that we have to make our mark on the shoreline. On this trip together—our 25/60 adventure, marking two important birthdates in our lives—we have spent days walking Athens's Acropolis and the even earlier Minoan culture on Crete. It pleases me to know that over the millennia, other men have stood here with their sons.

we face globally are urgent. They want to understand these problems deeply and contribute toward making the world that they are about to inherit safer, more accepting, and more equitable. They are ready for a curriculum that is rich in historical context, interdisciplinary connections, and demonstrable purpose—a curriculum that provides them with what they need to be powerful agents of change. They are ready for Da Vinci.

CHAPTER TWELVE

~

Putting Theory into Practice— New Schools, Schools within Schools, and Curriculum Renewal

DuFour and Evans 101

It is easier to move a graveyard than to change a school's curriculum.

—French Statesman George Clemenceau

There is nothing more difficult to take in hand, more perilous to conduct, or more uncertain in its success, than to take the lead in the introduction of a new order of things.

—Machiavelli, *The Prince*

Making It Happen

A User's Guide to Comprehensive Curriculum Change
Chapter 12 examines how to make change in secondary schools. It focuses on four key aspects of the change process: professional learning communities, resistance to change, program evaluation, and the elements needed to accomplish change in an organization.

Anyone who has tried to change a school's curriculum will agree: changing a school's curriculum is not for the fainthearted. Schools are inherently conservative places—they exist, in part, to preserve cultural heritage. As Dewey said, "Ours is the responsibility of conserving, transmitting, rectifying and expanding the heritage of values we have received (1934)." In most schools, there tends to be more conserving and transmitting than rectifying and expanding. Everyone wants to see change—change in other departments, other grade levels, and other teachers' classrooms. Many teachers are more comfortable teaching the same courses that they did last year, in the same room, with the same colleagues and the same curriculum.

It's hard to blame them. As society has changed, schools have been buffeted with an unrealistic degree of change over the last twenty-five years. The changing family and community have impacted every teacher. America's bold experiment to extend civil rights opportunities to all students has changed the very population we serve. Federal and state legislation and regulation has had an impact on every school. The graying of our society has impacts on budgets and programs. In the 1960s, 70 percent of families had students in school. Today the figure has dropped to 30 percent.

The growing discrepancy between rich and poor and the "Great Recession" have deeply affected schools. Meanwhile, education has been in a transition from a grossly underpaid cottage industry requiring minimal preparation to a unionized, research-based, selective profession requiring extensive preparation, testing, and licensure. Given this relentless change agenda and teachers' natural resistance to change, how should a group of teachers and/or administrators go about incorporating the Da Vinci Curriculum—or any other change—in their school?

Although charter schools might form around these ideas, few existing schools are likely to be ready for a wholesale adoption of the ideas in this book. For most, it would be wise to begin with a pilot program with a subset of the population or a school-within-a-school. The program should be fully optional for students and teachers. We know a lot about change in organizations. Here are a few basics on school change.

Before you begin, it is worth thinking about your reason for making change. Do you have a clear rationale for why you are thinking about changing your school? What kind of school are you? Are you considering whole school change or creating an optional program for students? Do you have others on board? You will need to build a community of change agents, a Professional Learning Community.

Professional Learning Communities (PLCs)

Rick DuFour and others tell us that schools need to create Professional Learning Communities (PLCs) in order to create and maintain change. PLCs share six characteristics (DuFour 2004, 2006, 2007):

- Shared mission, vision, and values.
- Collective inquiry—practice is influenced by research that is shared among colleagues. Research should include quick and dirty action

research within the school setting and reliable juried research from outside of the school (from journals)—both are important. It is great that you talk and share your expertise—this is one important source of ideas—but it is not enough. PLCs inform themselves from outside of their circle as well as from within.

- Collaborative teams—change occurs when colleagues candidly support one another. It's not about superstars—it's about teamwork.
- Action orientation and experimentation. Leaders tend to fire before taking careful aim. Teachers could spend a whole career getting ready to aim. Effective change teams get ready, take aim, and fire. Then they approach the target, see where they shot, and take aim again with the new information. Effective PLCs are not afraid to act with limited but reliable knowledge.
- Continuous improvement—Ready, aim, fire, look at the target, aim again, fire again, reevaluate, and so on.
- Results oriented—it all comes down to kids. How are they doing academically using many different conventional and authentic measures, and how is their well-being? Are you sure? How do you know? What are you watching for? What are you measuring? What gets measured is what gets attention.

DuFour asks the simple but powerful question, "How does your school respond when students do not learn?" In asking this, he acknowledges that, despite the faculty's best efforts, many students do not learn. They also shift the focus from the student to the school by asking what the school plans to do when many students do not succeed. This leads to a conversation about pyramids of intervention.

The text *Learning by Doing* (DuFour et al. 2010) is an excellent handbook for a team hoping to make large-scale change in their school. The DuFour team is available at conferences throughout the United States. Schools are unlikely to change without their faculty embracing the concepts of PLCs.

Resistance

Resistance is a natural part of any working group—even a self-selected, everybody's-on-board group. At some point, each of us will resist aspects of the changes that we hope to make. Consider the following.

During change, "people no longer know what their duties are, how to relate to others, or who has the authority to make decisions. The structural benefits of clarity, predictability and rationality are replaced with confusion, loss of control and the belief that politics rather than policies are now governing everyday behaviors" (Bolman and Deal 1984).

Well-meaning people resist change. People who want to see change occur resist change. It can get ugly when the old rules no longer exist and what was once comfortable—even complacent—begins to feel chaotic, rudderless, and like everyone is scrambling for power. Clear lines of authority will help, but you will not be able to foresee every possible circumstance. Trust, improvisation, and anticipating resistance will help. Evans (1996) is a must read for anyone attempting organizational change.

Elements of Change

It takes at least five elements in place for change to occur. There must be a clear and persuasive *vision for change*. Lots of authors have written about vision. Rick DuFour is as good a source as any since he distinguishes between mission (why your school exists), vision (where you are going), values (what you believe in), and goals (specific steps to reach your vision). I hope that this text will give you a good start for building your vision. Without a clear and moving vision, there will be confusion and lack of commitment. People must know why they are participating and why it is important for them to do so.

Second, those implementing the change must have the *skills* that they will need. Lacking skills to do the job that they are asked to do will be frustrating and ultimately anxiety provoking. "I'd like to help, but . . ."

There must be *incentives*. Incentives do not have to be monetary; they may be kind words of support, recognition at an event, or something else. The most important thing is that the incentives are meaningful to those involved. How do you find out what someone needs to feel appreciated? Tell them that you appreciate their contribution and would like to thank them in a way that they would enjoy. Ask them what they would like. Whether for staff or supporters, incentives are important and should be understood. After you have given your staff and supporters what you know they enjoy, then do a little more to show that their participation really means something to you beyond what you have agreed to. Handwritten cards are always meaningful. E-mail thank-yous are cheesy.

What can you expect without incentives? Resistance. "Why should I help her with her pet project? Doesn't mean a thing to me." Remember that how you treat your staff is how you are teaching your staff to treat their students. Be generous, but not gratuitous, with your appreciation.

To effectively carry out change, there has to be adequate *resources*. Most schools are practiced at doing things on the cheap—it's one of the things we do best. I can think of dozens of projects I have seen nickeled and dimed in schools over the years that have (predictably) failed, leaving teachers cynical about the idea, which may have been good, had it not been starved to death. We are especially good at underfunding training and we almost never fund program evaluation. These are big mistakes.

Here are two common examples of inadequate resources. A principal I worked with wanted to see Teacher Advisories (TA) incorporated into the school. He saw them operate well in another district and was hot on the idea. He set up a new schedule, asked a few teachers what they thought, and implemented a new TA program. A year later he went around to visit TAs and saw something that looked an awful lot like the old homerooms that the school used to have. Students were listening to announcements, doing homework, and socializing while the teacher was polishing a PowerPoint for her first-period class. What happened to this great idea—to the principal's vision of Teacher Advisories?

It doesn't take a brain surgeon to figure this out. Teachers know how to teach—they have been trained to do so. They know how to supervise a homeroom—they had supervisory duties when they student taught. But they have not necessarily been trained in *advising* students. These are new and complicated skills that take training and practice. If you want teachers to become teacher-advisors, you must provide them with the training to do so. This training must be ongoing since some people will come and go and others will simply need to refine their skills.

Another common training mistake concerns schedule changes. One school principal I worked with saw imaginative, engaging, and sustained learning in a block-schedule format and decided to change the traditional school schedule to eighty-minute blocks. She thought about union issues—teachers will have the same number of preparations per year and will teach the same number of total minutes. No problem! Yet like with the TA change, block schedules do not work if teachers simply extend their didactic teaching from forty-three minutes to eighty minutes. They need to be retrained so that they will use the new block schedule optimally. More of the same could actually be worse. The bottom line is that if you don't have the resources to make the change—particularly to train people well—don't take it on or take more time to build up the resource base. Lacking resources will lead to frustration, failure, and cynicism.

In order to effectively make change, groups of people need a clear vision, relevant skills, motivating incentives (perhaps intrinsic ones), appropriate resources, and an action plan. If any element is missing, the change process is likely to be derailed. For example, without a clear vision, there will be division and confusion. Without the appropriate skills, there will be anxiety as people struggle to do what they are not trained to do. Without incentives, there may be resistance. Without resources, people will be frustrated. And without an action plan to guide them, people are likely to feel that they are running on a treadmill without making forward progress. You might talk about these things with your study group to develop a common understanding about the elements of change and to build a common vocabulary with them.

Program Evaluation

Program evaluation is almost universally nonexistent as a routine activity in schools. At best, it is a once-a-decade activity carried out under the threat of an imminent visiting accreditation team with laptops and sour demeanors. Occasionally it is done after the fact. Almost never is program evaluation built in from the start. It is an expense, but does it have to be a debilitating one? No. Program evaluation is really no more complex than asking the following:

1. What are we trying to accomplish?
2. How will we know if we were to accomplish this?
3. Where will we look to find data that will help us understand the degree to which we have accomplished what we set out to do?
4. Who will be able to help us find and analyze date objectively?

Program evaluation should be closely linked to the program's goals and should be simple and manageable. It should be ongoing. It should be objective.

If change is to occur effectively, there must be an *action plan*. Vision is great, but all the vision in the world does not implement a program. Think about your staffing—some people are best at creating a vision; others are best at implementation. Rarely is one individual equally competent in doing both. As many philosophers have said, "Know thyself." In a small staff, "knowing each other" is also important. Encourage frank discussion of strengths and weaknesses in your team. Beware of anyone who claims no weaknesses or claims no strengths.

Table 12.1. Approximate Timeline for Planning, Creating, and Implementing a Da Vinci Option within an Existing School

Events	Approximate Time	Notes
1. Assembly of Study Group	Four months	Do not ask people to sign their names in blood at this stage. You are simply looking for a working group to do some preliminary research and begin a conversation. Think about who needs to be at the table for this to be successful. Establish a spirit of open-mindedness and other working norms. Be tight on facilitation and loose on outcomes.
2. Establish the Da Vinci Study Group's Vision	One month	Read DuFour on mission, vision, and goals.
3. Develop the Study Group's Action Plan	Six months	Be sure to include resource procurement, authority discussions, and a concrete time line that neither jumps ahead without research nor gets mired in inaction and perpetual study. Articulate clear goals. Include program evaluation and retuning in your plan. How will you know if your program is successful?
4. Carry out the Action Plan	Year Two	Start small. Expect resistance. Listen and learn.
5. Implementation	Year Three	Take action however imperfect. Begin your program evaluation immediately.
6. Refine and Improve	Year Four	Goal is improvement, not perfection!

Closing Thoughts

School change is difficult business. It *is* more difficult to move a graveyard than to change a school's curriculum. Yet the curriculum that we have has not always existed. Universities, prestigious study groups, impressive experts, politicians, and time itself have created the American curriculum that we all know and love. It has changed before and it can change again (Kliebard 1987; Gibboney 1994). It *will* change again. I invite you to be a part of that change rather than leave it to the nonschool "experts."

To do so requires courage and vision. You can create a school that the large majority of your students look forward to attending. You can create a school where the relationship between teachers and students shifts from one of coercion and compliance to one of shared intellectual enterprise. You can create a renaissance in your school.

Chapter 12 Summary

Putting Theory into Practice—New Schools, Schools within Schools, and Curriculum Renewal: DuFour and Evans 101

- Professional Learning Communities (PLCs) are a potent vehicle for school change.
- Resistance will inevitably be present.
- Improvement never ends.
- There must be a clear vision for change.
- The resources needed to change must be present.
- There must be effective action planning.
- Second order change is deep rooted.
- Curriculum is central.
- Program assessment is central.
- It takes, vision, skills, incentives, resources, and an effective action plan to make change.

References

ACT, Inc. "Reading between the Lines: What the ACT Reveals about College Readiness in Reading." 2006. In ACT, Inc. [database online]. Iowa City, IA. Available from http://www.act.org/research/policymakers/pdf/reading_summary .pdf (accessed September 6, 2011).

Advanced Placement: U.S. History. Available from http://www.smithsonianeducation .org/idealabs/ap/index.htm (accessed October 6, 2011).

Creation Myths from Around the World. Available from http://www.amazon.com/s/ ref=nb_sb_ss_i_2_14?url=search-alias=aps&field-keywords=creation+myths+from +around+the+world&sprefix=creation+myths (accessed September 29, 2011).

Aristotle. 1943. *Aristotle's Politics.* Translated by Benjamin Jowett. New York: Modern Library.

Atalay, Bülent, and Keith Wamsley. 2008. *Leonardo's Universe: The Renaissance World of Leonardo da Vinci.* Washington, DC: National Geographic.

Bacon, Francis. Novum Organum (1620). Available from http://www.constitution .org/bacon/nov_org.htm (accessed September 13, 2011).

Bacon, Francis. 2004. *The Instauratio Magna Part II:* Novum Organum *and Associated Texts.* Edited by Graham Rees. Oxford: Clarendon.

Barth, Roland S. 2001. *Learning by Heart.* San Francisco: Jossey-Bass.

———. 2003. *Lessons Learned: Shaping Relationships and the Culture of the Workplace.* Thousand Oaks, CA: Corwin Press.

Barth, Roland S., and Linda Sand Guest. 1990. *Improving Schools from Within: Teachers, Parents, and Principals Can Make the Difference.* San Francisco: Jossey-Bass.

BBC. "A History of the World: *Standard of Ur.*" Available from http://www.bbc.co .uk/ahistoryoftheworld/objects/cVczEWH0RVm_dFZtJBAjRw (accessed September 25, 2011).

Beane, James A., and Association for Supervision and Curriculum Development. 1995. *Toward a Coherent Curriculum: The 1995 ASCD Yearbook*. Alexandria, VA: The Association.

Benn, M., and N. Cornell. 2007. Conversation regarding two on-line digital curriculum programs and their possible adoption at Addison northeast supervisory union. Personal communication.

Bennis, Warren G., and Patricia Ward Biederman. 1997. *Organizing Genius: The Secrets of Creative Collaboration*. Reading, MA: Addison-Wesley.

Big Picture Learning. 2011. In Big Picture Company [database online]. Available from http://www.bigpicture.org (accessed September 6, 2011).

Bloom, Benjamin Samuel. 1956. *Taxonomy of Educational Objectives: The Classification of Educational Goals. Handbook 1: Cognitive Domain*. New York: McKay.

Bolman, Lee G., and Terrence E. Deal. 1984. *Modern Approaches to Understanding and Managing Organizations*. San Francisco: Jossey-Bass.

———. 2001. *Leading with Soul: An Uncommon Journey of Spirit*. San Francisco: Jossey-Bass.

Boorstin, Daniel J. 1992. *The Creators*. New York: Random House.

———. 1998. *The Seekers: The Story of Man's Continuing Quest to Understand His World*. New York: Random House.

Boorstin, Daniel J., Clare Boothe Luce, and Daniel J. Boorstin Collection (Library of Congress). 1983. *The Discoverers*. New York: Random House.

Börner, Katy. 2010. *Atlas of Science: Visualizing What We Know*. Cambridge, MA: MIT Press.

Brady, Marion. 2008. "Cover the Material—or Teach Students to Think?" *Educational Leadership* 65 (5) (2002): 64–67.

Bransford, John Douglas, National Research Council (United States), Committee on Developments in the Science of Learning and National Research Council (United States), and Committee on Learning Research and Educational Practice. 2000. *How People Learn: Brain, Mind, Experience, and School*. Washington, DC: National Academy Press.

Brooks, Jacqueline Grennon. 2004. "To See Beyond the Lesson." *Educational Leadership* 62 (1) (2009): 8–12.

Brown, Dan. 2004. *The Da Vinci Code*. New York: Doubleday.

Business People—Vermont. "The Headmaster's Tale" [The Gailer School]. Available from http://www.vermontguides.com/2000/7-jul/jul1.htm (accessed December 15, 2010).

Casas, Bartolomé de las, and George William Sanderlin. 1992. *Witness: Writings of Bartolomé de las Casas*. Maryknoll, NY: Orbis Books.

Center for Science, Mathematics, and Engineering Education, Committee on Development of an Addendum to the National Science Education Standards on Scientific Inquiry. 2000. *Inquiry and the National Science Education Standards: A Guide for Teaching and Learning*. Washington, DC. Available from http://www.nap.edu/openbook.php?record_id=496 (accessed February 25, 2012).

Clarke, John H. 1990. *Patterns of Thinking: Integrating Learning Skills in Content Teaching*. Boston: Allyn and Bacon.

Clarke, John H., and Arthur W. Biddle. 1993. *Teaching Critical Thinking: Reports from across the Curriculum*. Englewood Cliffs, NJ: Prentice Hall.

Coles, Robert. 1989. *The Call of Stories: Teaching and the Moral Imagination*. Boston: Houghton Mifflin.

Costa, Arthur L. 2008. "The Thought-Filled Curriculum." *Educational Leadership* 65 (5) (2002): 20–24.

"Critical thinking." Available from http://www.criticalthinking.org (accessed November 2, 2007).

Daggett, W. R. 2011. International Center for Leadership Education. In International Center for Leadership Education [database online]. Rexford, NY. Available from http://www.leadered.com/ (accessed September 6, 2011).

da Vinci, Leonardo. 2004. *The Wisdom of Leonardo da Vinci*. Translated by Wade Baskins. New York: Barnes & Noble.

da Vinci, Leonardo. 1956. *Leonardo da Vinci*. New York: Reynal.

da Vinci, Leonardo, and Carlo Pedretti. 1978. *The Codex Atlanticus of Leonardo da Vinci: a catalogue of its newly restored sheets*. [New York]: Johnson Reprint Corp.

de Bry, Theodor. 1976. *Discovering the New World*. Edited by Michael Alexander. London: London Editions.

DeKuyper, Mary Hundley. 2003. *NAIS Trustee Handbook*. Washington, DC: National Association of Independent Schools.

D'Epiro, Peter, and Mary Desmond Pinkowish. 2001. *Sprezzatura: 50 Ways Italian Genius Shaped the World*. New York: Anchor Books.

Developmental Biology 9e Online. "Anton van Leeuwenhoek and His Perception of Spermatozoa." Available from http://9e.devbio.com/article.php?ch=7&id=65 (accessed September 9, 2011).

Dewey, John. 1934. *A Common Faith*. New Haven: Yale University Press.

———. 1938. *Experience and Education*. New York: Macmillan.

———. 1963. *Experience and education*. New York: Collier Books.

Diamond, Jared M. 1998. *Guns, Germs, and Steel: The Fates of Human Societies*. New York: W.W. Norton & Co.

"Did Leonardo da Vinci paint the Salvator Mundi?" *The Telegraph*, November 7, 2011. Available from http://telegraph.feedsportal.com/c/32726/f/617107/s/19e5facb/l/0L0Stelegraph0O0Cculture0Cart0Cleonardo0Eda0Evinci0C88750A310CDid0ELeonardo0Eda0EVinci0Epaint0Ethe0ESalvator0EMundi0Bhtml/story01.htm (accessed March 8, 2012).

Donaldson, Gordon A. 1991. *Learning to Lead: The Dynamics of the High School Principalship*. New York: Greenwood Press.

DuFour, Richard. 2004. *Whatever It Takes: How Professional Learning Communities Respond When Kids Don't Learn*. Bloomington, IN: National Educational Service.

———. 2007. "In Praise of Top-Down Leadership." *School Administrator* 64 (10) (2011): 38–42.

———. 2010. *Learning by Doing: A Handbook for Professional Learning Communities at Work*. Bloomington, IN: Solution Tree Press.

Eisner, Elliot. 1978. *Reading, the Arts, and the Creation of Meaning*. Reston, VA: National Art Education Association.

Engelbert, Phyllis. 1997. *Astronomy and Space: From the Big Bang to the Big Crunch*. Available from http://newarrivals.nlb.gov.sg/item_holding.aspx?bid=7767590 (accessed September 29, 2011).

Evans, Robert. 1996. *The Human Side of School Change: Reform, Resistance, and the Real-Life Problems of Innovation*. San Francisco: Jossey-Bass.

Farrington, Benjamin. 1964. *The Philosophy of Francis Bacon: An Essay on its Development from 1603 to 1609*. Liverpool: University Press.

Florida, Richard L. 2002. *The Rise of the Creative Class: And How It's Transforming Work, Leisure, Community, and Everyday Life*. New York: Basic Books.

Foundation for Critical Thinking. Books, Conferences, and Academic Resources for Educators and Students. Available from http://www.criticalthinking.org/ (accessed September 13, 2011).

Friedman, Thomas L. 2007. *The World Is Flat: A Brief History of the Twenty-First Century*. New York: Farrar, Straus and Giroux.

Glasser, William. 1986. *Control Theory in the Classroom*. New York: Perennial Library.

Gardner, Howard. 1983. *Frames of Mind: The Theory of Multiple Intelligences*. New York: Basic Books.

———. 2006. *Five Minds for the Future*. Boston, MA: Harvard Business School Press.

Gibboney, Richard A. 1994. *The Stone Trumpet: A Story of Practical School Reform, 1960–1990*. Albany, NY: State University of New York Press.

Given, Barbara K. 2002. *Teaching to the Brain's Natural Learning Systems*. Alexandria, VA: Association for Supervision and Curriculum Development.

Green, Tim, Loretta Donovan, and Kim Bass. 2010. "Taking Laptops Schoolwide: A Professional Learning Community Approach." *Learning & Leading with Technology* 38 (1) (2008): 12–15.

Gursky, Daniel. 1990. "This Teacher Started His Own School." *Teacher Magazine*. September 1990.

Henry, Gary T. 2005. "In Pursuit of Social Betterment: A Proposal to Evaluate the Da Vinci Learning Model." *New Directions for Evaluation* 106 (Summer 2005): 47–63.

High Schools on the Move: Renewing Vermont's commitment to Quality Secondary Education. 2002. Montpelier, VT: Vermont High School Task Force, Vermont Department of Education.

Hirsch, E. D. 1987. *Cultural Literacy: What Every American Needs to Know*. Boston: Houghton Mifflin.

Hockney, David. 2001. *Secret Knowledge: Rediscovering The Lost Techniques of the Old Masters*. New York: Viking Studio.

Hoff, Benjamin. 1983. *The Tao of Pooh*. New York: Penguin Books.

International Center for Leadership in Education. Bill Daggett. Available from http://www.leadered.com/aboutdaggett.html (accessed March 7, 2012).

———. Rigor/Relevance Framework®. Available from http://www.leadered.comRef. (accessed February 24, 2012).

Jackson, Philip W., and American Educational Research Association. 1996. *Handbook of Research on Curriculum: A Project of the American Educational Research Association*. New York: Macmillan.

Jacobs, Heidi Hayes, and Association for Supervision and Curriculum Development. 1989. *Interdisciplinary Curriculum: Design and implementation*. Alexandria, VA: Association for Supervision and Curriculum Development.

———. 2004. *Getting Results with Curriculum Mapping*. Alexandria, VA: Association for Supervision and Curriculum Development.

Jacobs, Heidi Hayes, and Ann Johnson. 2009. *The curriculum mapping planner: templates, tools, and resources for effective professional development*. Alexandria, VA:

Jernstedt, C. 2008. *Learning and the Brain*. Vermont Leadership Academy.

King, Ross. 2000. *Brunelleschi's Dome: How a Renaissance Genius Reinvented Architecture*. New York: Penguin Books.

———. 2003. *Michelangelo and the Pope's Ceiling*. New York: Walker & Co.

Kliebard, Herbert M. 1987. *The Struggle for the American Curriculum, 1893–1958*. New York: Routledge & Kegan Paul.

Knefelkamp, L. L. 2003. "The Influence of a Classic." *Liberal Education* 89 (3) (Summer 2003): 10–15.

Kohn, Alfie. 1993. *Punished by Rewards: The Trouble with Gold Stars, Incentive Plans, A's, Praise, and Other Bribes*. Boston: Houghton Mifflin.

Kuhn, Thomas S. 1962. *The Structure of Scientific Revolutions*. Chicago: University of Chicago Press.

Kuralt, Charles. 1990. *On the Road with Charles Kuralt*. CBS News.

Kurtén, Björn. 1995. *Dance of the Tiger: A Novel of the Ice Age*. Berkeley: University of California Press.

Landing of Columbus. Available from http://www.aoc.gov/cc/art/rotunda/landing_columbus.cfm (accessed September 13, 2011).

Lehrer, Jonah. 2010. "The Truth Wears Off." *The New Yorker*. September 2011.

Lester, Toby. 2012. *Da Vinci's Ghost: Genius, Obsession, and How Leonardo Created the World in His Own Image*. New York: Free Press.

Loertscher, David V., Richard DuFour, Rebbecca DuFour, and Robert Eaker. 2010. "Revisiting Professional Learning Communities at Work: New Insights for Improving Schools." *Teacher Librarian* 37 (4) (2004): 75–.

MacCurdy, Edward, ed. n.d. *The Notebooks of Leonardo da Vinci*. Old Saybrook, CT: Konecky and Konecky.

Machiavelli, Niccolò. 2004. *The Prince*. London: Penguin.

Mansilla, Veronica Boix, and Howard Gardner. 2008. "Disciplining the Mind." *Educational Leadership* 65 (5) (2002): 14–19.

Marzano, Robert J. 1992. *A Different Kind of Classroom: Teaching with Dimensions of Learning*. Alexandria, VA: Association for Supervision and Curriculum Development.

Math Forum Discussions. Available from http://mathforum.org/kb/thread .jspa?messageID=195215&tstart=0 (accessed September 15, 2011).

McLeish, John. 1994. *The Story of Numbers*. New York: Fawcett Columbine.

McLuhan, Marshall. "McLuhan Hypothesis." Available from http://deoxy.org/media/ McLuhan (accessed March 8, 2012).

McTighe, Jay, Elliott Seif, and Grant Wiggins. 2004. "You Can Teach for Meaning." *Educational Leadership* 62 (1) (2009): 26–30.

McTighe, Jay, and Grant P. Wiggins. 2004. *Understanding by Design: Professional Development Workbook*. Alexandria, VA: Association for Supervision and Curriculum Development.

Meier, Deborah. 1996. *The Power of Their Ideas: Lessons for America from a Small School in Harlem*. Boston: Beacon Press.

Mendeleyev's Periodic Table, 1869. Available from https://www.sciencephoto.com/ media/227211/view (accessed September 13, 2011).

Menzies, Gavin. 2003. *1421: The Year China Discovered America*. New York: William Morrow.

———. 2008. *1434: The Year a Magnificent Chinese Fleet Sailed to Italy and Ignited the Renaissance*. New York: William Morrow.

———. "1434"; "1421"; "Chinese voyages"; "Renaissance history"; "Medieval history"; "Martitime exploration"; "Chinese exploration"; "Admiral Zheng He"; "Chinese junks"; various articles available from www.gavinmenzies.net (accessed September 13, 2011).

Michlewitz, Debra. 2001. "Eloquent Images—Using Art to Teach History." *American Educator* 25 (4): 12–21.

National Association of Secondary School Principals. 1996. *Breaking Ranks: Changing an American Institution: A Report of the National Association of Secondary School Principals in Partnership with the Carnegie Foundation for the Advancement of Teaching on the High School of the 21st Century*. Reston, VA: The Association.

———. 2004. *Breaking Ranks II: Strategies for Leading High School Reform*. Reston, VA: National Association of Secondary School Principals.

———. 2004. *Supporting Principals Who Break Ranks: Recommendations from Breaking Ranks II for Creating Systems That Support Successful High Schools*. Reston, VA: National Association of Secondary School Principals.

National Governors Association, Council of Chief State School Officers. 2010. Available from http://www.corestandards.org/ (accessed September 6, 2011).

National Research Council (U.S.). 1996. *National Science Education Standards: Observe, Interact, Change, Learn*. Washington, DC: National Academy Press.

National Research Council (U.S.), Committee on Learning Research and Educational Practice. John Bransford, James W. Pellegrino, and Suzanne Donovan. 1999. *How People Learn: Bridging Research and Practice*. Washington, DC: National Academy Press.

Nicholl, Charles. 2004. *Leonardo da Vinci: Flights of the Mind*. New York: Viking Penguin.

Nichols, Peter. 2009. *Evolution's Captain: The Dark Fate of the Man who Sailed Charles Darwin around the World*. New York: Harper Collins.

Noddings, Nel. 2008. "All Our Students Thinking." *Educational Leadership* 65 (5) (2002): 8–13.

O'Toole, James. 1995. *Leading Change: Overcoming the Ideology of Comfort and the Tyranny of Custom*. San Francisco: Jossey-Bass Publishers.

Paul, Richard, and Linda Elder. 2009. *Critical Thinking: Concepts and Tools*. Tomales, CA: Foundation for Critical Thinking.

———. 2009. *Understanding the Foundations of Ethical Reasoning*. Tomales, CA: The Foundation for Critical Thinking.

———. 2010. *The Thinker's Guide to the Art of Asking Essential Questions*. Dillon Beach, CA: Foundation for Critical Thinking.

Paulos, John Allen. 1988. *Innumeracy: Mathematical Illiteracy and Its Consequences*. New York: Hill and Wang.

Pearce, J. M. S. 2007. "Malpighi and the Discovery of Capillaries." *European Neurology* 58 (4): 253–55.

Pedretti, Carlo. 2004. *Leonardo: Art and Science*. Cobham, UK: TAJ Books.

Perkins, David. 2004. "Knowledge Alive." *Educational Leadership* 62 (1) (2009): 14–18.

Perry, William G. 1999. *Forms of Intellectual and Ethical Development in the College Years: A Scheme*. San Francisco: Jossey-Bass Publishers.

"Philosophy." The National Paideia Center. Available from http://www.paideia.org/about-paideia/philosophy/ (accessed September 9, 2011).

Pink, Daniel H. 2009. *A Whole New Mind: Why Right-Brainers Will Rule the Future*. New York: Riverhead Books.

———. 2009. *Drive*. New York: Riverhead Books.

Pollio, Vitruvius. 1960. *Vitruvius: The Ten Books on Architecture*. Translated by M. H. Morgan. New York: Dover Publications.

Popham, W. James. 2008. *Transformative Assessment*. Alexandria, VA: Association for Supervision and Curriculum Development.

Posner, George J. 2004. *Analyzing the Curriculum*. Boston: McGraw-Hill.

Prown, Jules David. 1995. "In Pursuit of Culture: The Formal Language of Objects." *Journal American Art* 9 (2): 2–3.

Rabb, Theodore K. 1993. *Renaissance Lives: Portraits of an Age*. New York: Pantheon Books.

Resnick, Lauren B., Leopold E. Klopfer, and Association for Supervision and Curriculum Development. 1989. *Toward the Thinking Curriculum: Current Cognitive Research. 1989 ASCD Yearbook*. Alexandria, VA: Association for Supervision and Curriculum Development.

Reynal and Company. 1956. *Leonardo da Vinci*. New York: Reynal.

Ritchhart, Ron, and David Perkins. 2008. "Making Thinking Visible." *Educational Leadership* 65 (5) (2002): 57–61.

Roberts, Terry and Laura Billings. 2008. "Thinking is Literacy, Literacy Thinking." *Educational Leadership* 65 (5): 32–36.

Royal Society for the encouragement of Arts, Manufactures, and Commerce. "RSA Animate—Changing Education Paradigms." YouTube video. Available from http://www.youtube.com/watch?v=zDZFcDGpL4U (accessed September 6, 2011).

Schaef, Anne Wilson, and Diane Fassel. 1990. *The Addictive Organization*. New York: Harper & Row.

Schlereth, Thomas J. 1982. *Material Culture Studies in America*. Nashville, TN: American Association for State and Local History.

Senge, Peter M. 1990. *The Fifth Discipline: The Art and Practice of the Learning Organization*. New York: Doubleday/Currency.

Sergiovanni, Thomas J. 1992. *Moral Leadership: Getting to the Heart of School Improvement*. San Francisco: Jossey-Bass Publishers.

Sertillanges, O.P. 2008. *The Thoughts of Leonardo da Vinci Editions du Clos Luce*. Amboise, France.

Seymour, Mike. 2004. *Educating for Humanity: Rethinking the Purposes of Education*. Boulder, CO: Paradigm Publishers.

Shelley, Mary Wollstonecraft. 2006. *Frankenstein*. London: Bloomsbury.

Shuh, J. H. "Teaching Yourself to Teach with Objects." *Journal of Education* 7 (4): 8.

Slave Narratives: An Introduction to the WPA Slave Narratives. Available from http://memory.loc.gov/ammem/snhtml/snintro00.html (accessed September 13, 2011).

"Smithsonian Education—Idea Labs: Artifact and Analysis." Available from http://www.smithsonianeducation.org/educators/lesson_plans/idealabs/artifacts_analysis.html (accessed October 6, 2011).

Snow, C. P., and American Council of Learned Societies. 1998. *The Two Cultures*. Cambridge; New York: Cambridge University Press.

Steadman, Philip. 2001. *Vermeer's Camera: Uncovering the Truth behind the Masterpieces*. New York: Oxford University Press.

Stiggins, Richard J., and Assessment Training Institute. 2005. *Classroom Assessment for Student Learning: Doing It Right—Using It Well*. Portland, OR: Assessment Training Institute.

"Strapped Schools Ax Foreign Languages." *Journal Sentinel* online. Volume 2012. Available from http://www.jsonline.com/business/105580973.html (accessed September 15, 2011).

Swartz, Robert J. 2008. "Energizing Learning." *Educational Leadership* 65 (5) (2002): 26–31.

Taylor, Raymond G., and Richard H. Card. 1985. *Power Sown; Power Reaped*. Augusta, ME: Felicity Press.

Thiers, Naomi. 2008. "EL Study Guide." *Educational Leadership* 65 (5).

Tishman, Shari. 2008. "The Object of Their Attention." *Educational Leadership* 65 (5) (2002): 44–46.

Tomlinson, Carol A. 1999. *The Differentiated Classroom: Responding to the Needs of All Learners*. Alexandria, VA: Association for Supervision and Curriculum Development.

Tomlinson, Carol A., and Jay McTighe. 2006. *Integrating Differentiated Instruction and Understanding by Design: Connecting Content and Kids*. Alexandria, VA: Association for Supervision and Curriculum Development.

Trust for Representative Democracy: "Civic Education Quotes." Available from http://www.ncsl.org/default.aspx?tabid=15386 (accessed September 9, 2011).

Tufte, Edward R. 1983. *The Visual Display of Quantitative Information*. Cheshire, CT: Graphics Press.

———. 1990. *Envisioning Information*. Cheshire, CT: Graphics Press.

———. 1997. *Visual Explanations: Images and Quantities, Evidence and Narrative*. Cheshire, CT: Graphics Press.

———. 2006. *Beautiful Evidence*. Cheshire, CT: Graphics Press.

United States Congress, Senate Committee on the Judiciary, Subcommittee on Technology, Terrorism, and Government Information. 1998. *The Nation at Risk: Report of the President's Commission on Critical Infrastructure Protection: Hearing before the Subcommittee on Technology, Terrorism, and Government Information of the Committee on the Judiciary, United States Senate, One Hundred Fifth Congress, First Session . . . November 5, 1997*. Washington: US GPO.

Vasari, Giorgio, Julia Conaway Bondanella, and Peter E. Bondanella. 1998. *Lives of the Artists*. Oxford: World's Classics.

"Vinland Archeology." Available from http://www.mnh.si.edu/vikings/voyage/subset/vinland/archeo.html (accessed September 13, 2011).

The "Vitruvian Man." Available from http://leonardodavinci.stanford.edu/submissions/clabaugh/today/perfectman.html (accessed September 13, 2011).

Webb, Norman L. 2007. "Issues Related to Judging the Alignment of Curriculum Standards and Assessments." *Applied Measurement in Education* 20 (1) (2001): 7–25.

Wenglinsky, Harold. 2004. "Facts or Critical Thinking Skills? What NAEP Results Say." *Educational Leadership* 62 (1) (2009): 32–5.

Widmer, T. 2007. "Navigating the Age of Exploration: And Restoring Our Capacity for Astonishment." *American Educator* 31 (4): 42–48.

Wiggins, Grant. 2011. "Moving to Modern Assessments." *Phi Delta Kappan* 92 (September 2011): 63.

Wiggins, Grant P., and Jay McTighe. 1998. *Understanding by Design*. Alexandria, VA: Association for Supervision and Curriculum Development.

———. 2005. *Understanding by Design*. 2nd ed. Alexandria, VA: Association for Supervision and Curriculum Development.

Wikipedia Contributors. "Theodor de Bry" in Wikipedia, The Free Encyclopedia. Available from http://en.wikipedia.org/wiki/Theodor_de_Bry (accessed September 15, 2011).

Wineburg, Sam, and Daisy Martin. 2004. "Reading and Rewriting History." *Educational Leadership* 62 (1) (2009): 42–25.

Wineburg, Samuel S., and Pamela L. Grossman. 2000. *Interdisciplinary Curriculum: Challenges to Implementation*. New York: Teachers College Press.

Wolk, Ronald A., and Blake Hume Rodman. 1994. *Classroom Crusaders: Twelve Teachers Who Are Trying to Change The System*. San Francisco: Jossey-Bass Publishers.

Zhao, Yong. 2009. *Catching Up or Leading the Way: American Education in the Age of Globalization*. Alexandria, VA: Association for Supervision and Curriculum Development.

Zull, James E. 2004. "The Art of Changing the Brain." *Educational Leadership* 62 (1) (2009): 68–72.

Index

Roosevelt, Eleanor, 65
Roth, Kathleen, 37

Saint Anselm of Canterbury, 60
Saint John's College curriculum, 29
Santa Croce Church, 151
Santayana, George, 89
school skills, traditional, 55–56
science: art illustrating, *134*, 134–38;
 faith struggle with, 62
science education: in DVC, 37; stories
 for, 38
Science Literacy, 64
Scientific Method, 59, 63
scientist, historian *v.*, 37
*Secret Knowledge: Rediscovering the Lost
 Techniques of the Old Masters*, 126
seminars, 76–79; leading, 77–79
sensory stimuli, 114–15
service learning, 170
seventh grade, inductive teaching,
 112–15, *113*
simple ideas, 22
skills: in Bloom's Taxonomy, 65; for
 change, 182; traditional school,
 55–56; in Webb's DOK, 65
slave narratives, 132–34
SLOOH Space Camera, 75
"Snowflake Bentley," 114
soccer game, 173
social process of eating, 14
sociocentric thinking, 63
Socrates, 76
Socratic method, 76–79
Spanish, 170
speaking: in CCSS, 55–56; in DVC, 72
special educators, 82–83
spoils of conquest, 137–38
sports, 171, 173
Standard of Ur, 115–18, *116*, *117*
standards-based reform, 12–13
state standards: CCSS acceptance, 14;
 existing, 12; reform of, 4, 12–13

Steadman, Philip, 126
stories: in DVC, 38; examples of, 33–
 34; for teaching, 20–22
strategic thinking, in Webb's DOK, 65
The Structure of Scientific Revolutions,
 140
students, DVC role of, 45–50, *46*
"subject matter learning," 48
survey courses, 66
syllogism, 60
synthesis: in academic disciplines, 38–
 39; art creation and, 55; in Bloom's
 Taxonomy, 65
synthetic functions, 54

Tacoma Narrows Bridge Collapse, 75
Taxonomy of Knowledge, 52–53, *53*
teachers: conventional role of, 50–51.
 See also Da Vinci Teacher; DVC job
 of, 50–51; redesigning role of, 82–83;
 UbD role of, 48. *See also* educators
teaching: stories for, 20–22. *See also*
 inductive teaching
technical centers, 28
tenth grade, inductive teaching, 123–
 26, *144–45*
Terman, Lewis, 96
text efficiency, 56
Thales, 20, 59, 62
Theodoric of Freiberg, 91
Theory of Everything, 40
thesis writing, 63
thinking: in academic disciplines, 31,
 38, 40; art creation and, 55; content
 acquisition *v.*, 15; deductive, 60, *61*;
 divergent, 7–8, 96; in DVC, 38–40,
 39, 72; egocentric, 24, 63; empirical,
 62; extended, 65; inductive tower
 and, 68–69; right-brain directed,
 54; sociocentric, 63; strategic, 65;
 words and, 72–73. *See also* creative
 thinking; disciplinary thinking;
 inductive thinking

~

About the Author

Dr. Harry Yeo Chaucer grew up playing on weekends in his great aunt's school in New Haven, Connecticut. The school was on the first floor of his father's family home. He enjoyed a progressive college education at Goddard College and continued on to complete his master's in botany and his doctorate in education at the University of Vermont.

Chaucer recently returned from a sabbatical in western Europe, during which he followed the life and works of Leonardo da Vinci. This research has resulted in writing and presentations about renaissance and societal change, curriculum development and the Common Core, the life of Leonardo, and the future of education.

Chaucer has been recognized as a White House Distinguished Teacher; Teacher of the Year for the National Association of Biology Teachers and the American Association of University Women; a Klingenstein Fellow at Columbia University; an Apple Fellow, a NEA Dorros Peace Trophy recipient, and as a recipient of many local awards. He designed the Da Vinci Curriculum as highlighted by *Teacher Magazine, Business People Magazine,* Charles Kuralt's *CBS News,* and the text *Classroom Crusaders.* He was head of the Gailer School for over a decade. Chaucer has lived the change that he describes. He is designing a school in Shanghai, China, that will blend the Western Common Core with Eastern values and traditions.

Chaucer is currently a tenured professor of education at Castleton State College, where he designed and directs the Woodruff Institute for School

Leaders and the ACT II Post-Baccalaureate Program. He currently sits on an independent and a public school board.

This spring, Harry and his treasured wife, Kathleen, are looking forward to the birth of a granddaughter and dozens of spring lambs. Kathleen is a nurse family practitioner and school nurse. They live at the end of a dirt road in Vermont.